Walt's Utopia

Walt's Utopia

Disneyland and American Mythmaking

PRISCILLA HOBBS

McFarland & Company, Inc., Publishers
Jefferson, North Carolina

11-18-15
LB
$35.00

LIBRARY OF CONGRESS CATALOGUING-IN-PUBLICATION DATA

Hobbs, Priscilla, 1980–
    Walt's utopia : Disneyland and American mythmaking / Priscilla Hobbs.
        p.   cm.
    Includes bibliographical references and index.

ISBN 978-0-7864-9836-9 (softcover : acid free paper) ∞
ISBN 978-1-4766-2213-2 (ebook)

    1. Disneyland (Calif.)—History.   2. Disney, Walt, 1901–1966.
3. United States—Popular culture—History.   4. Cold War—Social
aspects—United States.   I. Title.
GV1853.3.C22D57337 2015
791.06'879496—dc23   2015017991

BRITISH LIBRARY CATALOGUING DATA ARE AVAILABLE

Printed in the United States of America

Front cover images © iStock/Thinkstock

McFarland & Company, Inc., Publishers
    Box 611, Jefferson, North Carolina 28640
        www.mcfarlandpub.com

For Stephen

Table of Contents

Acknowledgments

A lot of people helped birth this book, which began as my doctoral dissertation. Without their help and support throughout, this book may have remained a Disney dream.

Thanks are owed the faculty of the Mythological Studies program at Pacifica Graduate Institute, and to my immediate cohort and those I adopted along the way, for the encouragement and feedback from the earliest conception of this project. They helped me root the topic, which could easily have floated away like a Disneyland balloon. From early concept, thank you to Patrick, Art, and Laura. Thank you to my dissertation committee: Glen, Addi, and Adam. And special thanks to: Leslie, who read several drafts of my concept and dissertation; Rebekah, for the lengthy discussions about postmodernism and Boomers; and Dori, my Disney Dolly, for the numerous research trips to Disneyland.

Thanks also to my family for their continued support and encouragement, because one should always thank their family. Even when I did not fully believe I could complete this project, their excitement about finishing it encouraged me to move forward, day by day, step by step.

Thanks to Deb and Mary, who have been wonderful cheerleaders. They always knew what to say and how to say it, no matter what I was whining about.

Thanks to those who contributed to my GoFundMe campaign to help me through a rough transition: Nikki, Marina, Jay, Keith, Rebekah, Malia, Sandi, Nina, Alyson, Lanette and R.J., Leslie, Elizabeth, Katie, Mary Anne, and Daddy.

A lot of churros were consumed in this process. I would like to thank the Disney fan community (the D23, Mouse Planet, and all who

Acknowledgments

have posted HD POV videos on YouTube of Disneyland attractions), for keeping the magic of the Mouse real.

Thanks and kisses to my kitty, Tangaroa, for the cuddles and nips when I wasn't paying enough attention to him.

Thanks to Alice, for just being awesome. I look forward to someday sharing Wonderland with you.

Finally, the most special thanks to my husband, Stephen, for standing by me (sometimes in the lines of Disneyland) through Graduate School Limbo and the Follies of Adulthood and Parenthood, for believing in my work, and for being my number one fan. If I could give you a petrified tree stump for our anniversary and place it in my theme park, I would.

Preface

Walt Disney once quipped, "We just make the pictures, and let the professors tell us what they mean." Many a project about Disney begins with this quote, as though its existence gives the writer permission to critique Disney. Whether analyzing the man, Walt Disney, his company, or their creative products, scholars—or "the professors"—have been analyzing the Disney opus for decades. Early analyses were laudatory, creating the illusion that Disney is above criticism. By the 1960s, commentators grew critical about Disney, recognizing the lasting influence of the films, cartoons, theme parks, and other products on the American public, especially children. The trend of Disney criticism has continued ever since, with some analyses criticizing Walt as "Hollywood's Dark Prince" or of the "Disney Version" of stories for bastardizing beloved stories and corrupting the minds of children.

Among the Disney "professors," there are also those who write about Disney from a loving perspective. These professors don't necessarily believe that Disney is some sort of messianic demigod above criticism, but in response to the negative voices, act as sort of academic apologists preserving the magic of Disney's opus, the memories of childhood, and see Disney's social influence from a positive angle.

I am one such "professor."

Additionally, this book does not seek to bury Disney, but to celebrate the man, the company, the works, and, especially, the first theme park.

I can't say when I realized my love for Disney. Having grown up with the first generation of the Disney Channel, all of my memories involve Disney in some way. I can remember, however, when we temporarily parted ways during the summer when *Tarzan*'s soundtrack got tiring, and when we became friends again in part thanks to *Pirates*

1

of the Caribbean: The Curse of the Black Pearl. I can also identify the exact moment when I became a self-identified Disney Apologist. I have to give credit to my friend and fellow mythologist, Dr. Dori Koehler, for the title.

Sitting in a graduate seminar at Pacifica Graduate Institute, my professor made a comment that if we, as a class, took a field trip to Disneyland, we would observe that everyone is unhappy. To which, I raised my hand, and commented that they're unhappy because they are experiencing the wrong myth. My rationale is that Disneyland is meant to be a place of fun and entertainment. There is no reason to be unhappy—tired/exhausted, yes, but not unhappy—unless it is truly not a place in line with a person's personal myth. Disneyland is not for everyone, but we have constructed the illusion that it is, that a trip to Disneyland is like a pilgrimage to one of America's holy places.

In the years since that class, I have had many opportunities to "defend" Disney in discussions ranging from Disney nostalgia and utopian vision, to the benefits of the princesses as role models, to why the theme parks are worth their high price tag.

Disney is as American as apple pie, baseball, and Ford. The company, its founder, and the Mouse are significant recognizable icons to Americans, and they all invite different interpretations and analyses. I offer this book to the larger conversation of Disney, America, and, perhaps, the entire world, looking at the place of Disneyland as a text, then analyzing it from a mythological perspective, an interdisciplinary perspective that allows me to analyze Disney using the tools of literary criticism, socio-cultural observation, and psychological interpretation.

This is not just another book about Disneyland; it is a book about the Cold War, the Baby Boomers, and the development of contemporary America. It's about the American quest to construct Utopia, globalization as the new Manifest Destiny, and the nostalgia for a lost era. It's about consumerism, reassurance, and the permanent impact of the mid-century on the collective American mind.

It all started, as Walt Disney was fond of reminding people, with a Mouse.

Introduction

"To all who come to this happy place, welcome!"
—*Walt Disney, "Dateline Disneyland"*

After the sun has set, a hush falls upon the crowd, many of whom have been sitting on the concrete with screaming, tired children, eating churros and popcorn, and appreciating the reprieve from all the standing and walking. They started arriving an hour or two earlier to secure the best vantage point. Other people follow suit, and the Plaza is full long before the magic is scheduled to begin. A voice comes over the loud speaker welcoming them, followed by familiar music and then the fireworks begin. The spectacle sucks the people in, inspiring many collective "oos" and "ahhs." Then, another, more familiar voice speaks, welcoming all who have come to this happy place. Everyone knows who belongs to the voice, and instantly the attitude of the crowd changes. It is as though God has spoken, wiping away the exhaustion and touching each person with the magic, happiness, near-ecstasy of an encounter with a god. This voice is not really that of God, but of an inspiring entrepreneur who passed away many years ago, Walt Disney, and the spectacle is the Disneyland nightly fireworks show, often the punctuation to a very special day. As the spectacle continues, the audience is held in rapture until it is time for them to disperse. The show is calculated to give a specific experience to the viewers, a mythic experience to elevate the crowd into a realm of transcendence that helps them forget their weariness and join collectively in the Disney fantasy, in the American dream.

Disneyland was the first theme park that sought to place all park visitors, or "guests" in Disney parlance, directly into the story by creating

3

Introduction

a controlled space full of attractions, restaurants, and shops that all have connection to the Disney theme, and by shutting the outside world off from the overall experience. A theme park is not a simple place of amusement; it does not rely on thrills to entertain. A theme park, instead, is a place that evokes other times and places, whether real or imaginary.[1] The theme park is composed of the narratives of culture that speak to the deeper recesses of a guest's frame of experience. The theme park speaks on a mythic level, acting as an interactive space where the myths of the guest or the culture can come to life. The stories that permeate Disneyland are not only the familiar ones culled from the Disney canon, but also from the stories that have defined America and her mythos, past and present, historical and idealized. Much of the Disney canon has become the preferred version for generations of Americans—Davy Crockett, Zorro, and the fairy tale films, to name a few—in some cases displacing "traditional" stories and histories, to the chagrin of some Disney critics.

Disneyland provides a place of escape from larger cultural issues while also fueling our country's consumptive behaviors. Some Disney critics are quick to scrutinize Disneyland as a place of consumerism and capitalism. But doing so overlooks the experience. Americans need places like Disneyland to reassure us in troubling times and to reaffirm our American-ness (or, for non–Americans, to participate in the myth). Each themed area, or land, of the park exposes us to different aspects of America's mythology, historical and contemporary. A full day in the park, jumping from land to land, attraction to attraction (the Disney term for the rides, restaurants, or events in the park) will assuredly rejuvenate even the most exhausted guest with a sense of magic, reinforcing the American Dream that is in danger of fading in today's doubt and struggles.

America has been in a state of constant change since the end of World War II. Popular culture has responded by establishing a firm interplay between entertainment outlets and the myths that shape culture. Walt (as he is called in Disney research to distinguish him from the company that bears his name), his Imagineers (the Disney division responsible for theme park design), and the entirety of the Disney corporation have responded by providing Americans with tools to process and cope with these changes, from short cartoons to "edutainment" films, to animated fairy tale features to a world-wide network of theme parks. These tools use familiar images, stories, and values to project hyperrealities that simulate a traditional mythic experience. The design of Disneyland facilitates this experience by imagineering American archetypes, drawing inspiration from the patterns of culture and engineering them to become defining images.

The Cold War and the more recent War on Terrorism have ushered a new era for American mythology. For the first time in her relatively young life, the United States is faced with a truly globalized world in which peoples from all over now have access to each other's culture and its beliefs and behaviors. Between newfound global relations and an unsteady doubt inspired by the events surrounding World War II and the nuclear bomb, America has been in a sort of crisis that has led to increased levels of consumption of simulated environments and modes of entertainment that have, in turn, lead to increased cravings for entertainment and extremism in all modes of consumerism, manifest and latent.

These tools for coping with American flux utilize familiar images, stories, values and mores to project archetypal hyperrealities that simulate a traditional mythic experience. In this book, I explore these tools, noting that each land, or uniquely themed area in the park, highlights a different mythic motif. Looking closely at how each land treats the motif reveals how they reflect the inward patterns of the present modern American culture while romanticizing the past and future, getting updated, or "plussed," to coincide with generational shifts in culture.

Recognizing American Myth

One term that is used several times throughout this tour of Disneyland is "myth." Just what is a myth? The word "myth" has come to mean at least three different things depending on its use. One, a pervasive definition, is that a myth is a lie or a falsehood, as in, "it's a myth that all Americans prefer driving pick-up trucks." Two, the one used in grade schools, is that a myth is a story of an ancient people, such as the Greeks or Romans, that describes the gods or goddesses they believed in or to explain natural phenomena. Third, thanks to the

Introduction

efforts of Joseph Campbell and similar scholars, myth refers to the collective soundtrack of humanity. These myths could be the stories of a hero or a culture; they could be the description of a particular experience, such as a religious one; or myths could be teaching tools to spread culture from one generation to the next. By this understanding, anything can constitute a myth, from a popular film to Grandmother's stories (or even her quilt collection!). It is this third understanding that is used throughout this book as we go through the myths of Disneyland, the myths of America, and their points of overlap with each other.

The myths of America communicate cultural ideals. These myths, deeply embedded in American history, reveal to us what it means to be an American, what makes America great, and what composes the American Dream.[2] Because of the unique nature of America's development, it cannot be looked at from the same approaches as traditional myth, nor does it follow a literary formula. American myth is tied closely to the three main channels that influence it: America's history, the land from sea to shining sea, and in popular culture, which includes the sometimes-legendary stories of the people and events that gave birth to the country. Although my focus is on the latter, all three are nonetheless inextricably combined and work together to bring richness and depth into the culture's mythology. The historical events that shaped America are imbued with a desire to fashion a nation after the Enlightenment principles of reason and reasoned knowledge in pursuit of a utopian ideal. America was, and in some ways still is, perceived as a land of infinite wealth and opportunity for anyone who wants to reinvent themselves, immigrant and citizen alike. The source of this wealth and opportunity could be found in the land itself: gold, silver, tobacco and other cultivated crops, and new wildlife whose furs and meats were valuable sources of income. More so than any other modern nation, Americans self-identify more with the land or their local region than they do with family or profession. This is especially emphasized in certain regions, such as Texas, whose identity seeps deeply into one's individuality.[3]

The stories of the land and history take on mythic proportions when they enter the popular sector, which is constantly defining the natural purpose and reevaluating it with each new generation.[4] These stories pursue a Heroic Ideal[5] and tell the tales of the pioneers, the explorers, the frontierspeople, politicians, and the selfless, self-sacrific-ing individuals who were driven by perceived destiny, a Manifest Des-tiny, to push westward in an unspoken covenant with an unspoken god to secure the New World's place in the global imagination. Although the phrase was not coined until the 1850s, Manifest Destiny refers to the mission of American settlers to spread civilization to the "savage," untamed wilderness of the land they felt entitled to as an extension of the original colonies.

Because of America's separation between church and state, some scholars—namely, Joseph Campbell—have suggested that myth in modern American culture is deeply buried and asleep, overlooking the potential housed within popular culture, preferring the more tradi-tional, academic approach to understanding it. C. G. Jung echoes this observation, but also suggests alternative places to look for myth, observing that modern expressions of archetypes, or the images of myth, might now be found in an object to lead us into new, different aspects of myth.[6] However, it should be noted that to work with Amer-ican myth, one needs to contextualize the popular culture with the spe-cific era of investigation, because of influence by factors beyond culture. Although other areas are given credence, the focus of this book is ultimately on the Cold War as a cultural "game-changer." The events leading up to and surrounding the Cold War reshaped America's rela-tionship to its mythology, and the effects of this shift are still struggling to be recognized and understood. With the Cold War, the mission of Manifest Destiny changed, the boundaries of the frontier realigned, and a new interdependence on a fully globalized world emerged.

The events of the Great Depression and World War II have held the American culture in an arrested state of fear ever since,[7] resulting in a destabilizing doubt about different aspects of culture. Rather than address that fear, Americans have sought ways to bury it in material goods, suburban utopias, and technology to distract us from interacting with each other, which can be described as the "Chronic American Way."[8] Other commentators have explored the effects on individual behavior and psychology. For our purposes here, I will focus on how popular culture—specifically, the Disney brand—speaks to these behav-iors on a collective level.

In the loosest definitions, popular culture is recognized as the

Introduction

culture of the people, in contrast to the culture of religion or the aristocracy. To be "popular" once meant to appeal to the lower classes, and was thus equated with vulgarity and the grotesque. In the United States, however, which claims to recognize itself as a classless society, "popular culture" refers to any cultural event that accords mass-recognition. Popular culture still undergoes an academic treatment in an attempt to debase its significance, but it is pervasive and captivates across economic status, gender, race and ethnicity. While there are many demographic-specific examples of popular culture that are aimed at and appeal to that group, these demographics have earned a different understanding today than they did thirty years ago when the advents of cable television and the Internet promoted and continue to promote a unified country (even if this unification is only for the purposes of achieving higher ratings).

Regardless of social politics, popular culture has always carried a culture's mythos, buried and embedded in fantastic settings, buried even deeper than the values and mores of a culture. From Homer to Shakespeare to the Brothers Grimm, stories and other areas of art have transmitted culture from one generation to the next. In the last century, with the explosion of new technology, popular culture not only serves to communicate to the next generations, but also serves as a reminder to recent generations, broken into twenty year units. The older a unit, the "older," more "vintage" it is recognized to be.

An experience of myth, no matter its mode of delivery, occurs when someone has a powerful connection to a myth. This might also be called *mythopoesis*, or the creation of personal myth in relation to the psychological individual experience. An inner, mythic experience occurs when the individual's experience affects a transformation. The myths behind Disneyland induce individual transformation because they are the latent cultural myths of America applicable to all settings. In other words, Disneyland is not just composed of the stories and fairy tales of America, but of a literature of perception, filled with stories full of themes of nostalgia and progress, for example, that affect how we interact with the larger society. Disney's motivation for Disneyland is the hope that everyone will have the same experience. This can be seen as counterproductive to any sort of individual transformation, but should not be seen as the dominant motive. If this were the case, any possibility for transformation would disappear from the park.

The components for the inner, mythic experience are similar to those of ritual, including separation, liminality, and *communitas*.[9] Separation entails removing the individual from his/her daily life, essentially to free the person from the daily stresses of work, children, and other civic duties. Or, in the case of younger people, separation also includes removing the individual from his/her parents. In the latter case, this removal coincides with a rite of passage to usher this person into adulthood. Following separation, the person is taken into a liminal space. The liminal space—or the state of liminality—is a place between worlds, neither "here" nor "there," where it is believed there is no passage of time, no illness or disease, no life or death; this is the land of "once upon a time." It is a place of transformation. When a person emerges from the liminal state, he/she will no longer be the same person, and her new state of being is determined by the success of the ritual performance. If the ritual is performed successfully, one experiences not only a societal transformation recognized by the larger community, but an inner transformation that changes one's self-perception forever. Exiting the liminal state, one experiences *communitas*, re-entry and re-acceptance by members of the community who have experienced the same transformation. From all of this, one writes another page of one's personal mythology, shaping who we are at any point of time.

Joseph Campbell describes four functions of mythology: cosmological, social, religious, and psychological.[10] The ideal myth will accomplish all four functions, but a sacred myth must necessarily fulfill the cosmological and religion function, whereas a secular myth can only truly fulfill the social and psychological functions. As such, Disneyland is a secular myth and its impact is felt on a sociological and/or psychological level. But the impact is so strong that it seems on a latent level to be both cosmological and religious. The legend of how Walt conceived of Mickey Mouse acts as a kind of cosmological myth that tells not where we came from, but, rather, tells of the establishing of a particular world order, one filled with magic and Mickey. It becomes religion-like in the sense that people participate in the Disney experience with the same fervor as any religious practitioner, adorning vestments, making a pilgrimage, and celebrating icons. In this sense, Disneyland is archetypal, though not an archetype.

There are a few sub-categories of myth that I consider in this book, all of which are held in tension against their counter-part. There are several tensions at play throughout the American culture, easily reduced into binary parts, with some halves being more manifest than others. For example, there is the aspect of culture that is driven towards assimilation and that of diversity. At various points in American history, one—usually assimilation—has clearly dominated over the other; however, in contemporary culture the two are at odds. In schools and work places, diversity is preached and narrated, but the more manifest spectrum promotes homogeneity, for no matter how happy with oneself one can be, that value judgment is still based on a comparison to someone else and the ongoing quest to either "be like" or "be better than" someone else—either to wear the same styles, or to have the greener lawn or better toys. The myths under discussion include: nostalgia versus innocence, adult versus child, progress versus doubt, and frontier versus wasteland.

Nostalgia/Innocence

As any person ages, nostalgia sweeps over them. They reminisce on "the good old days" to anyone willing to listen. The time and events they remember have been filtered through the layers of memory, sometimes to the point of no longer resembling what really happened. Some stories, those of a particularly happy or overly traumatic time, recur, often with small changes between versions, such that family and friends can and will start correcting the storytelling. But there is another aspect to nostalgia, one prevalent in western, American popular culture, and this is nostalgia for "days of yore." Things that are "retro," "vintage," "retro-esque" or "vintage-esque" are among the most popular among youth culture, to the point that contemporary producers of culture and product intentionally set out to recreate the past and market it to the present. Psychologist James Hillman calls this *pothos*, after the Greek term described by Plato as "a yearning desire for a distant object."[11]

To add another component to the discussion is the cultural nostalgia for an era that seemed more naïve, innocent, clean and simple. An era when data was not stored digitally, when children could still trust their neighbors, when the gruesome nature of humanity was not broadcast on television, or if it was, it was done with a sensitivity to the viewer and not to boost ratings through sensationalism. This is remembered as an era of sock hops and street dances, hamburgers and road trips, free love and shared community. Various events since World War II and Vietnam have altered the reality of American ideals, and, collectively, the culture yearns to return to that feeling of security experienced only in the comfort of home of when things are going just right.

The prevalence of recycled culture on DVD and cable television, iTunes and CDs, allows newer generations to discover the films and music of previous generations. What was once considered groundbreaking and innovative now blends into the endless soundtrack of the individual American life. "Innovative" sounds and sights are compared to their forebears, blending together into a sort of homogeneity stagnating ever closer to identical sameness.

Cultural nostalgia includes remembering innovators, such as Walt Disney, who helped define the cultural iconography both then and now, and how the work they did then was truly magical, as though the work and their results possessed an archetypal spinal tap that fed off the collective unconscious. Few are capable of such innovation now, according to the voices of the reminisces, who are capable of such change: "Something happened to our education systems." "Where did all the artists go?" "The community and nuclear family are in danger of falling apart." And so on, ad nauseum.

Despite the Great Depression, a World War, the Red Scare, and the Vietnam draft, the years between the turn of the century and 1970 are seen as a time of innocence: there was no sex on film, no pointless murder, no poisoned Kool-Aid ... at least explicitly. The shadow side of culture was consciously cut from film. So those who wax nostalgic about the past also long for a return to an innocence now perceived as lost. Indeed, although the post–1980 generations did not suffer a major life-altering event on the national level—even 9/11 is glossed over by many—these generations have come to the conclusion that pure innocence is lost, and though they would like to regain it, it might not be possible. It is difficult to rile the youth; they pass through life like "sheeple," as obedient as sheep following an unknown shepherd. No one knows who the shepherd is. Jesus? The President? Big Brother? Mickey Mouse? Nor do they realize they do it.

It is just how life is.

Adult/Child

Walt Disney embodied much of the archetypal eternal child, easily one of the dominant archetypes post–World War II. He knew the language of the youth as well as grown-ups. Hillman describes the eternal child, or *puer*, as

> that archetypal dominant which personifies or is in special relation with the transcendent spiritual powers of the collective unconscious. Puer figures can be regarded as avatars of the Self's spiritual aspect, and puer impulses as messages from the spirit or as calls to the spirit. When the collective unconscious in an individual life is represented mainly by parental figures, then puer attitudes and impulses will show personal taints of the mother's boy or fils du papa, the perennial adolescent of the provisional life.[12]

Furthermore, Hillman continues, the eternal child is impatient and does not like to work. This is someone who would rather live in the realm of fantasy than be confronted with the realities of everyday life. The grown-up, or *senex*, is everything the child is not: responsible, dedicated, hardworking, and controlling. Hillman's description of the eternal child aptly describes Walt Disney, who understood what stories could communicate and how to ensure they did. He re-told and re-visioned heroic stories, such as the early life of the man who would become King Arthur in *The Sword and the Stone*, or the heroism and defiance of Robin Hood. He reminded us how to love in Snow White, Cinderella, or Sleeping Beauty, or that a little mischief is a necessary good thing for one's overall well-being, as in Alice in Wonderland or Peter Pan, and he reminds us not to get ahead of ourselves in "The Sorcerer's Apprentice." Walt also embodies the archetypal grown-up. Shortly after establishing the Disney Studio, Walt quickly removed himself from production and settled into a role of delegation and negotiation. He personally oversaw every project being done by Disney, including shorts, features, marketing, and the parks, and his employees quickly developed a love-hate relationship with Walt. They loved him because he nurtured creativity, never (or rarely) telling someone they were not good enough. But they hated him (or at least some did) because of his powerful perfectionism and involvement in everything. If something was not perfect, it was likely that Walt to ask for the entire project to be re-done in favor of making it perfect. Walt could not accept any form of "no," whether from critics, financiers, and certainly not from his employees. Those who loved him still speak of him with reverence, referring to him as "Uncle Walt," while those who did not defected to a competitor, such as Universal.

Progress/Doubt

This particular dyad plays with and complements another one running throughout American culture: that of progress versus doubt. Much has been written in recent scholarship about the problems of unrestrained progress on society,[13] but the looming doubt has not been given equal focus. It is evident that the doubt is there by the unrest and activism of fundamentalism in the religious sector, the Tea Party in the political sector, and in the face of every college student who realizes that their college work no longer guarantees them a job that will actually pay the debts they have accrued. It is further evident in the paranoia and fear that has arisen since 9/11 with half the country supporting the ideological War on Terror while the other half has lost all faith and trust in the government's competency. The looming doubt remains in the shadow of progress, whose effects have become so central to the culture that it has a blank check to continue to run amok, evidenced by ongoing scientific experiments—stem cell research and the Super Collider—and constant technological advancements and "improvements." Just below the surface, doubt threatens to topple progress, to overthrow the tyrannical leader and lock it into a mythological Tartaros, hopefully bringing about a paradigm shift, ideally believed to be for the greater good of the people. Into this tension is yet another duo: utopia versus decay. Because of the unparalleled success of progress, the world is painted as though nothing is wrong: every-

Introduction

one and everything is clean, safe, successful, and progressive. In the utopia, the decay of reality is ignored: the dirty streets, the disagreeable citizens—who really struggle for their piece of the pie—lack of success is viewed as laziness, and anything that hinders progress is seen as a colossal inconvenience.

The myth of doubt emerges at any time when things either never seem to get better (i.e., during Medieval Europe around the time of the Black Plague) or when things seem to be going a little too well. It is marked by a rise in cultural tension and fundamentalism, during which the factions on any side of the issue stand at an absolute opposition, without willingness to compromise. The modern world has been swimming in its own doubt, operating on an unconscious level for at least the past several decades. The Modernists who ushered in the 20th century responded to cultural tension by conveying their doubt in their art, literature and philosophy, relying on realistic images that stand for what they are, and not what they could be. There is no romantic resolution, or, at least, it is suppressed. The Postmodernists restore a hope for the Romantic view, reminding us of the possibility of a happy ending at the core of Disney mythos.

But there is a severe contrast between the happily-ever-after ending of a Disney film and the evening news broadcast. Post-postmodernists just do not know what to think anymore. They are doubtful, skeptical, and cynical of culture and society as a whole.

The modern myth of doubt is conjoined to the myth of progress, the myth that keeps us moving forward towards new, improved, better lives through scientific and technological innovations. This dichotomy emerged as a result of the Cold War, where the culture, as a whole, lived in constant fear of nuclear attack or Russian ("Commie") invasion. To prove to ourselves that we were and are superior, we unleashed the monster of Progress and did not hold it back.

Now we realize that the monster needs to be contained, brought to light by the fact that corporations, despite their involvement in all aspects of our lives, cannot even stop an oil leak in the Gulf of Mexico or prevent the homelessness of many who misunderstood their loan agreements; and brought further to light by a seemingly never-ending war on ideology for a precious resource we believe we need to keep our society functioning. The sad part is that the monster has become

14

so embedded in our cultural psyche that we do not really know how to tame or cage it without sacrificing our plushy lifestyle.

Frontier/Wasteland

Many scholars have recently commented upon the United States' ancestral heritage borne from Judeo-Christian roots. These roots give us a cultural programming of both the need for constant movement—a culture founded by pilgrims and explorers—and the quest for God's chosen people to find New Jerusalem, or Zion. Additionally, the myths we inherited from our immigrant foreparents point to quest and adventure as critical aspects of our lives. Logically, then, it would seem that our country is one of questing nomads trying to find the perfect new life through relocation.

The American West was particularly attractive for early Americans. The lands west of the Mississippi are rich in resources and full of vast amounts of space, waiting for cultivation. In the West, where even the poorest could strike it rich, one could create a new life and identity. The Western terrain begged to receive settlers' projections. The West became equated with perennial success and adventure. By the early 1900s, the West was populated and by the mid–1950s, there was not much left to the mystique. Hollywood, which attracted new adventurers to Southern California who sought to make it big in the movies, responded to the collective psyche's need for an empty expanse to project onto by making stories of the West. John Wayne, Zorro, Davy Crockett and others became cinematic mainstays of the Western Frontier. Today, astronauts have replaced cowboys and Outer Space has become the new West. The notion of the Western Frontier is now regarded with nostalgia, and projections are now on the stars. Both the Frontier and Outer Space point to what is described as the Wasteland. This is a land where all the life has disappeared. It is the ghost towns of the Old West, full of ramshackle buildings and tumbleweeds. The mythic imagery has moved on to other things, leaving us to cultivate new myths. The problem lies in the fact that we have a hard time letting these images go because they are so deeply ingrained in our psyche/collective unconscious to the point of collective neurosis.

Introduction

Disneyland/Everything Else

Into this, Disneyland resides, embodying one half of the conceivable binaries, while the other half resides just below the surface, threatening to manifest and topple Disney's delicate utopia. Illustrating this is the Disneyland of 1955—the year it opened with every aspect being closely monitored by Walt Disney—and the Disneyland of 2010—the year this research project began. In the months leading to the first rough draft of this, a classic ride "mysteriously" was renovated to include safety rails that were not needed over the fifty-five years of the ride's history, a female cast member sued claiming discrimination because Disney would not allow her to wear a hijab at work, a twenty year old was hospitalized for falling twenty-five feet out of a queue, and a couple Disney employees were fired for insider trading.[14] From Main Street (the land of Utopia) to Tomorrowland (the land of Progress), Disneyland of 1955 captured the idealistic mythos arresting America, and projected it out into the greater cultural spectrum, to the point that its images are those illustrating the mythos—that Main Street is a utopia and that Tomorrow is a step of progress, linear and vertical—not cyclical, round, or any other direction and shape other than forward and up. In this way, Disneyland both embodies the cultural mythos and imagineers it; images are given to abstract ideas while simultaneously becoming the images we expect to see.

Disneyland of 1955 and Disneyland of 2010 are two entities, separated not only by time, but also by the culture influencing the Imagineers and the culture they seek to influence. In the immediate aftermath of Walt's death in 1966 until the 1980s, Imagineers tried to continue Walt's dream, often asking themselves, "What would Walt do?" From the 1980s until the 2000s, Disneyland was driven by profit and a severe business model designed and overseen by CEO Michael Eisner. Now, under the leadership of Bob Iger, Disneyland is in yet another new era trying to restore its image and reputation with major expansion and renovation. Each of these four epochs of Disney life—Walt, Post-Walt, Eisner, and Iger—influences the tone of the park and the conveyance of the park magic. Other outside factors also contribute to the park's tonality: Vietnam and Sixties counterculture, Recession and fuel crisis (Reaganomics), the stratosphere of perceived success in the 1990s, and 9/11, its aftermath, and the economic stress of debt and bad mortgages.

Why Disneyland?

Disney is ubiquitous to the American experience for a couple of reasons. First, Walt Disney and the Disney Corporation are heavy contributors to the evolution of popular culture. A little piece of Disney is present in all aspects of American culture, and Disney is at the forefront of spreading American culture to others across the world. Whether one grew up watching the construction of the park on television, living in the shadow of the park, or anxiously anticipating that coveted trip to Anaheim, Disneyland has touched many, if not all, Americans somehow. Second, Disneyland defines the hyperrealistic, four-dimensional experience that is embedded in a simulated reality. Not only are the myths and fairy tales held beloved within American culture brought to life, but the guest is placed directly into the story alongside the characters. Stories, print literature, and cinema are confined to the second dimension. Depth is added by the individual imagination. At Disneyland, those previously flat stories are brought fully into a three-dimensional experience. The imagination now becomes a fourth dimension, an abstract level that utilizes the three material dimensions to build a new imaginal realm.

The potency of Disneyland lies in its attempt to remove vestiges of reality from within the property. It accomplishes a fully encapsulated microcosm that simulates reality through fairy tale, making the fairy tale seem more real than reality. Indeed, fanatics of Disneyland perceive the park as the model for a perfect world—a utopia—and spend as much time as possible there. The same is also true of the park's Florida sister, Walt Disney World, whose property is twice the size of Manhattan Island. For non–Disney fanatics, the park is on the "bucket list" of places to visit before one's death, and is seen as a pilgrimage to be made at least once. Its cultural significance holds rank as an exemplar of America's splendor, along with New York City and its wonders, Las Vegas and its nightlife, New Orleans and its celebrations, and Hawaii and its paradise.

Furthermore, Disneyland showcases the plot of American culture. This version of the American story is built on the myths of the people who helped create the country: the pilgrims, the founding fathers, the frontiersmen and women, and the business moguls who industrialized and technologized the country. This is represented in the map of Disneyland in that the hemispheres of the past (Frontierland, Adventureland, New Orleans Square) and future (Tomorrowland) are bisected by Main Street and Fantasyland, the realms of the present: an America built into cities and themed environments, which share the frontier myths and history that made us who we are, often overlooking disparities between communities. In a single location, one can touch representations of the events that define American experience and tradition.[15]

Critics of the Disney Corporation are quick to remark upon the shallowness of Disneyland, seen as both an extension of the vastness of the corporate empire or as a unique entity, and its ability to quickly separate a visitor from his or her money. Operating under the assumption that the American experience is fundamentally mythic, the question may be asked why this particular microcosm as opposed to one with greater historic significance or, at least, less perceived controversy surrounding the corporation's capitalist, consumerist goals? The choice for Disneyland is twofold. One, Disneyland reinforces an American optimism that attempts to keep up with the ever-changing aspects of myth today. Two, generations raised since 1955 have been raised almost entirely on mass media and popular culture, with VCR/DVD/Blu-Ray players, cable television, video game consoles, and personal computers touching a large part of the population. Disneyland utilizes the symbolic language of mass communication to construct its environment, using the signs and symbols that many Americans will recognize. In doing this, it makes enculturation fun and entertaining. This is not to suggest that other mythic microcosms are any less important to the American experience, but that they are all versions of the same story.

Reassurance

As mentioned previously, America suffered a debilitating sense of doubt and fear following the Second World War. Popular culture responded to these feelings by providing some sense of reassurance, a sense that everything would be okay as long as we maintain our Americanness and stood our ground against any enemy. It was not just that Americans were wounded by the attack at Pearl Harbor, but that we also witnessed just how easily we could destroy other people (a trait pervasive throughout the nation's history but one often overlooked) with the press of a button. How easily an entire way of life could be wiped out in a flash of light. How easily someone could turn this powerful weapon back on us. The adolescent nation no longer had a parent to turn to for reassurance; the world was now looking to us for guidance and support. So we built our own reassurance. The decades following the end of World War II included the suburban boom and the advent of television.

Disney also responded to this need for reassurance by continuing to release animated features, life-action films, short cartoons, and launching a television show, all reflecting the Disney Ethic. The Disney Ethic is a particular flavor all products and personnel across the Disney brand possess, reflecting a perceived innocence and simplicity, while simultaneously entertaining children and adults. The *Disneyland* television show brought the Disney Ethic into the home of all viewers, bringing us closer to the company that had defined childhood since the 1930s. This in itself was reassuring: to see Walt Disney introduce the show with a little history behind the character or story, or to narrate an episode about the construction and ongoing "plussing" of Disneyland. But television is a poor substitute for physical comfort; thus, *Disneyland* the show showed viewers that a place of reassurance could be built, and that it was an easy vacation away.

Disneyland accomplishes reassurance through its themeing. Each land is themed around a particular motif, and variations within each land are themed around a particular attraction. For example, when someone is in Frontierland, the cast member costumes are themed around the Old West. As one moves from Big Thunder Mountain Railroad to the Golden Horseshoe, the landscape transitions from an isolated mining zone into a frontier town. As one leaves Frontierland and enters New Orleans Square, the landscape gently shifts form the Old West to New Orleans, avoiding the sharp contrast that will likely disorient a guest.

Introduction

The architecture of Disneyland is also designed to reassure. The ground floor of all show buildings is built to a standard adult scale, but each story above that is reduced by a small proportion to give us the illusion that the building is taller than it really is. This is called forced perspective, and is applied liberally throughout the park. For example, the ground floor of a building in Main Street, U.S.A., is regular height, but the second floor is to ⅝ths scale and the third floor is ⅜ths scale. Neither of these upper floors is used. Exceptions to the scaling are made when the upper floors are used for office space or, in the case of the Fire Station, living space for Walt so he could spend as much time in possible at the park. Forced perspective achieves reassurance by not dwarfing the guest with the buildings.

The characters also provide reassurance. We love them on screen, and at Disneyland can hug them in person. John Hench, Disney Imagineer, once described the reassuring nature of Mickey Mouse and the use of circles. In fact, straight lines at Disneyland are used only when necessary. Mickey's head is a circle topped with two circles, which, when viewed in a certain way, recalls an image of the archetypal Mother image ingrained in all of us. Being close to Mickey, then, is like being close to Mother. When Mickey hugs us, it is as comforting as a hug from our mother (or mother figure).

Moving Beyond the Consumption Myth

Americans lead the world in consumption in many different ways, consuming everything, including commodities, food, entertainments, education, office supplies, clothing, cleaning and beauty products, to construct a short list. One could even argue that we consume our pets, children, loved ones, and families. Additionally, there are indirect acts of consumption, such as the dishes and appliances we use to consume food, the electricity and water we consume to use gadgets or to maintain a quality lifestyle. Then there are the means of consumption such as credit cards, shopping malls, online retailers, none of which we consume directly, but are all facilitators in our consumptive behaviors. Disneyland is an example of all of the above enacted in a single place.

Disney critics are quick to claim that the only thing Disney offers is stuff to consume, thus Disney cannot provide anything of significance beyond that. On the individual level, the Disney products we consume have the potential to become avatars for how we choose to present ourselves to the world. How we wear or incorporate Disney products into our daily lives establishes publicly our relationship with Disney. On the cultural level, there are two main components to Disney consumption: Disneyfication and Disneyization.

Disneyfication occurs when a story or fairy tale is adapted into a Disney-style visual program (such as a film or television show) that is perceived as sanitized, trivialized, and remarkably less "Grimm." Critics note that this process also removes conflict and imagination making the story cute and literalized, and often the version recognized by Americans. This process takes a story and makes it acceptable for the American disposition, including emphasizing cultural mores that are not otherwise present in the "original" story. In addition to consuming the original program, Disneyfied consumption is further enhanced by merchandise tie-ins, spanning from toys to DVDs to clothing.

Disneyization refers to the impact of the Disney Corporation's business model on the larger society. Alan Bryman describes four components of Disneyization: *theming*, which entails clothing an entire environment in the same theme; *hybrid consumption*, which assumes that the form(s) of consumption is linked to the act of consumption; *merchandising*, which is the production and sale of items bearing the logo associated with the themed consumption environment; and, finally, *performative labor*, which controls and scripts the frontline employee performance to contribute to the ambiance of the experience.[16] Coupled with the McDonald's/Ford assembly line, Disneyization has created two delivery systems for consumption: the themed environment, in which a particular theme is maintained throughout the entire experience from the attitudes and behaviors of the employees to the general ambiance of the place; and the notion that consumption is a fun experience. Increasingly, businesses have turned to the specialized theme environment to compete for our attention, and increasingly they have gone out of their way to entertain us. This is, according to social commentator George Ritzer, one of the reasons why small businesses are failing in the shadow of Big Box stores; they just do not have the ability to keep us amused while we consume.

Introduction

Disneyfication functions in American mid-century culture as a normalizing force that retells familiar stories (often coming from the Old World) as versions suited to the values and norms of the contemporary American. The lasting effect of these versions of the story is not the destruction of the imagination as some critics have argued, but rather the conveyance of specific cultural values for subsequent generations, using the preferred mode of storytelling of the modern era—film. This could, perhaps, be seen as an oversimplification of Disneyfication, and no doubt many scholars in the literary community would disagree with this perspective.

Rather than criticize Disney for its modes of consumption, I would argue that consumption is a key part of the modern American experience, and one that is not going away any time soon. A connection between American democracy and consumption as a mode of empowerment dates back to the early eras of American history. From the first landings of pilgrims on the Atlantic coastline, Americans have been consuming the land. Manifest Destiny can be interpreted as a theory of consumption that pushed Americans west under the guise of a "civilizing mission." First we consume the land, and then we consume the industries that make it possible to enjoy the land, such as running water, gas/electrical power, and public transportation. Then, we begin consuming stuff. Early Mickey Mouse merchandise was not limited to only toys, but also included items people use: watches, writing tablets, drinking glasses, among many others. Tourists come to this country to buy these symbols of empowerment, such that corporations started sending their respective consumption modes abroad to simplify consumption-qua-empowerment for foreign peoples.

The danger of the Consumption Myth comes when the act of consumption turns into an addiction. This has gotten easier in the past thirty to forty years with the push of credit cards and other debt channels onto younger and younger people, thus giving them a false sense of power mixed with a permanent cycle of debt. In this respect, Disney and other major corporations are only partially to blame. At the core of our modern Manifest Destiny lies a precarious link between consumption and empowerment, the need to consume is necessary to self-definition, and educators fail to stress the risks of such attitudes and the consequent struggles of never-ending debt.

Chapter Overview

The organization of this book is inspired by the layout of Disneyland, following the assumption that the map of the park is a map of the American psyche,[17] with each land representing a particular aspect of current social/mythological/psychological trends. Any visitor of Disneyland comes with a prescribed plan for tackling the park. Some guests go straight toward their favorite attractions, while others may stroll along the paths, drinking in the Disney experience down to the very last detail. This book is arranged according to my own plan, one that has unintentionally become the primary way I approach the park. If I don't go straight to Fantasyland to ride Peter Pan's Flight or Alice in Wonderland before the lines get long, I always go into Adventureland or Frontierland first. Disneyland's West is home to some of my favorite attractions (Pirates of the Caribbean, The Haunted Mansion, The Big Thunder Mountain Railroad) but it's also home to the Rivers of America, which somehow calls to me every time I'm there.

The park experience begins with Main Street, U.S.A. (chapter 1), which reflects the current American condition, emphasizing reassurance through consumption. The American elements of doubt (New Orleans Square, chapter 3), Manifest Destiny (Frontierland, chapter 4), and Utopia (Fantasyland, chapter 5), three crucial components to the cultural identity, are separated from Main Street by expressions of the spirit of adventure (Adventureland, chapter 2) versus the spirit of progress (Tomorrowland, chapter 7). The map suggests that in order for the core elements of the American psyche to make it to Main Street and American consciousness, they must first pass through a hyperreal transmutation that likely distorts or obfuscates their true nature, yielding simulated experiences that have become real, and thus mythic, in the American consciousness.

Chapter 1, "Dreaming, Designing and Building: Background," looks at the history of Walt Disney, his studio, and their role in contemporary American myth. The intent of this chapter is to provide some background and to further introduce my method and approach to analyzing Disneyland.

Chapter 2, "Main Street, U.S.A.: The Myths of Reassurance and Nostalgia," concentrates on both the imagery of an idealized utopian

Introduction

Main Street and the myth of innocence envisioned in the small town idealized by Walt as a cultureless, sterile zone where many backgrounds come together enhancing a nostalgic memory of turn-of-the-century America. As the first land one enters, it is meant to reflect the hustle and bustle of a small town, designed to reassure the guest while simultaneously exciting typical American consumptive behaviors. Also at play in Main Street is a nostalgic feeling for an innocent past, one continually influencing American utopian ideals. This chapter also considers the impact the myths of innocence and nostalgia have had on the "Disneyization" of utopia. All three of these factors (consumption, nostalgia, and utopianism) are modern manifestations of Manifest Destiny and reflect a longing for an idealized past in the face of ever-present change in American myth. All guests must pass through Main Street, U.S.A., in order to embark on the great adventure ahead, one only accomplished by leaving home—a prevalent theme in American hero's journey.

Chapter 3, "Adventureland: The Myth of the Spirit of Adventure," defines hyperreality and establishes its context within Disneyland's interpretation of Nature. Through this understanding, the question of Disney's approach to realism is considered. This chapter also considers how Disney personifies the Spirit of Adventure and how this figure helps establish control over Nature, taking into consideration the extent to which Disney manufactures the natural atmosphere of the jungle and how it impacts the guests' relationships to nature.

Chapter 4, "New Orleans Square: The Shadow of American Doubt," looks at two of the most popular Disneyland attractions, the Pirates of the Caribbean and the Haunted Mansion, and how they provide relief from fear and doubt through caricature. Both attractions play on American shadow imagery, but do so in a way that presents it without fear. In fact, they encourage us to laugh and to love the darker aspects of culture. However, as this chapter seeks to demonstrate, the accomplishment of our amusement is a way to deal with the shadow by making it easier to consume without directly dealing with it. Befriending America's shadow, which influences doubt and promotes anxiety, Disney again provides reassurance to the anxious culture. Finally, Disney characterizes the shadow through the imagery of New Orleans, whose rich history, described below, represents a duality between the culture's perception of the city as a romantic, antebellum Southern port city opposed to a reality immersed in class and racial differences at the core of the American shadow, or the psychological locale of forgotten or selectively overlooked cultural traits.

Chapter 5, "Frontierland: The Myths of Frontier and Destiny," explores the American romantic ideal of the Western Frontier and how it was laid waste by the consumptive behaviors of Manifest Destiny, as well as how the imagery of the West reinforces American nationalism during the Cold War. Frontierland serves as homage to a crucial aspect of the American identity, one steeped in the Westward expansion and the hopes of achieving the "American Dream." By the 1950s, American imagery of the West relied on nostalgia to construct a collective memory of the legends that shaped modern America. Disneyland presents Frontierland as a tribute to these legends while also providing reassuring imagery that reinforces individualism and cowboy heroism. This chapter also considers the West and its relationship to Hollywood and how modern images of the West have transformed the Old West into a Cold War myth. By Disneyizing the Cold War through images of the Old West, Disney offers a way to conquer America's fear and anxiety.

Fantasyland represents the Myth of Utopia, which is discussed in two chapters. Chapter 6, "Fairy Tales and Happily Ever Afters," looks closely at the fairy tales that provide the central core to the Fantasyland mythos: *Sleeping Beauty, Snow White, Peter Pan, Pinocchio, Alice in Wonderland,* and *Wind in the Willows.* The Disney version of these stories maintains their fantastical settings while conveying story arcs that are relevant specifically to American culture. Each of these stories represents a conception of utopia that Americans hope to construct in their Main Streets, while demonstrating the ways in which Disneyization of fairy tales is beneficial to America and not the negative force it is perceived as by critics. Chapter 7, "Disneyfication, Disneyization and Globalization," looks at the intersection between Fantasyland's fairy tales, American utopia, and the Cold War. This chapter also considers "it's a small world" and how it functions as a fairy tale image of global culture.

Chapter 8, "Tomorrowland: The Myth of the Spirit of Progress," explores the impact of technology on selected mythologies of the culture, and how these help facilitate the construction and perception of simulated environments. To accomplish this, this chapter looks at Disney's personification of the Spirit of Progress, whose fascination with technology helped created a digital hyperrealistic world that increasingly separates Americans from the natural world and each other, making the realm of fantasy and imagination tangible in the minds of modern Americans who know of no life without computers. This chapter also addresses technological progress as a component of anxiety and its role as a homogenizing force. When Progress poses a threat, Americans get nostalgic for older technology, and this is expressed in Tomorrowland. Rather than assume that the technologies present in this land will be integrated into the daily American life, the technologies now romanticize an inner world whose images are influenced by those from outer space.

Epilogue, "After Walt: Critter Country and Mickey's Toontown," looks at the two newest lands of Disneyland and how they represent a version of America developed after Walt Disney's death in 1966, one that gives preference to a post-identity mindset and attempts to celebrate American nationalism. Critter Country and Mickey's Toontown are comic renderings of nature and Main Street, respectively, and it is through their lens that we can effectively discern new avenues of hyperreality while unveiling a renewed doubt about the possibility of the American Dream. This chapter also considers in what ways Disneyization and hyperreality affect the transition of American myth and what happens next for Disney.

1

Dreaming, Designing and Building
Background

"It all began with a mouse."—Walt Disney

Inevitably, an exploration of any aspects of Disney starts with an overview of Walt Disney's life and career. Consensus among scholars is that the two discussions (Walt Disney the man versus Walt Disney the brand) are indistinguishable because Walt was known for his micromanagement and involvement in all Disney projects to some degree. Because Disneyland was one of Walt's last undertakings, his role should not be ignored. For the purposes of my discussion, the biography of Walt Disney is a small, albeit crucial, facet for understanding the Disneyland experience and its impact on American culture: "understanding him may also enable one to understand the power of popular culture in shaping the national consciousness, the force of possibility and perfectionism as American ideals, the ongoing interplay between commerce and art, and the evolution of the American imagination in the twentieth century."[1] Very few other visionaries in American popular culture have been able to not only tap into the archetypes of the culture and give them a potent voice that many prefer over the alternatives, but to also create a feverish desire to possess, or even hoard, representations of them. He did this by creating idealized worlds that played on American utopian fantasies, from Never Land to Wonderland to Disneyland, in which "wish fulfillment prevailed, Disney has consistently concretized the ideal and provided the pleasure of things made simple and pure the way one imagined they should be, or at least the way one imagined they should be from childhood."[2] In short, Walt Disney represented a myth, both as a Horatio Alger hero and as a name associated with reliable entertainment.

Walt Disney emerged as a Hollywood-based successful animator in the 1920s. In 1923, his vision for a successful studio characterizes the Modernist era, typically described as lasting from the late–1800s through World War II in 1946, and this era's drive toward progress in reference to innovations in science, philosophy, politics and economics that both idealized and idolized industry, reflected in the attempts to abolish the "old ways" and rules of the previous eras. Walt used these new tendencies toward progress to emerge as the head of a successful animation studio.

To Walt, animation was an art form and not simply the novelty others, such as animation pioneers Windsor McCay and the Fleischer Brothers, perceived it. He regarded animation as a medium of both animation and entertainment, limited only by the animator's own imagination—and Walt's was limitless. Shortly after establishing the Disney studio, Walt Disney quickly removed himself from production and settled into a role of delegation and negotiation. As mentioned above, he personally oversaw every project of the studio, including shorts, features, marketing, and the parks, such that his employees quickly developed a love-hate relationship with Walt. They loved him because he nurtured curiosity, rarely telling someone they were not good enough. But they hated him, or at least some did, because of his powerful perfectionism and involvement in everything, perceived as creatively stifling. When Mickey Mouse was introduced in 1928, animation was already a twenty-year-old industry, but The Mouse, as he was called, was one of the most family-friendly characters offered at the time. To take animation to the next level, Walt Disney's studio was the first to synchronize sound to cartoons when he added a soundtrack to Mickey's short "Steamboat Willie" in 1929, two years after sound was added to film.

In the late 1930s, before American involvement in World War II and the release from the Great Depression, Walt again stretched the boundaries of animation by producing and releasing the first feature-length, colorized cartoon, *Snow White and the Seven Dwarfs*, based on the Grimm fairy tale. He wanted children and adults alike to enjoy it, and altered aspects of the story to make it seem less grim, partially because of budget limitations and the concerns of the animators for the types of images the viewing public would find acceptable. This started the tradition of family-friendly, literalized fantasy storytelling with concrete images that has been much criticized by modern theorists. Walt and his studio revisioned the story of Snow White into an optimistic message for the era: Snow White, symbolizing the USA, is demoted from her status of wealth by the Queen, her stepmother, representing the stock market crash. She is poisoned by the harbinger of that loss of status, the Queen turned into the Old Witch, representing the Great Depression, and is revived and rescued by a new hope characterized as her Prince Charming, the forthcoming post–War growth and baby boom.

As the Disney Studio grew in popularity during the 1930s and 1940s, fans began to ask if they could visit the studio and meet Mickey. Disney responded in 1941 with a tour of the studios in the short film, *The Reluctant Dragon.* Throughout the 1930s, Mickey Mania was sweeping across the country, inspiring the first Mickey Mouse Clubs. Disney merchandising allowed fans to own a small piece of Disney's mythos—a watch, a writing pad, hand soaps, among other household items and toys. It became clear that the interest to meet Mickey was not simply a matter of idle fascination, but, rather, a form of idol worship. In the American fashion, fans wanted to witness the embodiment of their favorite cartoon character, similar to the fanaticism of celebrity worship. The faces on the movie screens were the American gods. Mickey, a cartoon character, illustrates the anthropomorphic mythological Everyman, symbolically relatable by people and metaphorically significant as more than "just" a cartoon character. A mythological god needs a temple, and the studios were unable to satisfy this cry for myth.

At the same time, Disney legend notes, Walt was raising two girls. On Saturdays, he would take them to the park to play, but the design of the park discouraged him, a playful fellow by nature, to play with them. His thoughts on the subject "meandered along many paths before arriving at a park with the types of activities families could share in the location that we know today. His plans started out relatively small, but like all of Walt's ideas, they grew and grew and grew...."[3] He set out to create an experience: one that he believed would never be finished as long as "there is imagination left in the world."[4] Sitting on a park bench, watching his daughters play and frolic, Walt hatched a plan for a place where adults and children could play together, a place for the young and young at heart.

These two questions—where Mickey lived and where adults and children could play together—helped inform the building of Walt's utopia.

In response to the post–War anxieties that characterized the 1950s, in contrast to the popular image of this decade as a sanitized, utopian decade, where everyone is happy with their social station, completely ignoring the shadows of racial tension and Cold War, Walt Disney offered Disneyland as a utopian community of fairy tale and fantasy, allowing guests to be fully submerged into the stories of actual characters in the story, offering an escape from their fears and anxieties. Walt Disney's storytelling is controlled and contrived with the hope that each guest will experience the story in more or less the same way. Regardless of whether or not this is "good storytelling" or "a massive corporate agenda," the younger generations of Americans are exposed to this form of storytelling to a larger degree than imaginative, individual experiences, in large part because of the prevalence of mass-media culture gaining increasingly more power over the cultural psyche.

When Walt set his mind to a project, he would make it happen by any means possible. At first, he kept his plans secret from potential naysayers, nurturing his plan with only a few key people. Two challenges needed to be overcome: where to build and how to finance it. Walt hired the Stanford Research Institute to suggest some locations, until finally settling on its Anaheim home, which was then remote farm land that had yet to be sucked into Los Angeles sprawl. The design of the park evolved into its familiar form the weekend before Walt was going to meet with some investors. Locked into a studio with future Imagineer Herb Ryman over a single weekend, Walt dictated his vision to Herb while Herb committed the vision to paper, becoming the first design plan for Disneyland.

In an agreement with ABC Studios, Walt raised funds in exchange for a weekly television show. The first episode of *Disneyland*, "The Disneyland Story," aired on October 27, 1954, introducing the park and showcasing the four themed lands that would inform the content of the show: Frontierland, Fantasyland, Adventureland, and Tomorrowland. Each week's episode would show a film, series of cartoons, or an original show that would demonstrate the weekly theme. One notable example was the Frontierland-themed *Davy Crockett* serial that aired from December 1954 to February 1955, sparking the extremely popular Crockett craze and demonstrating the influence Disney had on young Boomer children.

On July 17, 1955, Disneyland opened with the festivities broadcast live on ABC. "Dateline: Disneyland," hosted by Ronald Reagan and Art Linkletter, showed Walt's dedication of the park and the various lands, introduced characters and attractions, and brought the celebration of the park into the homes of *Disneyland* viewers. Although the initial day had some kinks to work out (Tomorrowland wasn't finished yet, and vendors ran out of water), it was enough of a success to secure Disneyland's place in the American imagination.

Walt's biography is significant to unlocking the mythic function of Disneyland, because he was a character in the mythology he created. He was both author and auteur. Schickel writes that Walt Disney should be taken seriously, "because whatever the literary content of his works, however immature his conscious vision of his own motives and achievements was, there was undeniably some mystic bond between himself and the moods and styles and attitudes of this people. He could not help but reflect and summarize these things in his almost every action."[5] In sum, Walt Disney's offerings are crucial contributions to America's story that the corporation has continued to emulate since his death. Disney as a whole has provided not only entertainment, but also optimistic alternatives to the messages of crisis in the culture, attempting to maintain the American dream.

Imagination's Playground

Just a little background: I am a child of post-modern popular culture. I could identify Mickey Mouse, Ronald McDonald, and similar animated, branded characters before I could recognize the religious and political iconic images of my family and country. I am one of many such Americans. Corporations have received criticism for programming entire generations to "worship" their logos, but these same logos have molded and shaped how these generations, such as my own, look at the world and, similarly, define their mythos. This is a large centralizing factor as to why I defend Disneyland as a "sacred" space. In no other single place, except for other Disney theme parks, are the values of post–War America collected into a single bundle of energetic surroundings. Walking through Disneyland is like walking in an alternative reality. The Disney experience can be overwhelming: all aspects of the park are meant to manipulate the senses.

The trek from the parking structure to the front gates is a type of pilgrimage threshold crossing, the call to adventure for each and every guest who is brought to this specific location to start their adventure. Among the first exposures to the park are the shops in Downtown Disney: the possible souvenirs one may take home, the smells of potential meals and treats, and the music that creates an ambiance that maintains the ebb and flow of visitor traffic. All of these help root the guest into the Disney experience. From there, it is a foot walk to the ticket gates, through which one enters a liminal space. Greeted by a botanical Mickey, which is modified each season to suit the park's overall theme, guests are welcomed into the Disney space, then shepherded through two tunnels leaving the world of today and entering the world of "yesterday, tomorrow, and fantasy," completing the threshold crossing. On the other side of the tunnels is the sanctuary of Disneyland, the place where dreams come true.

Disneyland does not have a hidden narrative *per se*, but it does have the agenda for exciting the imagination. Outwardly, Disneyland is all about the commercialism, capitalism, and the bottom-line. Attendees are encouraged to interact with the products they are consuming in order to fully engage with the Disney magic despite already being totally immersed. This experience has the power to incite a general awe among those who attend and to connect guests with the Disney mythos, which collects America's values and constructs a narrative that underscores Walt's own populist and utopian vision for the country.

The Imagineers describe the park as "the physical embodiment of all that our company's mythologies represent to kids of all ages."[6] The park is an embodied experience of these myths, bringing them alive and giving them dimensional substance with which guests can interact, from getting the autograph of a beloved character to going on a ride through the story alongside the hero. Viewers' imaginations are awakened by the "Disneyfied" myths and fairy tales. Walt capitalized on a collective need for fairy tales for children and adults, and Disney brings these tales to life by attempting to illustrate them with timeless and cultureless images. For example, Mickey Mouse is essentially an animated actor, but it is his animatedness that makes him otherworldly and mythic, and able to transcend the boundaries of culture. He is an image of the imagination, and becomes idolized in Mickey-related merchandise.

One criticism would be that there is a problem to the lack of mythologizing Disneyland allows. Being such a controlled environment, there is little flexibility for the imagination to supplement Disney canon, but this should not be seen as a negative. "Prefabricated myths," as I have come to describe them, are ubiquitous in the modern era, forming the core of how stories are communicated to the culture and what we do with the story elements once we embrace them. Prefabricated myths are the stories and experiences that, regardless of their origin, have been corporatized, concretized, and transmitted across various media.

The language of myth enhances the magic behind Disneyland. It gives a language to the overwhelming connection one may feel when visiting the park and helps the guest filter through the barrage of sensory exploits, and this invites repeat visits. Instead of being a "family vacation," the visit is now an "embodied experience"; or, rather than a "consumerist capitol," Disneyland is a "mythic pilgrimage site." It is essential to observe that Disneyland draws upon all of the standard techniques of establishing a sacred space, so absolute, filed with the same images and icons necessary to "worship." While most guests can recognize that Walt was not a god, many would observe that he was a visionary, a master storyteller, who tapped into the collective imagination to fulfill the hunger of the people, so far removed from the traditional stories that satisfy their hunger for mythic narrative, provide an understanding of their role in the universe, and give an experience of the transcendent.

To best appreciate the power of Disneyland, it helps to consider that the mythmakers in any society are often the artists and poets who are able to understand the symbolic language of myth and the imagination. They are the ones who take this subject matter and make it more palatable for the average person. Mythmakers throughout human history have always "Disneyfied" stories, including or excluding story elements that may or may not be relevant to their audience. In contemporary America, the mythmakers are now the manufacturers of popular culture, and pop images now fulfill the role that myths and stories once did. Disneyland allows the myths to leave the screen, the toy store, and the page. Disneyland is only one big toy; it is also the dollhouse, play-place, and imaginal backyard all in one.

Disneyland as Mythic Space

For the American, raised in a century founded upon the rugged individualism of pilgrims, Disneyland is one of the most genuine mythic spaces. As Americans composed and compiled their mythos, our founding parents emphasized the simplicity of life and the need for hard work, rooting ritual to the family living room. Local church congregations served core as a place for social gathering. The notion of the church as solely the place of ritual and worship was left in Europe. As the country grew, local myths and spaces cropped up. The idea of mythic spaces that brought together all things American as pilgrimage sites was a new development of the 20th century. Disneyland helped serve such a purpose, because it was composed of national stories and it was transmitted to the American people through the magical ubiquity of television.

The most recent generations of American children were taught the stories of the country through media, which has long faced the challenge of what narratives to convey. These recent generations on the whole take the validity of a god image for granted, but do have a longing for the feelings of ecstasy that are a part of the religious experience. For a growing number of Americans, the most accessible myths where ecstatic feelings are found are those in popular culture, because these images are more potent and resonate loudly to our imaginations due to their familiarity from our childhoods. With everything else constantly under debate (including the validity of god, the reliability of the government, and the security of the future), pop culture images are the only images that remain constant, which offers security and is a good place for projections of the notion of religiosity.

In order to have a new mythology, we must first have a poet to express it: "A poet, in his capacity of the mediator (messenger) between sky and earth, between Gods and men, is continually bringing things into the open, showing them in their imaginal essence."[7] By this understanding, Walt Disney is such a poet as are all of the employees within the studio who work in tandem to produce the myths. The imaginal space constructed by Walt and his Imagineers is one full of images of fantasy constructed in an unnatural way, providing a detachment between the guest and the imagery that gives the mythos "autonomy, self-referentiality, and simultaneity"[8] by separating them from everyday experience while simultaneously drawing the guests' attentions to them, bringing them into the open, or conscious, realm. These images are those of the American mythos and culture that have become deeply rooted, in part, because of Disney's films: images of beloved fairy tales, idealized images of the frontier or small town, or romanticized images of the future. Disneyland allows us to experience all of those images. When coupled with the thrill aspect of some of the rides, and the playful aspect of others, the park experience brings about catharsis, and the anxieties and tensions of a culture confused about its own mythology are released by the drops and twists of roller coasters or in the story rides that insist that there is a better tomorrow on its way.

Disneyland constructs its narrative by controlling, or attempting to control, every aspect of the experience, and thereby limiting how we interact with the environment. This aspect of control raises the question whether Disney actually provides a mythic experience, or if it only provides the illusion of such an experience. If it indeed provides a mythic experience, how can we have an individualized experience in a commercial environment that is based entirely on familiar images taken from the studio's opus? There is evidence throughout the park of guests attempting to assert their independence against the control. One notable example can be found in the trees that line the queue of Indiana Jones Adventure: Temple of the Forbidden Eye. The first half of the queue is situated outside the ride entrance, and is decorated to look like the jungle surrounding a ruined temple. All along this stretch of the queue, people have carved various messages, mostly their initials, into the trunks of the bamboo trees growing there. For some of these trees, this has resulted in entire patches of missing bark. This idle destruction of the trees is evidence of how we "prefer to busy ourselves in asserting our identity against the world without realizing that this self-assertion, this search for identity, is nothing more glorious than a futile attempt to remain the same from moment to moment...."[9]

One scathing critique against Disney is that they trump the imagination by providing literalized images of characters and settings of familiar stories. Disney and Disneyland have literalized images, and that cannot be denied. When hearing a fairy tale, those raised on the Disney imagery imagine the story using the same visualization as the Disney film, and are often surprised to find the stories are not the same. This should not, however, be seen as a negative reflection on Disney, but rather a negative reflection on American culture as a whole. For instance, the recent generation now labeled the Millennials is one raised on static, literalized images from major corporations and the Internet, the outlets transmitting cultural myths. The imagination is discouraged in all educational sectors from running free on the perception that an imaginative person cannot find a well-paying job.[10] The Internet is full of examples of people using their creativity, because the demands of society and the restrictions of corporate control cannot stifle the fundamental need of humanity to play. The need for play emerges from a necessity, which forms an "essential component of the imaginal psyche itself."[11] This necessity, inherent in the images we play with, is tied to their essential nature. They emerge to fill an archetypal void created by suppressing play. But with enough suppression on a cultural level, literalized images are necessary to remind us how to play and dream.

Disney's efforts have helped breathe new life into images that have resisted change for generations. It is an error to suggest that the only way to restore a perceived golden era is to adhere to the older images as some sort of symbolic Truth. There are no rules as to how archetypal images manifest, but they do need new faces in order remain relevant. Relying on the same faces that are 3000 years old is arguably what led us to the existential crisis of the twentieth century in the first place, and we would not be having this discussion if the older images still had relevance.

Mickey Mouse and friends do not possess religiosity in the traditional sense, but they nonetheless fulfill the need for some sort of figure to be in their place. Archaeologists could dig up artifacts from this culture, thousands of years from now after our documents and records are long gone, and will encounter toys and figurines of Mickey Mouse, or even Barbie or Star Wars toys, and what will they think? The only logical conclusion is that they are objects of religious importance (similar to how modern archaeologists have interpreted prehistoric artifacts), and that they were probably worshipped as some kind of god. It is for this reason that it is important to embrace new mythologies of all categories, since they are the ones that will be remembered. Disney is only one mythos among the many emerging these days.

Because of this control, Disney constructed an environment that is not natural. Although it may appear natural, the plaster and wood, concrete and foreign plants, serve as reminders that nothing is natural about Disneyland. One could even argue that Disneyland is one of the most unnatural places in the United States. From the second a guest drives onto the Resort or steps off the tram, he or she is inundated with images, music, and this highly controlled—hyperrealistic—environment designed for the purpose of eliciting a good time. Granted, it can be observed that several people, especially parents and their children, look unhappy, but this is more due to exhaustion and sensory overload than actual unhappiness, which is not allowed by design. Disneyland is not simply a popular place for family vacations, but it is the one place, a kind of Mecca, for people to engage with the imaginal worlds of their childhood. In short, it is the hot spot for the projections of the American imagination. In being such an unnatural environment, it becomes the most natural American playground.

As with the phenomenon of the mirage, which is an illusion of displaced and distorted natural images, the reality of the place differs from the perception of it.[12] The Disney park is not itself an illusion, but the design of the park and its play on the senses is. Through the efforts of the Imagineers, it sometimes appears as though magic really does happen, that birds can talk and sing, or that a little fairy dust can make one fly to Never Land. It is thus necessary to read Disneyland as a fairy tale, as a narrative with all of its literary and metaphorical implications, not just as an abomination of nature, as critics are wont to proclaim. Disneyland may embody capitalism, but the park is a playground for the imagination. It allows people to interact with the stories and characters they love, themselves the products of imagination, and thus embody the closest thing to a mythological canon American culture has to offer.

Perhaps one of the most essential aspects of Disneyland is that it allows a person to fully embody and be submerged into fantasy fairy tale such that the stories not only become a three-dimensional reality, but the guest actually becomes a part of the story. This experience of embodiment is a missing element in modern American society.[13] Americans have culturally become so removed from nature that our behaviors do not readily support any degree of return. We recognize the body as a well-oiled machine and technology as a means of enhancing that machine. As we become more and more reliant upon technology as a society in the modern era, Americans value nature less and less. Similarly, myths and fairy tales have been likewise distanced from us, perceived, at least until the recent resurgence in children's and young adult fantasy, as escapes from reality, not as significant contributors to imaginal life. The revival of fantasy and fairy tale is seen in the mid-twentieth century as a necessary component for a healthy imagination. Depth psychologist Marie-Louise von Franz, a student of C. G. Jung, suggested that fairy tales are essential for connecting with the archetypes of the unconscious, because they are the most fundamental manifestations of unconscious material. Mythologist Joseph Campbell makes a similar argument for the study of mythology as more than a literary form, elevating the stories to a sacred level by underscoring their importance as roadmaps of human history, humanity, and humanistic thought. While the faces of fairy tale and fantasy have changed since the mid-century, bridging the gap between anonymous short story and epic-proportioned mythology, they nonetheless continue to bear the essential element of an Other World where animals talk, magicians roam, and the laws of natural science are ignored, which is precisely what Disneyland tries to achieve. If the fairy tale is fundamental to the imagination, and nature is an essential part of the human experience, it stands to reason that by revisioning the natural experience,

1. Dreaming, Designing and Building

Disneyland is essentially fulfilling the needs of the entire individual in mind and body.

Each land is designed to accomplish a specific atmosphere that conveys the stories in an environment closely related to their themes. Walt's vision was that each guest could step into another time or place during their visit to the park. He charged the Imagineers with creating each of these lands to be an imaginal microcosm. Guests are supposed to be unaware of the other lands while being fully focused on the one they are in, while also not feeling too cramped, crowded, and, ideally, overwhelmed by the experience. The following chapters look at each of the lands from symbolic perspective, but for understanding the natural experience of the park, we can place the lands into three categories: Imaginal Ecosystem (Adventureland), American Mythos (Main Street, U.S.A., Frontierland, and New Orleans Square), and Imaginary Times (Fantasyland and Tomorrowland). I am excluding from this list two lands, Critter Country and Mickey's Toontown, because they are designed more as merchandising tie-ins to Winnie the Pooh and Mickey Mouse, and hold little imaginal connection with guests beyond getting to meet one's favorite character.

Imaginary Ecosystem The rides in Adventureland were inspired by a series of adventure-themed films produced by Disney in the 1950s, and they represent a conscious opposition to "urban-industrialism," or "the willful withdrawal of our species from the natural habitat in which it evolved."[14] Assuming that archaeological theories are true, and humans evolved in the African savannah, then Adventureland takes us back to that environment, protected by a large landscaping budget from the horrors of global warming. The major point of criticism on this point is that hardly anything in Adventureland is, in fact, real. All of the animals are audio-animatronic, or computer-controlled robots that can mimic actions and mannerisms of humans and animals, because that would ensure the same performance for every guest. Many of the plants are imported, but are balanced with domestic Southern California foliage, rooting the experience into familiarity, some of which are completely artificial and designed to look real. None of the stone is real, and can never erode. To fully embrace Adventureland, and this is also true of the entire park, one has to look at it through an aesthetic eye: look "at the whole appreciatively, historically, synthetically … as a spectator watches a drama."[15] Overlooking the unnaturalness, we see in Adventureland a jungle microcosm not found elsewhere in the United States.

American Mythos Civilized man "is in danger of losing all contact with the world of instinct—a danger that is still further increased by his living an urban experience in what seems to be a purely manmade environment. This loss of instinct is largely responsible for the pathological condition of contemporary culture."[16] This is precisely what the three lands of the American mythos attempt to remedy. By recreating the frontiers of the American legends, these three lands remove us from our urban existence and transport us into the imagination. That these three lands are human-made is a testament to how far American culture has evolved from the original environments that inspired these lands, and is a testament to how much the culture has changed, in that we have to consciously reconstruct these environments because they no longer exist or have faded into memory.

Main Street, U.S.A., is designed to reflect an idealized image of Small Town, U.S.A., modeled on Walt's childhood home in Marceline, Missouri. This area is forever locked in that transition between a pioneer town and a more industrialized city, and is the first guests pass through upon entering the park. Main Street, U.S.A., was conceived by Walt and designed by Imagineer Herb Ryman to reflect something they remembered from their childhoods. That Walt felt he had to build an entire street, excluding the rest of the park, reflects Walt's and America's drive for grandiosity that emerged after World War II and has become the mythic stereotype of the 1950s, one that entitles all families to own a house, have at least one car, abundant toys at Christmas, and the expectation that everyone should receive an education. At least, that was the projected ideal, and far from the actuality. This degree of grandiosity emerges when the imagination has to compensate for reality. As the world was recovering from the War and the Great Depression, it became more important for the imagination to compensate for all of the hardships experienced during those events. Opening in the summer of 1955, Disneyland was built in the midst of this collective compensation.

Frontierland harkens to a mythologized time in American history: the movement west. It glorifies mining towns and the Romantic view of an America only slightly touched by technology and unaffected by the Civil War and tensions with Native Americans and Mexico. The land is in response to the popularity during the 1940s–1970s of Westerns on television, weekend games of Cowboys and Indians, and the idolization of Davy Crockett, King of the Wild Frontier. The search for gold and other ores taint the otherwise unbroken expansiveness of the Western frontier. By projecting its ideal onto empty terrain, the American imagination sees possibility for development of itself through the development of the land, activating a "negative interiorization of nature" to the point that nature "becomes sublated in soul, the space of interiority opened up through the application of domination of itself."[17] Furthermore, the mines are images of going into the depth of the Earth and extracting pieces of her soul for our own benefit. It is important to note that the human body possesses as "irrevocable kinship to nature,"[18] and it can be alluded that by mining the earth, we are desperately trying to mine ourselves, and this is more the reason why glorification in Disneyland of the frontier serves as a reminder of the buried treasure within the imagination.

New Orleans Square imagines a more gothic side of the American mythos: the collective shadow as projected onto the port city, New Orleans, Louisiana. Since nature encompasses all archetypes, then it also encompasses negative archetypes including the shadow. New Orleans is a good setting for this because the port city brought together traders from the Mississippi, the Caribbean, and Mexico. It has never had a reputation for being a "clean" city. The primary attractions in New Orleans Square feature pirates and Grim-Grinning Ghosts, infused with a comic light-heartedness so as to not frighten guests. Nonetheless, these reflect America's shadow. The greed and conquest of pirates represent the driving force behind capitalism and globalization, and the ghosts represent the fear of death and a quest for immortality. The fear of death further reflects a cultural psyche that is "trapped in the desolation of an infinity where it finds no consolation, no remorse, no response to its need for warmth, love, and acceptance."[19] The attractions in New Orleans Square place the desolate, trapped imagination into a warmer context, especially when in conjunction with Fantasyland, which, through its immersion into fairy tale, satisfies our need for pure imaginal experiences.

Walt's Utopia

Imaginary Times The Universe "has been reaching forward toward finer orders of complexity, toward realms so subtle and complex that they can be fabricated only out of the delicate dynamics of the human imagination.... It embodies the full potentiality of all that has gone before, realizing it, expressing it. It occupies the frontier of the cosmos."[20] Fantasyland and Tomorrowland reflect time out of time. Fantasyland is not tied to any particular era, but the facades suggest imaginary pre-industrial European villages that have become the iconic settings for fairy tales: an imaginary past. Tomorrowland, conversely, imagines the technology of the future.

Fantasyland is mostly designed with children in mind and has more attractions than any other land. Visiting Fantasyland is about having an experience, rather than just a thrill. This experience helps people feel happiness and is associated with the essential experience that makes us human. The land offers a stronger flow of experience, creating an exceptional moment in life in which what guests feel, wish, and think are in harmony. One can do a literary analysis of each of the rides, as I demonstrate in a later chapter, breaking them down into their fundamental elements, indicating the totality of this land's storied attractions. This experience is indicative of the life-world, or "the world of our immediately lived experience, as we live it, prior to all our thoughts about it."[21] Guests do not necessarily pay detailed attention to the minutiae of the rides—there is a lot to take in during a short period—but they all recognize that an experience nonetheless occurs. Because of the nature of Disneyland, guests are permitted the inability to coherently describe the attraction, because the speed and detail affect a guest on a subconscious level, inviting multiple repeat visits to fully grasp the entire story. This is especially strong in the Fantasyland dark rides, which are gentle rides (i.e. not roller coasters) that transport the guest in a story-appropriate themed vehicle through the Disney version of a familiar story. There are five of these rides in Fantasyland: Snow White's Scary Adventures, Pinocchio's Daring Journey, Peter Pan's Flight, Mr. Toad's Wild Ride, and Alice in Wonderland. All but Pinocchio have been open since the early days of the park.

Tomorrowland has always showcased possible technologies of the future, and is constantly being updated to reflect technological trends. One of the lasting trends is the projected possibility of Outer Space as the new Frontier now that the historical West has, essentially, been fully claimed. One possible future in store for us shows more reliance on machines than not. Psychologist C. G. Jung prophesied that modern, Western civilization will either destroy itself or be destroyed by its over-reliance on machines.[22] Indeed, there is perhaps some truth to this doom-and-gloom future when one considers the growing (and potentially problematic) trend of the United States' gradual overreliance on machines, and how this further and further removes us from nature. It would seem from this view that there is little that can positively be derived from modern technology; however, Walt Disney was a visionary who embraced technology rather than feared it. He envisioned Tomorrowland to be at the top of attraction technology, including advances in three-dimensional video incorporated with ride-vehicles, the first indoor roller coaster that stimulates flying through outer space, and the first fully-operational American monorail. The park shows the positive use of technology for the purposes of providing a better, cleaner, safer future for the American people. This technology, the park suggests, is crucial to the success of Walt's utopian vision.

In his Disney-published series of young adult novels, *Kingdom Keepers*, Ridley Pearson describes what happens when one spends too much time in one aspect of the Disney imagination: that if one believes in something strong enough, then it can come to life through fantasy and fairy tale, and sometimes can cross into reality. In those fairy tales Disney brings to life, Pearson asks, what happens to the evil characters after the protagonists' life happily ever after? Pearson speculates that they remain active in the park after it closes, and he calls them the Overtakers. The Overtakers, bitter and hungry for revenge, threaten to engulf the park in their dark magic, the shadow side of Disney's magic. This highlights that for every positive thing, there must be some negative aspect, and that the two must be kept in balance. In the relationship between the imagination and nature, the fear is that we as a society have already crossed some sort of tipping point that has severed us from nature, from global warming to cyborgs to terrorist threats. In Disneyland, one can escape from these issues and spend some time in psyche's playground. In order to create this experience, Disney fabricated an environment completely removed from pure nature, but one built to satisfy the needs of the entire country.

2

Main Street, U.S.A.
The Myths of Reassurance and Nostalgia

"When you come to the main gate, past the railroad station, down the steps and across the band concert park, straight ahead lies a heart-line of America: an old-fashioned main street. Hometown U.S.A. just after the turn of the century. America was growing fast. Towns and villages were turning into cities. Soon the gaslight would be replaced by electricity, but that was still in the future. At this time, little Main Street was still the most important spot in the nation, combining the color of frontier days with the oncoming excitement of the new twentieth century."—Walt Disney, "The Disneyland Story"

"Main Street, U.S.A., takes you back to a turn-of-the-century small town modeled on Walt's own memories from his boyhood. It's a world at the dawn of the age of electricity, but still firmly rooted in a simpler time. Anything can be accomplished, and soon will be. It's a time and a place of boundless possibilities."—The Imagineers, The Imagineering Field Guide to Disneyland

From the turnstiles, guests face a large, manicured, botanical face of Mickey Mouse on the side of a hill on top of which sits a train station. To each side of the garden are two tunnels that lead under the train tracks, each topped with the same sign that proclaims, "Here you leave the world of today, and enter the worlds of Yesterday, Tomorrow and Fantasy." The two tunnels open into the same land, Main Street, U.S.A. Although this Main Street is clearly set in the

44

past, it looks familiar and reassuring, as though it is in fact our home-town.

Legend tells that Main Street, U.S.A., was borne from Walt's own nostalgic memories for Marceline, Missouri, a small mid-western community that housed his family for a brief period during his childhood and imprinted deep, lasting impressions on him of a feeling of home and community. Walt's memories provide the basis for his perfected Main Street. This area, while borne from Walt's childhood, represents Walt's projection about America. Many writers note that the parallels between Walt's biography and Main Street are eerily similar, but it should be noted that, in the end, the area is called Main Street, U.S.A. not Walt Disney's Main Street.

As the first area of Disneyland into which one enters, Main Street, U.S.A., is designed to root one firmly into the homely aspects of the small town before launching one on an adventure into the depths of the American Disneyfied mythos. To have the guests enter by the controlled means of the tunnels appears to have two purposes. One is the practical problem of crowd control. Walt had enough foresight to envision the potential disorientation and bedlam that greeted guests upon entry. By moving confused guests down Main Street to the Plaza Hub, he could avoid traffic build-up at the entrance of the park. The second strategy seems to be one of rooting the guests into a familiar environment before sending them forth into the unfamiliar "chimerical lands" that lay ahead.[1] By using turn-of-the-century, small-town architecture, Walt hoped to evoke a common, shared memory among the guests. If they themselves did not live in a small town, they would nonetheless be able to recognize one from family photos, television, or film. This recognition is expected to instill comfort. Art historian Karal Ann Marling calls this "the architecture of reassurance": through constructed environment Disney is able to achieve familiarity, making guests receptive to the unfamiliarity that lay ahead.[2]

Additionally, Main Street, U.S.A. serves as the conduit to the American imagination. This is why it is filled with images and architecture that evoke nostalgia and innocence. It provides a tableau of comfort onto which any person, small town or city alike, can cleanse the palette before embarking on the journey ahead while also evoking a perceived archetypal small town built on the image of a friendly community inherent in all of us.

Main Street, U.S.A., Key Attractions

- Great Moments with Mr. Lincoln (Town Square)
- The Disneyland Railroad (Town Square)
- The Cinema (Main Street)
- Shop Windows (Main Street)
- *Partners* (Plaza Hub)

Main Street, U.S.A., is a mid-century conception that best exemplifies the way in which nostalgia and innocence converge in Disneyland. On one hand, it was designed as a tribute to turn-of-the-century America, romanticizing a past that was pushed into hiding by the Depression and the post–War booms in technology, progress, and social principles. Disney was tapping into a mid-century ideal that romanticized the utopia as a clean, safe community in which one can raise children and die of old age in relative peace. This is further reflected in the attempt at suburban or urban communities that strive to make it simple to live, work, and play within the community, in contrast to the suburban sprawl that still necessitates a commute into the nearest urban center for work. This latter trend appears to be a response by recent generations for their lack of community as children and teenagers. Main Street, U.S.A., reflects a kitsch that stands as a monument that highlights the squeaky clean virtues of a simplified hard-working middle American, a past remembered only through the complicated lens of Nostalgia.

There are three subsections in Main Street, U.S.A., which have remained fundamentally unchanged since the earliest proposals for Disneyland[3]: the Town Square, which one enters first after crossing under the berm; Main Street; and the Plaza Hub at the end. There are few stand-alone, ride-based attractions inspired by turn-of-the-century transportation, but the attractions, shops, and restaurants do communicate to the guests the experience of American perceptions of home and community.

Town Square: The Culture of Consumption and the Consumption of Nostalgia

The Town Square is organized as the civic center of Disneyland. Here one finds a town square surrounded by a city hall, a firehouse, and a bank. The buildings of this area, and indeed the rest of Main Street, U.S.A., and most of Disneyland, apply forced perspective to make the buildings stand without dominating the landscape. They are tall enough to shield the guest from the rest of the park. Utilizing cinematic technique, Disney controls the guest experience as though the guest were a movie camera taking an introductory shot of Main Street, none of which is visible until Disney is ready for the guest to see it, transitioning a from narrow, focused shot to a long shot that culminates with Sleeping Beauty's Castle forming the backdrop of the Main Street vista. This strategy intensifies emotions of surprise and comfort that guests inevitably feel upon crossing the berm, the border separating Disneyland from the rest of the world, on top of which drives the Disneyland Railroad connecting all areas of the park by train.

The Town Square establishes the foundation for Main Street, U.S.A., as Disneyland's commercial center. In addition to the "administrative" buildings, the boundary between Town Square and Main Street is flanked with shops to purchase Disney memorabilia, positioned to lure guests on the way in and the way out to pick up the coveted Disney souvenir. Wearing Mouse Ears, for instance, or a t-shirt with a Disney character on it reinforces the guest's experience of the park.

Consumption and Experience In creating Disneyland, Walt created an experience. During the Michael Eisner era, as many critics note, Disney trended toward consumption, meaning that all entertainment channels from movies to the theme parks had to generate substantial merchandise revenue. Any product line that did not perform to par was quietly phased out. Eisner also oversaw the establishment of the Disney Stores and the initial construction of the foreign theme parks. However, under Bob Iger, the current Chief Executive Officer, Disney trends toward consumption as experience, which, it could be argued, is what Walt was aiming for all along. This mode of consumption still includes the push of key product lines (Disney Princesses, Pixar); yet, it also includes synergy of experience. Annual themed campaigns began with the 50th anniversary of Disneyland, which attracted a growth of visitors. They have since offered other campaigns that have included free park entrance on one's birthday or free park tickets for participating in a charitable event. For example, beginning with the 2010 season, the themed campaign, "Let the Memories Begin," encouraged families to upload their favorite Disney memory onto a promotional website. The pictures were then shown during a special show during the nightly fireworks. The consumption contained in this campaign is the idea of consuming memories before one has a chance to form them. This mode of consumption is further linked to the recent expansions of the Disney Cruise Line and the opening of their Hawaiian resort, Aulani.

The presence of these two levels of consumption at Disneyland, merchandising and experiential, suggests that the experience of consumption is a fundamental aspect of American culture, a byproduct of larger incomes coupled with more free time, such that parents are encouraged to connect the ideal of normal childhood with the act of consumption.[4] We have built a culture of consumption, and this culture is closely related to Disneyland.

In laying down his theories about consumption, philosopher Jean Baudrillard suggests a connection between a growth culture and consumption. A growth culture occurs whenever a society is focused on achieving collective Happiness. This is not an unworthy task—even Thomas Jefferson advocated for the pursuit of Happiness in the Declaration of Independence. Baudrillard observes, however, that the quest for Happiness turns into the quest to fulfill the "myth of Equality."[5] Within American society, the myth of Equality and its sister, the myth of Democracy, are transferred to "an equality before the object and other *manifest* signs of social success and happiness."[6] A growth culture, then, allows everyone access to the tools they need to achieve happiness. Consumption sociologist George Ritzer further expands the idea of consumption as a means of enchantment, keeping Americans entertained and consuming. Recently, modes of consumption have entered into a competitive race for American customers to the point that they have needed to become flashier and more elaborate. Building on the Disney model, non–Disney consumerist places have become more elaborate, from shopping malls to tourist attractions, to lure consumers. Because many of these places are destinations, they further blend happiness with consumption.

With the pursuit of happiness comes an imbalance between the proverbial "haves" and "have nots," which leads to a rise in a poverty defined solely on one's ability to consume the tools of happiness. It then becomes the goal of this society to eliminate poverty. But rather than revise social policies, the tendency according to Baudrillard is to ignore uncomfortable social issues, because acknowledging poverty forces us to evaluate the system by questioning its validity and whether it will work. Instead, it is far easier to maintain poverty as a *"visible phantom"* and preserve the consumerist myth of growth.[7] Disney caters to the visible phantoms of poverty through its merchandising practices. Owning Disney merchandise is meant to be an equalizing agent. While not all families can afford a fancy video game console or even a nice car, they can afford a Disney-related toy or clothing. There are some aspects of the merchandising that highlight disparities between social classes, such as collectable items, but that has never been a barrier to enjoying Mickey Mouse and other Disney friends. Beyond such acknowledgment, poverty does not play a role within the Disney universe, favoring a generic, middle- or upper-middle class to reinforce a homogenized utopian view of America.

Consumption and Nostalgia Nostalgia and utopianism are both Romantic concepts that play significant roles in American myth. Nostalgia is "a longing for a past that cannot be reclaimed and that possibly never existed in the first place. And utopianism is a longing for an ideal future that will never be seen and may never exist. Both nostalgia and utopianism therefore show evidence of a desire for transcendence, as well as an external anxiety concerning mortality and the present."[8] This anxiety stems from a cultural flashback of the events of World War II that fueled Cold War fears that insisted on recognizing the past, to look backward in order to find the moments that help explain the present.[9] Disney responded to these fears by constructing an Americanism that respects the past and becomes an instrument for the national identity.[10] Because Americans were hungry for the release from their anxiety, they fell to consuming expressions of nostalgia. Nostalgia suggests that the past is over and no longer exists,[11] but Disneyland reinvents and reimagines the past through the lenses of the present, intentionally presenting the past as a reassuring option to the present.

Much of the understanding of American nostalgia pertains to cultural memory: how we remember the past and the filters we build to keep the memories we treasure. While each person's memories are arguably unique to them, two dominant themes stand out: the memory of the past as a Golden Age when everything was "better" than it is today, and memory borne from trauma, remembering key events in a negative light. Both aspects are at play within the entire culture. Americans revere the Frontier or the Turn-of-the-Century as Golden Eras, even romanticizing the violence of cowboys and gangsters as contributions to the ambiance. These images serve to remind us that American myth is in itself a memory—"a memory of the lives and actions, the beliefs and efforts, of millions of human beings who have lived in American spaces, participated in an American social world, and died Americans."[12] Inherent within the persistence of American memory are the many perceived self-evident truths that help reinforce national identity, and explain the country's form, function, and the lives of its citizens. Through memories of the place and people, Disneyland helps also to communicate behavior,[13] through the architecture, emphasizing not only what nostalgia for America once was, but also what it is to be American and play a role in the overall dream.

The cultural memory that Disneyland recreates is a side effect of television, through which Hollywood was able to cheaply retell stories of the past such that the stories ultimately replaced the actuality of the memories. This is especially notable with Westerns and family television that built a sense of what Main Street should look like. In the 1950s, "our national longing, during those postwar years, was for [...] a fantasy that, with each successive year of removal of the postwar people from an ever-diminishing real thing, small-town America was mentally configured into a golden age."[14] This gave birth to the nostalgia craze that has grown and festered such that the cultural memory is dominated with images of what we wish had been rather than what actually was.

Cultural memory is built into the myths and legends of a particular social group. These stories may or may not be "true" in the historical sense, but they are often retold to convey a sense of culture to the new generation. This cultural memory bonds us together. Within the American memory, there are two levels of cultural influence: there are the myths and legends of westward expansion, rugged individualism, cowboys, and Native Americans, but there is also the immigrant culture, bringing with it memories of the Old World. These deep-seeded memories help shape our acceptance of some fundamentally American myths:

the image of the cowboy riding alone is an image in American heroic mythology. It is available to Americans: it comes to their minds easily, in many variations; it is rich in associated images and ideals; it grows from thousands of tellings and retellings—in stories, movies, television programs, history books, children's play—of cowboy stories which are part of life in America. Almost intuitively, Americans know it explains American loneliness, independence, conviction, and the need for approval, while at the same time it reconciles some of the contradictions among those characteristics.[15]

Absent are Native American myths, seen more as hindrances to the perceived natural order, thus they were shoved in corners and collectively ignored. This is not to discount their influence. The Native American connection to the virgin American landscape was a valuable tool in unlocking her secrets.

It was the myths and legends unique to the American experience that influenced and interested Walt Disney. Disneyland was created in response to cultural memory, housing many of the key memories that have now faded into the realm of myth and legend: Adventureland explores a native jungle, while Frontierland recreates a modern environment for guests to reenact the founding of the West. In Disneyland 1955, these memories included a tour of the Old West on mules or stagecoaches, an Indian Village with regular dance performances, and the Golden Horseshoe that showed Old West shows on a stage resembling an old saloon, all of which were housed in Frontierland. Main Street was always intended to evoke a turn-of-the-century Main Street right when America moved from gas light to electric light, playing on an American memory that by 1955 was already beginning to fade. Immigrant stories were mere distractions from the whitewashed pride and nationalism Walt poured into his work. Although many of the Disney stories, especially the feature films, are based on Old World stories, Walt offered a translation, sometimes by accident of circumstance, which made it an American story. The studio also retold American folk talks, such as Paul Bunyan and Pecos Bill, Johnny Appleseed and Zorro, idolizing historical figures such as Ben Franklin, Davy Crockett, and Daniel Boone. Historical or fictional, Disney celebrated and celebrates their contributions in shaping America, recalling images from the cultural memory to keep the memory alive.

Great Moments with Mr. Lincoln is an excellent example. Located in Town Square just northeast of the Main Street Station in the Opera House, Great Moments with Mr. Lincoln was commissioned by the State of Illinois for inclusion in the state's booth at the 1964–1965 New York World's Fair. Walt saw this project as an excuse to have his Imagineers develop audio-animatronic figures, robotic figures that move with the near fluidity and clear sound as human beings. He was inspired by toy automatons he had acquired in Europe, and saw the storytelling potential of these figures for his controlled, Disneyland environment. Beyond the Fair, Mr. Lincoln was conceived to be one among all presidents, a concept that eventually manifested as the Walt Disney World attraction the Hall of Presidents. The Illinois booth was also Walt's opportunity to also pay tribute to the other state he called home during his youth, and to a president who embodied many of Walt's ideals.

Abraham Lincoln was the sixteenth president whose historical legacy is for being the president in the unique position of governing a divided country through the Civil War, who oversaw the abolition of slavery, who spoke at Gettysburg, and who was assassinated by John Wilkes Booth while visiting the theater. He paved his own path, emerging from the Illinois countryside in pursuit of personal betterment and education. As a tall man, Lincoln is remembered as being larger than life. He demonstrated that the common person was indeed capable of greatness, something near and dear to Walt's own biography.

He was also a brilliant orator capable of stirring the masses using short, succinct speeches in which he was able to intuit the future of America, often making cautionary statements promoting the furthering of liberty. His greatest concern was for the best interest of America, and he demonstrated as much throughout his presidency. Through the technology of audio-animatronics, Walt and the Imagineers brought Lincoln back to life, but with an emphasis on his humanness. Great Moments with Mr. Lincoln recounts how the Civil War broke apart families, an ongoing metaphor for America, followed by a speech that is just as relevant in Lincoln's time as it is now. He is troubled by the state of the nation, struggling with it, finally taking a stand calling for union. The theme of union is prevalent throughout Disneyland, and it is a crucial element of the Disney Utopian Ideal. Lincoln's emotions are apparent through his delivery, and perhaps mirror emotions felt within the Disney studio. The Imagineers programmed subtlety into

Lincoln's facial expressions. He begins his speech tapping his fingers on his chair and sighing. When he stands, this is not only a triumph of technology, but also a triumph of America taking a stand to reinforce nationalism, and unite us despite of our differences.[16]

In creating this attraction, Disney fueled the Lincoln myth, giving expression to ever-present concerns in current American culture through Lincoln's words. Lincoln's voice became the voice of American nationalism, expressing the vision that the individuals were all a part of a whole, that the nation could be "all one thing."[17] Lincoln's speech, spliced together from several of his speeches, offers as much hope for Cold War America as it does for an America afraid of terrorism, opening at a time when Americans were searching for a unified national identity, a problem at the center of mid-century anxiety.[18] American nationalism projects this image onto the president, seen as a sturdy representative of American individualism.[19]

Whereas Great Moments with Mr. Lincoln speaks to a cultural memory, the Disneyland Railroad illustrates how nostalgia works on a personal level. Walt Disney was a railroad enthusiast. He adopted the hobbies of model railroading and miniatures collecting when his doctor told him that a hobby would help relieve some of his stress. This eventually led to a backyard garden railroad, which eventually supplied the inspiration for the Disneyland Railroad.[20]

By the time fan letters arrived at the studio asking to see where Mickey Mouse lived, Walt had been considering a mobile attraction of Old Timey miniatures on a railroad tour. To have a permanent home for people to visit, a park seemed a more practical solution to balance the flow of expected visitors projected from the fan mail and the cost of operation. Though the park concept grew and morphed over several years before construction was implemented, plans always involved a railroad.[21]

The Santa Fe and Disneyland Railroad, now simply the Disneyland Railroad, circles the park on top of the berm. The Main Street Station serves more as the park's front-piece sitting on top of the botanical Mickey that greets entering guests, and is experienced before one actually enters the park, and less as an integral part of Main Street, U.S.A. However, one finds that the Main Street Station is just as significant to the impact of the Main Street experience, as it is the first example of the "architecture of reassurance" that the guest sees, invoking an era when many towns were only accessed by train (or stagecoach), a time before highways and air travel. Many small towns, including Walt's Marceline, were built as service points for early modes of transcontinental transportation.[22]

The American mythos with its focus mainly on the present and the future to the point of omitting the "actual richness of American history,"[23] leads to a sense of rootlessness, noting the constant movement of many Americans, which in turn leads to loneliness.[24] This lack of historical connection makes a discussion about nostalgia seem paradoxical. Nostalgia involves a constant reflection on the past, the very thing we seem to be moving from; although, eventually, we reach a point, a "destined time," when the cry for myth, or when the nostalgia, leads to historical events in response to the restlessness of the people. A historical event helps root the myth and give it meaning.[25] There are plenty of incidents during the 1950s and 1960s to satisfy the cry for a multitude of mythologies. The history of the era testifies to a paradigmatic shift. Disneyland, it seems, set the parameters for a defined myth of nostalgia. Most of the Disney projects portrayed in the park were contemporary in tone despite their setting in "a land of long ago and far away." The disparity in setting is meant to allow contemporary themes and issues to stand on their own without the muddied perspective of their real-life settings, and this appears to be a completely unconscious endeavor by Walt Disney and his crew. As artists, the medium of animation allowed them to speak directly to and from unconscious material. So naturally, as Walt and his crew themselves began to experience nostalgic longings, they used the medium to explore it further, found it limiting, and created a new medium to explore it. This coincided in a cultural need for the same. Indeed, in the years following the war, American use of and reliance upon media shifted from either informational or entertaining to a fusion of the two, sometimes blurring the fact from the fiction. Walt called this "edutainment."

The need for nostalgia stems from America's constant search for utopia that, after almost 200 years as a sovereign nation, still had not been found. The conquest of America was made possible by the optimism borne from Renaissance humanism[26]: The founding of the United

States was the response to the cry for myth that brought the end of the Middle Ages and the beginning of the Renaissance. America became the symbol for the rebirth of western humanity, because it was a land without "the sin or evil or poverty or injustice or persecution which had characterized the Old World."[27] Our intentions for this New World utopia were made clear almost the second the first pilgrims landed on Plymouth Rock; however, the rugged terrain of America was unwilling to yield so easily. The harshness the pilgrims encountered threatened to debunk the idealistic hopes for the perfect utopia, but the myth was strong enough to move the country forward.

The nostalgia of the 1950s for a utopian America was fueled by a socio-political climate that cried for a reminder of the national identity. At the core of that national identity, however, lies individualism. America's rugged individualism, unique in many ways to this country within the larger context of world history, runs counter to aspects of the human tendency for a connection to community and ritual. The tension between community and individualism manifests as defiance. American myth is built on stories of defiance, because this "implies the challenge and the thrill of a child deliberately disobeying what must have been a parental injunction, or deliberately destroying something that the parent presumably treasures."[28] So pervasive is this plot that part of an American's identity formation hinges on an act of defiance, breaking away either from family or culture by destroying whatever ties hold them in bondage.[29] Without this defiance, rugged individualism cannot happen. American community is formed of individuals united to a common cause: the establishment of a democratic, free market, utopia. This is a theme that appears throughout Disney's work: the hero defies the expectations and commands of his or her supposed superior. In the case of Pluto (a dog who should always obey its master) or Donald Duck (who revels in his "innocent" malevolence), the defiance never ends well. For others, such as Mickey Mouse, the defiance can result in some kind of punishable offence ("Sorcerer's Apprentice") or it can result in happiness and romance ("Steamboat Willie"). Disney allows defiance to serve as a dominant theme throughout his live-action films inducing a major paradigm change, suggesting that it is fundamentally essential for social change to occur so we, as a culture, do not stagnate.[30] Furthermore, this defiance is linked intimately with the quest for success, or "the hoped-for outcome of the pursuit of happiness."[31] Success cannot occur without risk.

Our commitment to all things "new" enables constant change, leaving us hungry for the thing we left behind, or at least giving us a sense that we did leave something behind even if we cannot identify what it is, thus the feelings of nostalgia. Although automobiles and planes replaced the railroad as primary transports, it still carries a symbolism of being able to conquer a harsh terrain, of the promise for change and adventure, and of the memory of a historic past when travel was slower than it is now. The Disneyland Railroad, then, serves as a pastiche to the national past, but resonates with the longing of a personal change, of the constant movement of the lonely, rugged individual.

Main Street: Consuming Innocence, Building Utopia

Just north of the Town Square is Main Street, the busy turn-of-the-century small town commercial center of Disneyland. The attractions on Main Street are primarily shops and restaurants, places where one can purchase all sorts of Disney memorabilia, eat lunch and people-watch, or simply admire the décor, including the shop-front window displays that change every season and the Main Street windows that honor the Imagineers and others who contributed to Disneyland's development. In one corner, guests can overhear a man sing in the shower or take a nap. Transport vehicles such as horse-drawn surreys, horseless carriages, and an omnibus for sightseeing run up and down the street transporting guests from the Town Square to the Plaza Hub. While dozens of businesses have come and gone, this area has remained the least visually changed of the entire park.[32] Shops have ranged from traditional main street shops, including a lingerie store and a tobacconist, when outside businesses could sublet space to help finance Disneyland, to eventually becoming shops that are exclusively Disney.

Main Street has inspired other commercial districts. In recreating the main street Disney remembered, he embellished and improved upon it, creating an idealized locale where "everything sparkles, runs perfectly, stays fresh," much like bringing a movie set to life.[33] The cleanliness of Disney's main street gives it the feeling of safety that can induce a relaxed affect that can lead to carelessness, sometimes with the end result of pick-pocketing or lost children.[34] This sense of safety can also induce nostalgia for the innocence of a lost childhood.

The myth of innocence is linked to the myth of nostalgia, such that the two often go hand-in-hand. Innocence is associated with childhood, a lack of corruption, and ways of looking at the world with wonder. It is also associated with a lack of stress, calmness, and simplicity. As a social myth, it is played out in Disneyland through Main Street, U.S.A., and its architecture. Innocence here becomes the utopian ideal: the architecture, cleanliness, and cooperation in this area between pedestrians, automobiles, and commerce, have inspired non–Disney community development projects seeking to emulate Main Street, U.S.A. Innocence in Main Street also suggest a unified world in which all people are treated the same—as American consumers.

The evolution of Disney's portrayal of innocence is worth noting. The earliest Disney projects—*Alice Comedies, Oswald the Lucky Rabbit*, and the early Mickey Mouse shorts, a few of which are played repetitively at the Main Street Cinema—were made with the audience in mind. They were never sexually explicit in the name of good taste, but they do depict situations that would offend parents today, such as Minnie Mouse dancing cabaret, Oswald trying to sneak into a cabaret saloon, or characters actively pulling the pants off of other characters revealing that they are not wearing undergarments. Additionally, because they were products of this era, many of these old cartoons portray racial stereotypes that are not appropriate today, such that Leonard Maltin, series host of the *Walt Disney Treasures* DVDs, prefaces each of the cartoons with a disclaimer that their value today is to understand the past so we can see how far we have evolved as a culture. When the Hays Production Code was implemented in 1930, all film entertainment cleaned up its act, Walt took it upon himself to target the entire family with scenes of love, success, and reward, creating Mickey Mouse as a sort of Everyman figure, who was so popular that his short cartoons often were given top billing over the main feature.[35] This set the Disneyized standard of innocence to this day.

Corporate Responsibility Disney innocence is challenged by commentators such as Henry Giroux or Carl Hiaasen who consider the far-reaching nature of the corporation as reflecting less than innocent intentions. Giroux explicates a critique against the Disney Corporation suggesting that Disney innocence is in fact an illusion, conveying predatory practices, from advertising to merchandising.[36] In response, he encourages pedagogy that will help people become more conscientious consumers. This critique on Disney's perceived innocence stems from Giroux's own observation that while the images presented on the screen are perceived as wholesome and family-friendly, they are, in fact, riddled with innuendo and adult humor, and marketed to a demographic who lack the resources to tell the difference. The implication is that Disney's motives are only innocent on the surface, and should be better understood and recognized by an informed population alerted to Disney's corporate practices. Additionally, Disney's intentions seem fundamentally malicious and intent on taking over the global market.

While it is true that all corporations have designs on expansion, they can only do so when permitted by the people and government. In describing the mythology of corporations, American historian James Oliver Robertson notes that

> every giant corporation has been *created* by a single individual.... That myth lives still. The great corporation becomes, in the logic of the myth, the living, *immortal* extension of all the characteristics and dynamics which belonged to the individual who created it. A corporation is, in this American mythical perception, *a single individual*, able to act on a national, even on a worldwide scale, vastly powerful, ruthless, efficient, greedy, and ambitious. The individual is living metaphor for the corporation; and, in the peculiar way of myths, the corporation has become a metaphor for the individual.[37]

Robertson suggests a connection between the pursuit of happiness (inextricably linked with success) and corporations in that corporations provide the structure and organization of happiness.[38] This suggests that corporate expansion is fueled by the cultural psyche, that our happiness is tied to our success, which is further tied to the success of corporations, whose own success is tied to expansion and global presence. In this way, Disney's motives reflect the American identity and the mission of expansion through dedicated hard work and ideological conversion. Corporate greed and expansion are this era's Manifest Destiny. As long as the American people continue to support corporate globalism and personhood, all corporations will continue to thrive as though they were individuals. The Disney image of a unified culture resembles that of a corporation: all individuals play their part in contributing to the corporation's overall mission.

In a way, the Chief Executive Officer, the leader and representative for an entire corporation who successfully magnetizes the consumer to its product, can be seen as a sort of cult leader. In the case of Disney, this CEO is supplying us with images of a utopian paradise, filled with the immediately recognizable images of Mickey Mouse and his friends. The same hopeful image of a successful leader that was once placed on a president, that of an effective individual who maintains control over the fate of Americans,[39] is now placed on the CEO who is accountable for any actions of the entire company. CEOs are now recognized as heroes along with presidents, from Walt Disney to Steve Jobs, encouraging a devotional fan base; they are also villainized, some inciting a regime change in the corporate leadership (Michael Eisner) and others bringing down the entire company (such as Kenneth Lay of Enron).

Building Utopia When Thomas More published *Utopia*, explorers were sending home to Europe reports of the Americas. *Utopia* invited the possibility that a utopia could actually be built. The Americas, for their resources and wilderness, were perceived as potential places for a utopia, a perception that drove colonization projects.

By constructing a familiar, concrete place, Disney is acknowledging a relationship between Americans and the desire for utopia. Because the country was founded on utopian ideals, the optimistic image of a unified, peaceful Eden, has become enmeshed in the American imagination, informing our relationship to Main Street, U.S.A., as a modern Eden. Of course, this utopian ideal suggests that all peoples are welcome, but was constructed under a familiar paradigm for white, middle/upper class Protestants, without overt religious connotation. Indeed, there are no churches or other houses of worship inside Disneyland. This was a conscious decision, in order to keep Disneyland open to all creeds. The Main Street Cinema poses as the closest thing to a church within the park. From the outside, one is invited by the marquee and the old-fashioned ticket booth. On the inside, six screens run simultaneously around a circular platform, playing early Mickey Mouse shorts, silent and black and white. The room is almost silent, as though the cinema creates an almost church-like setting, inviting guests to revere Disney's beginnings and celebrate the Mouse, giving reverence to the archetypal figure Mickey Mouse. The silent Mickey shorts are a testament to the universality of this image in that they are not hindered by sound, language, or any other cultural barriers. They are pure cinema, communicating through pantomime to all viewers.

Utopia, however, cannot work in the "real" world, and many such experiments have failed largely because they suppressed the individual's quest of happiness in service to the society.[40] For a utopia to work, it needs absolute commitment from all parties involved, leaving no room for individual thought or expression. Popular culture since the turn of the century has questioned the utopian ideals of the American Dream versus America's individualism, ultimately concluding that a utopia could not work on grounds that it forces communal control on its population, describing this as the point when utopia turns into dystopia. Disney is infamous for its amount of control, from the strict dress and conduct codes of its employees, protection of the Disney brand, and its expected behaviors of the guests. Disney also exerts control over the guest's experience, guiding the paths one takes through the park, what souvenirs to buy, even, to an extent, when to use the restroom. This is why one cannot live in Disneyland, because it would fail as a utopia due to the amount of control it imposes over the experience. Disneyland residents would eventually want a return to the "real" world so they can experience their individualism. Plus, Walt's vision did not favor limiting the population to an elite; he wanted all to have the opportunity to benefit.

Towards the end of his life, Walt outlined plans for a utopian community that would have formed the basis for the Walt Disney World project. He called this community EPCOT, or the Experimental Prototype Community of Tomorrow. With Disneyland, he implemented the vision of ideal mythscape, but quickly became disheartened when seedy hotels plagued the area surrounding the park. When he bought the land in Florida, he purchased enough land to help him fully actualize his utopian dream. In the 1966 promotional film, *EPCOT*, Walt presents plans for his utopia. Borrowing from the image of a wagon wheel, EPCOT[41] was designed with the commercial center in the middle, with residential districts radiating off like spokes. Trash and traffic were kept away from the main view of the people with the intent of promoting safety and recreation, especially for children. Monorails and WED-Way People Movers would transport residents to and from school or work in the center or in the adjacent industrial area. His plans suggested a fully self-sustainable, eco-friendly, community-centered environment. These plans did not come to fruition, but many elements are at play within Walt Disney World, its nearby community Celebration, or have been implemented by city planners trying to achieve New Urbanist utopian communities.

The dream for EPCOT laid groundwork for bringing the myth of utopia into the real world, offering hope for a brighter, cleaner tomorrow. Whether because of the magic of television or because of ever-growing nostalgia, the idealistic dream that was EPCOT gained potency as people genuinely believed that utopia could be constructed in the real world: "what once sufficed no longer does. People used to be satisfied with an afternoon on Main Street, U.S.A. Now, they want to live there."[42] It is no longer satisfactory to suspend our disbelief temporarily, but, as Douglas Brode suggests, we need to suspend it permanently.

Walt's utopian visions have been credited for the Disneyization of community and cityscapes.[43] This movement, regardless of its Disney connection, is known as New Urbanism as "a reform movement emphasizing physical design as a tool to improve the quality of life of urban and suburban areas [...] promoting housing and urban development projects to mitigate sprawl, to facilitate infill development, to support regional development patterns that facilitate walking and transit, and to encourage sustainable growth sensitive to environmental quality, economy and social equity."[44] Ideally, a New Urbanist community places garages behind or separate from the house to keep cars off the same streets on which children frequently play. The houses are designed with inviting porches and the neighborhoods include community amenities that promote community interaction. Ideally, residents can walk or commute to work or school by a variety of public transport options. New Urbanist principles respond to the weakening influence of neighborhoods and the commodification of public space.[45] Unfortunately, the New Urbanist model relies on neighborhood control resting in the hands of an outside entity, or a limited association of homeowners, rather than trusting the individual homeowner to maintain the standard. This control is exemplified in an interview Walt gave concerning EPCOT: "there will be no slum areas because we won't let them develop. There will be no landowners, and therefore no voting control."[46] Indeed, Home Owners Associations utilize outside management companies to enforce their policies.

In an interview with Leonard Maltin for the *Tomorrowland* collection in the *Walt Disney Treasures*, Ray Bradbury, noted science-fiction writer and consultant for Tomorrowland and EPCOT, describes Walt as an "optimistic futurist."[47] Bradbury notes that the aftermath of World War II brought an influx of new technologies to the American consumer, amidst lingering social tensions that formed the crux of the Cold War. Additionally, America witnessed the first wave of decline in community, attributed to both new technologies that made home life more enjoyable (notably, air conditioning), and post-war suburban development and the ease with which families could purchase a house in exchange for removal from urban centers.

Walt Disney, on the other hand, firmly believed that his utopia could coexist with modern technology, calling for a separation of automobiles and industry from the central core of the community but not completely banned. He believed that we could have all of the modern conveniences while cultivating the community. There is some nostalgia at play in this ideal, and arguably this reflects Walt's own nostalgia for a small-town life eclipsed by his residence in Los Angeles, exemplar of sprawl. But, as one of the first New Urbanists, Walt believed in harmony between the two ideals of nostalgia and progress. We can observe that "a half century after Disneyland's inception, it is safe to say that few urban spaces remain untouched by the Disney effect. The effect constitutes a radical shift from one type of design and design vision to another: from effects-based (materials, physics, engineers) to context-based (human perception and values)."[48] For the rest of us, New Urbanism plays into the myth of nostalgia by suggesting that the widely accepted model of suburban and urban development does not have to result in alienation, or even that living in the cleanliness and newness of suburbia does not commit one to three hours of commuting in rush hour traffic on a daily basis. The importance is placed on a restoration of family values, themes that do not change with technology.

Plaza Hub: Consuming Idols of the Past

The Plaza Hub sits at the heart of Disneyland, and it is from here that all of the lands are accessed. The lands of adventure in Disneyland are firmly related to the past and lie to the west of the Hub. Frontierland and its ties to the American frontier logically reside in the West. Adventureland was placed next to Frontierland because of the proximity to the waterway; however, with the west being the cardinal point for sunset, the western location of these lands invokes the symbolic past by suggesting the sun is setting on a forgotten past. The frontier mentality is still very present in the United States, but the sun sets on it as science fiction, progress and innovation dominate. Tomorrowland in the east, aligned with the rising sun, suggests the newness of meaning expected form new invention, and with it the expectation of a "great, big, beautiful tomorrow," according to a Sherman Brothers song written for the Tomorrowland attraction, the Carousel of Progress, now closed. Bisecting these two is the North-South line bookended by Fantasyland and Main Street, when the nostalgic realm of middle America coincides with the imaginative realm of fairy tale.

The four primary cardinal roads radiate off the hub giving it the impression of being wheel-like. The Plaza Hub represents a mandalic image. Mandalas are circular images that appear in Eastern religious practices. The mandala is the center of the psyche and represents the self. It is the path of individuation.[49] Furthermore, as a rule, "a mandala occurs in conditions of psychic dissociation or disorientation."[50] The Hub, then, plays a crucial role in the mythic experience of Disneyland. It serves as a point to help orient the guest in what is otherwise a disorienting environment. Five of the eight total lands of the park are accessible directly from the Plaza Hub, providing pathways into realms of the imagination that beg to be explored.

On November 18, 1993, Mickey Mouse celebrated his sixty-fifth birthday. To mark the occasion, the statue *Partners* was unveiled in the

Hub. Sculpted by Imagineer Blaine Gibson, this bronze statue depicts Walt and Mickey Mouse pointing together toward the front gate. The placement of the tribute is significant because it places an icon of Walt and Mickey in the heart of Disneyland. Together, Walt and Mickey watch guests as they wander up Main Street, forever watching the present meet the past. Together, they stand as reminders of a past when Uncle Walt appeared on television, taking viewers on adventures to new and exciting parts unknown, a reminder of an idealized mid-century childhood. Walt and Mickey seem to be calling guests back to childhood.

Journalist Christopher Noxon observes that there is/are a "new band of grown-ups [who refuse] to give up things they never stopped loving, or [revel] in things they were denied or never got around to as children."[51] He calls them "rejuveniles." The goal of many rejuvenile is not to desperately cling to childhood to the point of neurosis, but, instead, to balance the hardships and monotony of adult life with the playful happiness they remember from childhood. Adults who return to some aspect of their childhood are looking for more than a simple regression. They are hoping to rejuvenate meaning using the tools available. The feelings they associate with their memories stem from a perceived loss of innocence, and this is where nostalgia emerges, especially in a society that has commodified rites of passage into superficial demarcations. Rejuveniles turn to play to instill meaning into their lives. It is this attempt to recapture, but not relive, the feeling of childhood that many, but not all, adults explore in their relationship to play. The "sense of a return to childhood is the basic appeal of the parks (as well as other Disney products) and is the essence of their sense of nostalgia."[52] This sense of nostalgia has no specific place, but a feeling one hopes to capture. Additionally, "there is an additional layer of nostalgia in the parks which is revealed in a longing for a return to the nation's childhood, as represented in turn-of-the-century settings like Main Street and the era of the conquest of the frontier."[53]

This goes beyond simply holding the past to an ideal memory. While it is true that American nostalgia does hold an idealized memory of the past, rejuveniles and their children idolize the past, giving it preference over anything to the point that present modes are revisions of those from the past. Indeed, corporations, including Disney, have responded to this trend by repackaging, rereleasing, and reselling the popular culture iconography from rejuvenile childhoods. For Disney, this entails releasing remastered collections of the films or cartoons with associated merchandise, reviving former park attractions, and celebrating the elderly Imagineers and animators who designed the imagery. For example, the cartoon shorts have been bundled by character into collections that are part of the *Walt Disney Treasures* series, which also include collections from the Disney television shows. One collection is themed around the opening day broadcast of Disneyland. For the rejuvenile who has strong ties to Disneyland, this show provides imagery of a forgotten Disneyland for those too young to remember it. Other non–Disney brands are part of this idolization trend as well. Many of the cartoons of the early–1980s have now been revamped for new audiences, many of whom are the children of first generation fans. While these new versions provide entertainment for new fans, they evoke nostalgia in older fans who hold an idealized memory of their cartoon idols.

The trend of remembering the past with shiny new things extends from collector circuits that have long been exchanging a wide array of pieces, from vintage to fine art, through auctions, trade shows, and antique dealers. But this is an elite crowd, willing and capable of paying large amounts of money for what originally cost a nickel. The response by modern marketing has been to place images of the idol on cheap consumables while simultaneously releasing an elite, "limited edition" line. For example, in 2009 Disney launched the D23, a high-quality Disney fan club. For several of the recent campaigns, Disney Marketing has released everyday merchandise, Disney Haute Couture merchandise (Disney's designer clothing and accessory line), and also a couple limited edition collectable figures only available to D23 members.

The Disneyization process, described by Alan Bryman, includes hybrid consumption, "a general trend whereby the forms of consumption associated with different institutional spheres become interlocked with each other and increasingly difficult to distinguish," and merchandising, "the promotion and sale of goods in the form of or bearing copyright images and/or logos, including such products made under license."[54] To accomplish this, merchandise is associated with the memories of one's trip. The basic intent behind Disney merchandising is to reference back to Disney messages of family, reassurance, nostalgia, and utopia, while also increasing visibility in daily use.[55]

Souvenirs are part of the Disney experience. Even if one goes to the park without the intent to buy something, one inevitably will. At Autopia, a Tomorrowland attraction that allows drivers of all ages the opportunity to drive a car, the guest is given a blank Driver's License before getting into the cars. At the end of the ride stand photo booths in which one can take his/her Driver's License Photo. At most of the restaurants and drink carts, guests can buy a reusable souvenir cup with their beverage that may include a light-up charm. Other little, seemingly innocuous items include pins, character autograph books, and reusable shopping bags. The ultimate Disney souvenir, however, is the personalized mouse ear hat. The ear hat comes in a variety of styles: traditional Mickey Mouse Club, seasonal/event, theme park attractions, and customizable/build-your-own. Some styles can be personalized with the guest's name or a short phrase while the guest waits. This hat allows any guest to dress in the Disney style, to become Disneylike at the parks or even at home.

Main Street, U.S.A., is both the main entrance into the park, but it is also the way out. Entering into the park, as described above, one simultaneously experiences the disorientation and the reassurance of Main Street to orient one into the park experience. However, upon exiting the park, Main Street, U.S.A. is transformed into a shopping district. The architecture is easily ignored as guests bounce from shop to shop trying to find the perfect souvenir or souvenirs for themselves or their loved ones. The quest for the perfect souvenir is disorienting itself, because the endeavor is an attempt to take something of Disneyland home, as though the souvenir is the proof that the trip was real and not just a magical dream.

Consuming our idols involves two modalities. One, especially applicable to school age children, is that wearing icons advertises one as a person. One's identity can be understood, even defined, by the brands one wears, an exercise in self-branding. The other is to surround oneself with images of comfort. Mickey Mouse, as Imagineer John Hench described, is a universal image of comfort. His two round ears and round head evokes primal images of the nurturing Mother.[56] Similarly, devoting a room in one's house, usually the office, as a shrine to one's childhood love, such as Disney or *Star Wars* collectables, creates an environment for work and play to function harmoniously.

The architecture of reassurance surrounds Americans on a daily basis and serves as a barrier between the real world of perception and experience, and the psychic fantasy hiding just below the surface. At a time when the national identity is destabilized, Disneyland reaffirms the meaning of "American" through nostalgic images that celebrate a homogenized past to construct a romantic utopian vision for the country. In the 1950s, this cry for myth was necessitated by the early terrors of the Cold War. Today, the same cry echoes throughout a post–9/11 country caught in the throes of terrorist threats and economic and environmental desirability. Though the ticket prices continue to rise, Disneyland continues to thrive because the place evokes the reassurance of Uncle Walt that was broadcast into the living rooms of many idealistic, hopeful, Boomer children. Perhaps the newer generation is more jaded and cautious than its parent/grandparent, but the hope of a utopia supplants even the grimmest outlook for the country's future.

The question being asked is not, what can utopia look like, as it was posed by Walt; rather, the question is, how can utopia be sustainable. Main Street, U.S.A., provides a model of a possible sustainable utopia, but as we have seen, it can only work if residents can continue their individual pursuit of happiness. Nostalgia emerges when this pursuit is less likely manifested in real life. Nostalgia emerges from the memory of a perceived better time, a time, perhaps, when Uncle Walt was still alive and appearing weekly on the television screen.

3

Adventureland
The Myth of the Spirit of Adventure

"Within Adventureland is the wonderworld of Nature's own design, her animal creatures, her fabulous plant life. Here too is a world of unusual people and far away places."
—*Walt Disney, "Dateline Disneyland"*

"Adventureland re-creates the eras and locales of great adventure stories. To Walt, it was a 'wonderland of nature's own design.' Here you'll navigate the tropical rivers of the world, explore Indian temple ruins, and climb into the tree canopy in the deepest jungles of Africa. Adventureland is for the young at heart and brave of spirit."—*The Imagineers,* The Imagineering Field Guide to Disneyland

When entering the Western half of the park from the Plaza Hub, guests have two options: they can enter the American West represented in Frontierland or they can enter Adventureland, a dense jungle of plants and animals that pay tribute to Nature, understood here as describing both the literal natural world and the idealized, Romantic concept of it, drawing inspiration from all mid-century conceptions of the "exotic." Disney's mini-paradise seems more real than real; it is hyperreal. All of the animals behave properly for guests all day, every day, and the plants are always green despite the time of year. They give the guest the perception of eternal paradise, even though the plants are meticulously manicured and not native to Southern California and the animals are audio-animatronic. Is Adventureland actually a little utopia or is it what Americans have come to expect of Paradise Gardens?

3. Adventureland

Initially inspired by the success of Disney's *True-Life Adventures*, the blockbuster non–Disney film *The African Queen*, and the mid-century popularity of Polynesian culture, Adventureland takes guests on an adventure into the exotic realms that are decidedly non–Western: African and Asian jungles and a Polynesian Tiki paradise. Adventureland represents the hyperrealistic realm of the Spirit of Adventure, and one that tackles the jungle or the ruined temples of ancient peoples as places to explore and eventually hope to conquer, setting the stage for Frontierland and the settlement of the West. An exploration of Adventureland reveals the American relationship to Nature as less a source for sustenance and more as an exploitable resource that simultaneously should be admired for its beauty. The created space of Adventureland further reveals the American disconnect between the form and function of Nature, which is why, I believe, Disney includes this hyperreal exemplar of the messy side of Nature, one so perfectly maintained as to distort our perceptions of the experience and to thus influence our expectations of the Great Outdoors.

Adventureland Key Attractions

- Jungle Cruise
- Walt Disney's Enchanted Tiki Room
- Indiana Jones Adventure
- Tarzan's Treehouse

The theme of Adventureland is not centered on a specific story or set of cultural ideals, but, rather, by the "wonderland of nature's own design."[1] The imagery for this "wonderland"[2] is derived from two main sources. The first source is the *True-Life Adventures* film series, documentary films showcasing animals in their natural habitats edited in accordance with Disney storytelling that gave each "star" an identity and a unique, fantastical adventure not unlike an extraordinary, if not fairy tale, American human experience. Although each film has a unique setting, the setting of Adventureland is generalized, a conglomerate of all of the *True-Life Adventures* settings, places, and times.[3] This mixing of setting creates in Adventureland an idealized, mysterious image of the exotic, particularly fascinating to post-war America that gained a new imagery of Africa, Asia, and the Polynesian islands during World War II. This fascination with exoticism, or transexoticism, is the second source for Adventureland's inspiration. Because Adventureland brings different locales together in a sort of "thematic melting pot" that represents a mixture—a stereotype—of the American image of exotic, it then becomes "the ultimate simulacrum of American primitivist desires."[4] Fascination with the exotic and the "primitive" is nothing new in America by the time of Disneyland's construction. The anti–Industry Romantics of the previous century left a legacy that inspires us to idealize "simpler" forms of civilization. For mid-century Americans, such civilizations are removed from the threat of nuclear chaos and other Cold War anxieties. It did not matter from which culture the "exotic" came. They are all the same to the American who seeks escape from the hustle and bustle of the American Dream, the Protestant Work Ethic, and fears of the unknown evil lurking in the recesses of American imagination.

Hyperreality, a term credited to philosopher Jean Baudrillard, occurs when the simulated reality, or "simulacra," seems more real than the actual reality. What occurs in Disneyland is "no longer a question of imitation, nor duplication, nor even parody. It is a question of substituting the signs of the real for the real, that is to say of an operation of deterring every real process via its operational double [...] that offers all the signs of the real and short-circuits all its vicissitudes."[5] All of Disneyland is a simulacrum, in large part because Walt Disney wanted a controllable environment in order to ensure that every guest has the same experience. Latent in that reasoning is that a simulated environment offers reassurance when designed well. In an era full of doubt and fear caused by the remnants of the Depression and World War II, and also the looming shadow of the Cold War, a simulated reality is preferable to the reality it sought to immolate. Similarly, "Disneyland tells us that faked nature corresponds much more to our daydream demands," and appears to tell us "that technology can give us more reality than nature."[6] The hyperrealistic imitation also gives credence to the myth of immortality,[7] because it constructs an immortal world, without the changeability of reality. By itself, the myth of immortality is a long-standing part of the mythos of the civilized world. When coupled with a fear of change in the face of rapid technology and nuclear onslaught, the myth of immortality can turn into apocalyptic motifs or it can lead to simulated environments that capture a moment in time when things were beautiful, the calm before the atomic storm Americans are convinced could happen at any time. Modern, post-war American culture is constructed as an expression of the hyperreal, such that Americans have developed a preference for the simulacra, and this promotes a worldview that is grounded in hyperreality, i.e., is fundamentally ungrounded, consumptive, expansive—and frustratingly fascinating.

Coinciding with the opening of Disneyland, American culture was undergoing a period of illusioned disillusionment. In the aftermath of World War II and in the face of the Cold War, American idealism was threatened, but it was easy to cover up and ignore with a façade of hyperreality. This was furthered by media efforts, notably television, that presented a simulated environment as a model for our own. Since the 1950s, the simulated environment has proven so effective that efforts are taken to transform the hyperrealistic world into the reality, thus playing into American romanticized utopian self-images.

Indiana Jones Adventure: The Spirit of Adventure, or Don't Look Into the Eyes of the Idol!

In the 1959 animated "edutainment" short, *Donald in Mathmagic Land*, Disney personifies the Spirit of Adventure. The spirit is present in Donald Duck, who is dressed as though going on a safari: hat, dungarees, and double-barrel shotgun. He stumbles into Mathmagic Land, with its number waterfall, trees with square roots, geometric figures that unite to recite π (pi), and a walking pencil that wins an impromptu game of tick-tack-toe in the sand. Scratching his head, Donald asks the ether, "What kind of crazy place is this?" And the ether answers, "Mathmagic Land." This disembodied voice introduces himself as the True Spirit of Adventure. He is not present on Donald's plane, but Donald faces the proverbial camera when addressing him. The Spirit, Mr. Spirit as Donald calls him, speaks with an (American) accent-less voice that commands authority and commands our undivided attention. As such, Disney's Spirit of Adventure is both the viewer, making the adventure experience personal, and the authoritative barrier between our own adventure and Donald's, as though enforcing the boundary that prevents Donald from coming into our world and us into his. In this character,

Disney both captures the curious spirit of adventure inherent in the American psyche, but prevents the adventure from delving too deeply into the realms of fantasy.

Disney's short appears at a time when America had explored the far reaches of the globe and was turning toward the new frontiers of space exploration and computer technology. These new frontiers offer new, exciting possibilities for both the expansion of American culture through a renewed, secular Manifest Destiny and some kind of transcendence from the humdrum of everyday life.

Three and a half decades later, Indiana Jones Adventure opened, reminding Americans of the mid-century Spirit of Adventure that was woven throughout Disney's work. The Indiana Jones Adventure is one of three attractions to reflect a partnership between Disney and George Lucas,[8] and was Disney's most ambitious attraction at the time it opened in 1995. Based on Lucas' popular *Indiana Jones* films, the attraction is filled with familiar images from the films and catchy lines recorded by Harrison Ford, the actor who played Indiana Jones in the films. The story begins at an archaeological dig site. Guests climb into jeep trucks that "whip guests through a perilous three-and-a-half minute journey inside the Temple of the Forbidden Eye. Snakes, fire, rats, bugs, blow guns, a collapsing bridge, that famous rolling stone, and sophisticated Audio-Animatronic Indiana Jones figures await."[9] The original design planned the jeeps to leave the dig site and entering the Forbidden Temple in one of three doors, with the reminder to "not look into the eyes of the Idol!" that is guarding the door, followed by different combinations of the following rooms, culminating in the near-squashing of the jeep by a giant rolling bolder, which we narrowly miss thanks to Indy's resourcefulness, ending with him self-congratulating for another successful, narrow escape with the treasure. Coupled with new technology in the ride vehicle that "dips, swerves, tilts, accelerates and brakes all along the 2,500-foot track, making the ride crazy and unpredictable," there are at least "160,000 possible variations of the experience."[10] Due to frequent breakdowns, however, the attraction has been simplified to a single story line, relying on the variations generated by the vehicle computers.

As a realistic attraction, Indiana Jones Adventure best captures the necessity of authenticity to the Disney experience. Because it is based on a popular, live-action film character, Disney had to maintain this character's humanness to reach the guests, while also creating him in audio-animatronics for reliability in the performance. As such, the audio-animatronic Indy looks like a wax replica of Harrison Ford in costume and make-up. Additionally, because the attraction is set in an ancient, forbidden temple, the environment has to include the same kinds of things Indy would have encountered in a movie, such as bats (recreated by sound), spiders (seen crawling on the wall while sound effects imitate their sound) and booby traps, which happen to "just miss" the ride vehicle, which also reinforces our trust in Indy. Although he is a tomb raider and engaging in illegal practices in the name of archaeology, he is a hero we can trust because he protects us from harm—a progressive notion in modern American philosophy, placing trust in national heroes and leaders, including politicians and heads of corporations, believing that they will protect us or attend to our needs, even if they have to undergo Machiavellian means along the way to fabricate the situation where we need their protection to enhance their heroic image.

The Spirit of Adventure is the voice of metaphysical wisdom and is able to run through the spectrum of time. Disney presents this figure without any negative attributes, identifying this Spirit as a loving guide and educator without any volatility. In fact, Disney is presenting this character as the voice or spokesperson for Nature, who communicates through wonder and beauty, not through the voice of reason and interpretation the Spirit's narration offers. These two voices (Adventure/Time and Nature) frequently tell the story of the earth through the *True-Life Adventures*: Earth offers the beauty of the natural world and the animals within it; while Adventure translates the story into the language of an experience we can understand. However, the narrative does not always match up with animal behavior, but instead personifies the animals' experience by twisting it to more resemble our own. Thus the Spirit of Adventure, as a storyteller, is reflecting a habit of the Disney Corporation takes full advantage of translating a story to make it better suited for the American situation and sensibility. Critics have noted that there is something fake about the *True-Life* films, given a false interpretation of reality, but of course, this is the very effect of existing in a hyperrealistic universe.

Disney's Spirit of Adventure controls the playful energy inherent in the nature of this spirit. When one is caught by the Spirit of Adventure, one assumes an uncontrolled, free-wheeling, playful experience ahead, but Disney's spirit restricts the play by constructing a control mechanism for how guests experience Nature: our attention is drawn from place to place along the Jungle Cruise by the captain, or each corner of the Enchanted Tiki Room is designed almost the same, with very subtle differences, leaving our attention focused on the immediate staging area above us, discouraging us from looking beyond our section and the center area. Disney's Spirit of Adventure is, then, a manager. This is perhaps a reflection on Walt Disney's own micro-managing style, but it also reflects the American desire to control our destiny. The movement West was a power-grab to control resources, regardless of previous claims to the land. Americans are known for our control over our environment, from our manicured lawns to earth-dominating architecture.

Within the Adventureland attractions, the Spirit of Adventure is embodied in the ride narrator: in the Jungle Cruise's playful spirit as we sail down the river, in the voices of Indy and his assistant as we navigate through the Forbidden Temple trying not to look into the eyes of the idol, and in the voice of Jose of the Enchanted Tiki Room. All three of these voices do not tell a story as other Disney narrators do, but they attempt to break down the barrier between us and the story, translating the scenes from nature into something the hyperrealistic American mind can understand. Within the berm of Disney theme parks, this accomplishes a breaking down of the "second screen," a phrase that describes the barrier of the movie screen that separates the viewer from the film. Yet, this nature is hyperrealistic in its use of audio-animatronics to simulate reality.

The Jungle Cruise and Hyperrealistic Nature, or: Hippos That Wag Their Ears

The relationship between hyperreality and nature is especially evident in Adventureland. Simulated or controlled environments are increasingly commonplace in American culture. As urban design and technology increasingly remove Americans from nature; thus, the construction of botanical gardens and simulated natural environments serve as reminders of the adventurous spirit that built the country. One example of hyperrealistic nature in Disneyland is the Jungle Cruise.

From the earliest designs of Disneyland, the Jungle Cruise was present in some form or another. The idea was and is to take a cruise along the rivers of the world's jungles, no single specific river, to give guests a safari experience. The plants of the jungle are dense, shutting out the outside world, giving the illusion of other-worldliness aided by the plants imported for effect, an adventure that begins as soon as one boards the boat. The attraction is inspired by the Academy Award-winning film, *The African Queen* (1951), a film set in East Africa during World War I about a couple of Americans who sail through the African jungle trying to find American forces while avoiding the Nazi troops, which thematically connects the Jungle Cruise to the nearby war-era Indiana Jones Adventure that opened forty years later in 1996.

Along the cruise, guests encounter playful elephants, hippos that wag their ears if they are angry, a stranded safari party trapped in a tree narrowly avoiding a rhino's horn, an abandoned temple, Schweitzer Falls (named after the famous Dr. Falls), and a head hunter offering two of his shrunken heads in exchange for one of yours. The Jungle Cruise is the one attraction that encourages cast members to write their own jokes, providing boatloads of entertainment for guests.

The safari is completely safe, even when the driver "shoots" at the angry hippos or when the natives throw spears at the boat. Although the ride was planned to showcase living animals, it was soon realized by either Walt Disney or an Imagineer[11] that live animals would not "perform" to Disney's standards, and early prototypes for audio-animatronics were developed, creating realistic-appearing robot animals that will always perform as expected during the brief seconds the boat is sailing by, barring mechanical failure, ensuring the same performance for each guest.

This imitation of nature pays tribute to the wonderland of Nature's design, honoring what is perceived as America's highest art form.[12] Because American mythos is tied so closely with land, it is logical for at least one Disney land to celebrate Nature. The choice of exotic locales represents a larger issue. Overtly, there is the fascination with exoticism already mentioned; latently, there is the suggestion that this fascination was a way for Americans to adopt the new understanding of these regions into our own culture. Cinema brought these places and peoples to life, no longer confining our knowledge to art and anthropological treatises. This fascination with the exotic culminated in 1959 with the statehoods of Hawaii and Alaska.

Hyperreality offers the tools to construct the utopian Main Street, and functions as a reinforcement of the globalism of Manifest Destiny by tapping into American romanticism and pulling the signifiers out of the realm of reality into the intangible realm of simulation and technology to create a more perfect world. This is "a vision of natural perfection in which everyone and everything lives in unwavering abundance and harmony and the cumulative effect of the forces upon it as a system of equal zero. Change is impossible."[13] Furthermore, within the Disney mythos, nature possesses elasticity akin to cartoon characters that can restore itself to its original condition, no matter what is done to it.[14] Thus, Disney's hyperrealistic nature is impervious to change, a reassuring comfort in light of man-made mechanisms of mass-destruction.

Walt Disney's Enchanted Tiki Room: Reality's Illusion and Disney Realism

Jean Baudrillard identifies three orders of simulacra:

(1) simulacra that are natural, naturalist, founded on the image or imitation and counterfeit, that are humorous, optimistic, and that aim for the restriction or the idea institution of nature made in God's image [the utopia]; (2) simulacra that are productive, productivist, founded on energy, force, its materialization by the machine and in the whole system of production—a Promethean aim of a continuous globalization and expansion, or an indefinite liberation of energy ... [science fiction]; (3) simulacra of simulation, founded on information, the model, the cybernetic game—total operationality, hyperreality, aim of total control.[15]

Disneyland belongs to this third order because it is "presented as imaginary in order to make us believe that the rest is real."[16] The overt presentation of Disneyland is to emphasize the reality of the rest of America, but since Disneyland's construction, more and more American locales have adopted a similar approach to reality, such that the real is no longer real and Disneyland is perceived as an American reality. It achieves this by not only constructing an environment of fantasy, but by presenting it as "genuine," not as reproductions, down to the souvenirs in the stores and the crying monkeys from the trees.[17]

Hyperreality is a reality that constructs a total environment such that the line is blurred between the authenticity of the simulacra and the re-imagining of the real. For example, the jungle environment is so total, that one is led to believe that the real jungle has no bugs, no rapid waterways, and the animals and natives will leave us alone in our boat. Unreality, on the other hand, does not attempt to dapple with realism from the outset, and leaves little room for doubt of its motives. Some moments exist when, during the Disneyland experience, one is awakened from the illusion, such as when an audio-animatronic malfunctions, or it rains, or fatigue and exhaustion put a halt on the day; however, the goal of the park in the totality of its theming is to offer enough changes of scenery to offset those factors that risk breaking the illusion. Timed like a rapid-paced movie, one does not have the time to think, but only to experience. Similarly, to be fake, a simulacrum has to distance the observer from it, such that the observer knows it to be fake. Thus, Disneyland is not fake, because its intention is to draw us in and make us part of its mythos. Because of the park's hyperrealism, we easily yield to the park's magic, because it speaks to our consumptive behaviors such that we know we are in the realm of the fake, but are willing to suspend our concepts of reality to fulfill a hungry need for a mythic experience.[18]

To further explicate Disney's hyperreality, it is helpful to look at Disney's portrayal of reality to provide grounding in the identification of the simulation. We can recognize three styles of realism in Disney cartoons that were likewise utilized in Disneyland's design: cartoon, realism and schematic, all three are especially evident in Adventureland.[19] Familiarity with these three styles helps us identify the intentional simulacra, separating it from the unintentional or mythic simulacra and its implications underlying the park experience. Operating under the assessment of Disneyland as a hyperrealistic environment places the park in the awkward position of being both the superfluous entertainment Disney critics claim it to be, and the tributary imitation that promotes reverence for the larger culture. The cartoon style is characterized by caricature and exaggeration. While this style can achieve a realistic sophistication, the exaggerations restrict it to an overall comic tone. For instance, "Animal characters were anthropomorphized. Human characters were generally drawn with head to body proportions that did not match those in real humans, and thus facial features were generally more rounded than in real life and displayed different proportions."[20] The realistic style covers a wider range of detail, and is reserved for more "serious" stories. For instance, animated characters "appeared more closely modeled after real world beings. Humans displayed body proportions consistent with those of real people...."[21] Finally, the schematic style is marked by the use of diagrams, maps, and figures. The schematic style may have either a humorous or serious tone, but its primary function is to indicate an educational or explanatory piece ("edutainment").[22] Within Adventureland, the schematic and realistic styles are meant to invoke the same Spirit of Adventure that was found in the *True-Life Adventures* films, and underscore exploration of Nature's wilderness as educational and/or the key for discovering a lost reassure. The cartoon style is notable among the anthropomorphic behaviors of the birds of Walt Disney's Enchanted Tiki Room.

Some of the first audio-animatronics were formally developed for the Enchanted Tiki Room, which served as a proving ground for the technology that Disney was hoping to showcase at the 1964 World's Fair. Originally designed to be a dinner showcase, the Tiki Room was intended to depict Polynesian culture, especially Hawaii: hula dancers, Polynesian foods and similar entertainment, but the idea was replaced with singing birds, flowers, and Tiki statues in response to Walt's fascination with robotics and to push more guests through the attraction.

The Tiki show is hosted by four caricatured international parrots: José (representing Mexico), Pierre (France), Fritz (Germany), and Michael (Ireland), creating a demographic slice of the American melting pot. The four hosts emcee the show with José in the lead, heckling the crowd–"pardon me, Madame, that whistle was for my good friend, Fritz!"–and leading the birds and plants in song, culminating in the Tiki statues drumming the house into a storm. Cut off from the outside world, the Tiki Room creates the illusion that a storm has brewed during the show, prompting José to exclaim, "The gods have been angered by all our celebratin'!" The gods to which José refers are introduced outside the house in a preshow and are inspired by Hawaiian and Polynesian mythologies.

Although the animals maintain their natural attributes, they are given human characteristics such as the ability to sing, or real human emotions such as vengeance and sorrow. This mode of caricature harkens back to the Disney tradition of *Bambi* or the *True-Life Adventures* (now Disney*Nature*), which explore the animal experience as though it followed the trajectory of an American average, middle-class life. Through this style, guests can relate to Nature via the animals, making the two realms equal rather than one subordinate to the other, reinforcing Disney's romantic view of the restoration and reinforcement of American myth through a return to a connection with Nature. The animals are realistic enough that they toe the line between the simulated illusion and the goal of the experience. The Disney experience aims to pull the guest into the cartoon as one of the characters, to be part of the story, and it is from this interaction that the mythic experience occurs.

Guests willingly suspend disbelief in Adventureland, allowing the Tiki birds to sing in part because the birds still look like birds, employing the realistic style. Mainstream Americans, however, loved Disney's fusion of the realistic and cartoon styles, because people "had grown weary of hallucinogenic fantasies that had no bearing on their interests and lives. The powerful familial themes in *Bambi* resonated with them. Rather than resist the laws of nature, Disney reconfirmed them."[23] Although the Adventureland attractions use the cartoon style predominantly to entertain guests, the realistic style is essential to the illusion, bringing it to the guests' experiential level. The cartoon style takes the experience into the absurd, potentially surreal, which, when not balanced with enough realism, can alienate a general public who do not want to be "forced to think" while on vacation. Entertainment, thus, needs to be obvious and clear. Any underlying messages must be conveyed through the latency of the experience so as to not turn the entertaining, amusement ride solely into an educational tool.

Realism is best represented in Disneyland by the audio-animatronic figures that appear throughout the park. Audio-animatronic technology fuses robotics that respond to a program that guides their gestures and expressions, with skins and costuming, creating a pronounced imitation of reality. Although the guest knows that the figures are not real, the timing of the attraction prevents guests from looking too deeply at the figures, which will reveal their inauthenticity, because guests are ushered from one scene to the next with no time to look back.[24]

Within the park, we see the schematic style utilized to provide a geography within the park. Characters, such as the jungle explorers or Indiana Jones, use maps to give a sense of direction in what can be an otherwise overwhelming tour of the imagination. All guests receive a park map upon entry, but the schematics built within attractions reinforce a sense of grounding, and reassure guests that they are not in fact lost. This is essential to the hyperrealistic illusion because direction is a construct of reality, used to help us navigate the complexities of civilization. Maps also provide a sense of movement toward something, such as an exit or a treasure. This constant forward movement reflects American rootless in the present, and the ongoing desire for tomorrow's improvements. The Spirit of Adventure thus guides Americans through unknown territories in a heroic quest that may never amount to anything. Americans are not fascinated with the end goal when we exit the attraction vehicle but, rather, with the journey along the way. Disneyland attractions frequently exit at or near the entrance; the journey only leads us back to where we began, but with the knowledge of a different story than before.

What simulation constructs is a parallel double universe, and this is the realm of dream and fantasy. As Disney markets "the Magic Kingdom" as "the place where dreams come true," the park crosses the line that divides this universe from its parallel. The risk is of oversimulation leading to overstimulation, which destroys both the image and the platform on which the imaginary exists, taking its seduction with it.[25] Indeed, this disillusionment has seeped into the larger society; we are so overstimulated with simulation that Disneyland's hyperreality is the vacation from hyperreality. Common places have been transformed into hyperreal worlds: malls, movie theaters, restaurants, educational institutions, religious institutions, among several others. Coupled with the onslaught of advertising, news, and other digital media outlets attempting to "amuse us to death,"[26] Disneyland's total environment becomes the escape of which Walt Disney dreamt.

Thus, Disneyland is neither real nor fake.[27] To be presented as real, the park has to emphasize the real and conceal the fake behind a guise of believability. Where this occurs is in the psychology of the guests who are motivated into atypical behaviors by the Disneyland environment, namely the consumption behavior pushed into hyper-drive. Disney makes liberal use of easily recognized symbols and makes them into commodities, but it does this with latent symbols that are not explicitly expressed within the parks.

Tarzan's Treehouse: Nature and Control

Tarzan's Treehouse is an updated version of the Swiss Family Tree-house that was portrayed in the film, *The Swiss Family Robinson* (1960), based on the novel by Johann David Wyss. This walk-through attraction was designed to give guests insight to the ingenuity of the Robinsons to construct a modernized, albeit "primitive," new life from the wreck-age of their ship. As though responding to the Cold War, Disney pre-sented a survivalist's model in case the American lifestyle is compromised. Metaphorically, we in fact do need to construct modern conveniences from the wreckage of our previous lives. The concrete Disney tree offers a lookout over the rest of Adventureland and the neighboring Rivers of America and Frontierland. A sign posted in the Jungle Lookout captures the Spirit of Adventure: "...In this compound we often pause to contemplate our small world.... Here adventure beck-ons ... with every view & every sound, the jungle & its river call out their mystery ... invite us to new discovery."[28] Through this relatively simple attraction, the Disney Imagineers re-discover the marvels of technology that shaped the modern world.

The Tarzan's Treehouse remodel was done in anticipation of 1999's animated feature, *Tarzan*. Since the two stories are set in different loca-tions (the Caribbean and Africa, respectively) radical changes were made in the Treehouse's design, including the addition of a "thin two-story tree" in the Adventureland walkway "with a rickety suspension bridge spanning above the crowds to lead guests to the main tree...," and period-appropriate English artifacts replaced the Swiss.[29] Though not at the center of the park, the Treehouse stands as a man-made

Tree of Life or *axis mundi*. It sits at the nexus for three lands—Adventureland, New Orleans Square, and Frontierland—tying together three seemingly diverse lands under the same umbrella, the Spirit of Adventure.

The return to nature, whether real or hyperreal, is perceived as a return to simplicity and innocence. This view, adopted by the Romantic writers and poets of the nineteenth century,[30] fueled the development of the social sciences that saw "primitives" as the models to help us understand child psychology (and vice versa) and as models for a naïve innocence untouched by technology and industry, exemplars for the pure state of the human condition. This childlike nature "dominated American consciousness through its vision of limitless progress, unshadowed idealism, endless growth."[31] In the mid-century, this idealism began to erode, fueling the efforts of entities such as Disney to create family fare fraught with play and is expressed throughout Adventureland by emphasis on a perceived natural order: representatives of the West are seen as violators of the natural order. In Tarzan's Treehouse, the relics of a Western safari are given new purpose by Tarzan and the apes who do not recognize the intended use of items, such as a gramophone or fine china dishes. This innocent misunderstanding of these inventions emphasize the disparity between the modern American mind and that of the less civilized "other," calling into question our reliance on technology and how it affects our relationship to nature.

The Spirit of Adventure assumes the innocence of the guests, and constructs the narrative accordingly. In Tarzan's Treehouse, we share the innocence of the apes, giving us the exposure to an anti-civilization narrative, promoting an eco-friendly dialogue about the impact of humanity on Nature. Disney has always promoted a romantic love for nature, and it was one of the primary influences for the *True-Life Adventures*. Although constructed from concrete and plastic, the treehouse represents Nature, while the ransacked rooms show how Nature may retaliate against human attempts to dominate and control, effectively putting us in our place about our role in the larger planetary ecosystem.

Disney's message is that humanity has lost sight of the bigger picture. Indeed, returning to nature no longer means a simplification of life and living on the land's resources, but to return to nature is seen as a challenge to see who will win: "man" or "nature." Conquering nature is seen as a heroic endeavor. Despite Disney's eco-conscious messages, the studio has nonetheless exercised a degree of control over Nature in the service of providing "quality" entertainment. This control is used to communicate a message of relinquishing control. For example, Disney's control over nature began with the *True-Life Adventures* films, whose narration constructed a different reality for the animals in the film, one anthropomorphized, than their experiences typically suggest. In one controversial incident, Disney's documentarians stage a mass lemming suicide by running them off a cliff into the ocean in *White Wilderness*, a staged event "'contradicts what scientists claim happens in real life.' As an expert into photofakery notes, 'thanks to Disney, several generations of Americans believe that lemmings do [commit suicide].'"[32] Disney was attempting to educate, but their emphasis was on entertainment and the *True-Life* films were some of the earliest experiments in "edutainment." To make Nature entertaining, Disney's people turned to standard storytelling techniques to construct their narratives, intentionally blurring the line between reality and fiction in service to the larger message to encourage viewers to rethink their relationship to Nature, especially relevant in cities falling increasingly victim to sprawl.

As Disney was designing Disneyland, a land of adventure was a natural choice to bring together the American love of control over the environment with the American fascination for the perceived simplicity of living in the natural world. More importantly, the natural world was one without economics and nuclear politics.

4.

New Orleans Square
The Shadow of American Doubt

"New Orleans Square is a captivating ode to the charms of the Crescent City. Here we set sail for parts unknown—on the open seas or in the hereafter. Sit for a spell and sip a sweet, minty cooler as you watch the world go by. The sights and sounds of this remarkable place leave an indelible impression."—The Imagineers, The Imagineering Field Guide to Disneyland

Situated at the crossroad between Adventureland, Frontierland, and Critter Country sits New Orleans Square. It is not a square, as the name implies, but rather a bowl-shaped area filled with crisscrossing streets that evoke the French Quarter in the Crescent City. The buildings are close together shutting the area off from the other lands, and creating an air of intimacy and relaxation that distinguishes the area from the other lands in the park. It is quiet and filled with quaint little shops. The area's restaurants serve Cajun-inspired cuisine and jazz street bands make regularly scheduled performances, weather permitting. The crossroads imagery invokes myths and legends from the world over, including famous "deals with the devil." As a mythic motif, the crossroads is a murky location with unknown creatures hiding in the shadows.

New Orleans has developed a reputation as an American crossroads. The city is both a port to the Gulf of Mexico and a port to the Mississippi; it is also a gateway to the Frontier for settlers coming from the East. More than any other American city, New Orleans exhibits bipolarity between its romantic and shadow nature.[1] On the romantic side is New Orleans's Old World ambiance, reminiscent of its French colonialist history, coupled with the charm of Antebellum Southern plantations. This romantic nature is tied into architecture and is a dominant tourist draw, notably in the Garden District and French Quarter.

New Orleans's shadow side[2] comes from three sources. The first lies in the city's founding. In 1717, John Law and his investment company secured proprietary rights, and established a population in New Orleans made of prostitutes, criminals, beggars, and orphans.[3] He created local inflation and deceived his wealthy aristocratic European investors, creating a place tolerant of criminality, poverty, and corruption. The second is found in the rift between the wealthy and the impoverished, made ever larger by the relatively small total square footage of the city. The poverty demographic is comprised in large part of African Americans, some descended from former plantation slaves. Despite the poverty, the African American subculture has also enhanced New Orleans' culture with jazz, a form of music that is derived from African American rhythmic melodies combined with the blues; soul food, often made from "cheap" cuts of meat and vegetables rejected by the elite; and superstition and voodoo, derived from west African traditions imported by slaves and Americanized by their progeny. The impact of jazz and cuisine has been incorporated into the romantic side of New Orleans. Voodoo and superstition, on the other hand, reflect a gothic fascination that delights in the shadow; except, for those who cannot control voodoo or superstitious belief, it can invite fear and terror, a necessary cathartic release for the shadow in some individuals.

The third shadow aspect of the city is inherent in its geography. Situated in the Mississippi delta, New Orleans is essentially composed of swamp, used in literature as a metaphor for depression, suffering, and death.[4] Additionally, the city is prone to flooding because it is situated below sea level. The inhabitants of New Orleans are aware of the dangers from flooding, but are otherwise lulled into "dreamlike unconsciousness" that can enhance creativity or induce madness: "In New Orleans, a visitor can be drawn strongly into archetypal fields that make him feel seduced or even possessed by the all-pervading spirits. He is open to dimensions of the sacred, encouraged to seek the occult, and brought closer to a conscious awareness of the shadow."[5] This "dreamlike unconsciousness" makes New Orleans a rich setting for the Pirates of the Caribbean and the Haunted Mansion, two of the most popular attractions at Disneyland, both of which induce dreamlike unconsciousness in their underground homes. Knowing that the city is prone to flooding, infrastructure and levees were constructed to keep the waters at bay in an attempt to control Nature to protect the people and the romantic architecture that defines New Orleans. This course of action, however, is only temporary as the Shadow cannot be ignored forever. Somehow, the Shadow will surface, often with catastrophic results, and when it does it raises doubt. Doubt is the response to a lack of confidence about a current status quo.

The United States found itself at a sort of crossroads after the War. The Cold War compounded fears and anxieties that extended from an ever-present crisis that shook American confidence, as Americans feared Communism as a destabilizing force of the American Dream, but also as the country formed itself as a central figure in the newly globalized world. Many concerns stemmed from "industrialization, standardization, and the development of worldwide communication."[6] Americans increasingly lost their trust in leaders to fulfill their promises for a better life, especially as the threat of nuclear attack loomed over the culture. Hollywood gave expression to American doubt through both horror and suspense thrillers, but also through romances and comedies that turned a blind eye to fear, offering escape and relief from the larger issues.

American doubt is arguably a critical aspect of the cultural identity; inherent in the entitlements of rugged individualism rests a doubt against the government and any establishment organization. This doubt was exacerbated by the Great Depression and a belief that the government was incapable of helping the people, but it was suspended during the War to return with full force with the detonation of the Bomb. For a country that found itself embedded in a period of wealth and prosperity, Americans were never secure in the permanence of that status.

Disneyland gives expression to American doubt by embellishing traditionally evil or shadowy characters with comic flavors. In New Orleans Square, the pirates are pillaging and plundering, but in the comic fashion of jesters, and the ghosts are grim and grinning, and may even try to go home with the guest. We are meant to sympathize with these characters that were initially the villains of legend and lore.

New Orleans Square Key Attractions

- Pirates of the Caribbean
- The Haunted Mansion
- Club 33

On a map of Disneyland, New Orleans Square is situated in the southwest. If the Main Street/Fantasy line bisects the park from Frontier and Progress, much the same way that the Mississippi River bisects America, then New Orleans sits at the crossroad between the untamed West and the civilized East. Unlike the rest of the Frontier, New Orleans brings with it a sense of mystery and macabre, derived from the city's own historical relationship to shadowy figures, from its voodoo culture to its annual Mardi Gras masquerades to an elaborate gothic culture. This history has saturated America's mythic understanding of New Orleans, making it one of the places in the country in which shadow elements exist in consciousness, especially made manifest in the aftermath of Hurricane Katrina, an event that brought issues American culture relegates to its shadow—poverty, racism, inefficiency of government aid—to the surface along with the bones of generations of the dead. Disneyland's New Orleans Square acknowledges and honors the city's mythos, while also encouraging us to laugh rather than scream at her shadowy offerings. Rather than a place of fright, New Orleans Square is a place of enjoyment, a caricature of its real-life counterpart.

As a nod to New Orleans's darker side, an audio-animatronic voodoo lady chants from one of the balconies, and the only two attractions in the land—and two of the most popular—celebrate the seedy side of humanity and highlight death. Philosopher Umberto Eco recognizes New Orleans Square as the perfect example of Disney's hyperreality: "The Pirates and the Ghosts sum up all Disneyland ... because they transform the whole city into an immense robot, the final realization of the dreams of the eighteenth-century mechanics."[7] In a land of fantasy and myth, Eco further notes, the characters of New Orleans Square represent "metaphysical evil" (the ghosts) and "historical evil" (the pirates), and it is in this that New Orleans Square holds any meaning,[8] or rather the Disney romanticization of New Orleans history that has made it the place to consider and re-enact the issues that lie buried in the American shadow.

Pirates of the Caribbean: Identifying the Shadow

When Pirates of the Caribbean opened in 1967, it incorporated technology that was new to the entertainment industry. Improving on the audio-animatronic technology first publically introduced in the 1964–1965 New York World's Fair, Disney Imagineers created a thoroughly encapsulated environment with a full cast of humanoid audio-animatronic figures. So much detail was put into the attraction that it invites multiple ride-throughs. Coupled with a catchy theme song and snazzy one-liners, Pirates of the Caribbean remains one of the most beloved attractions in Disneyland and has been recreated with some story modification at four of the other Magic Kingdoms around the world (Walt Disney World, Tokyo, Paris, and Hong Kong), with a fifth planned to open in 2016 with the opening of Shanghai Disneyland. Originally conceived as a walk-through wax museum of pirate and maritime history, it evolved into a boat ride to push guests through easier.

The ride begins on Lafitte's Landing, which is situated under the bridge between Adventureland and New Orleans Square. Guests are filed onto the bateaux and sent on a leisurely ride through a swamp. This introductory area shares its space with the Blue Bayou Restaurant, an upscale themed restaurant; Club 33, an elite club built under Walt's guidance as a Disneyland VIP lounge; and a river shack with an audio-animatronic river man rocking lazily while a banjo plays a lazy rendition of the traditional folk tune, "Oh Suzanna." Just when guests are lulled into a false sense of ease, the boat enters a tunnel and is dropped down a watery incline with a splash. A talking Jolly Roger warns us that "dead men tell no tales," a warning to the guests of the dangers ahead. The boat sails through a cavern before getting dropped down a second waterfall, and into a treasure cave filled with the skeletons of dead pirates who chose to live with their treasures than live at all. Dead men, after all, tell no tales, as the voice in the cavern echoes. There are vestiges of a shipwreck in the cavern, suggesting part of the reason why there are wealthy, dead pirates in the cave. As the boat leaves the cavern, guests pass through a cloud onto which Davy Jones, the pirate who rules the seas of life and death, is projected warning us again of the dangers up ahead.

The next scene is a battle scene. A pirate ship is attacking a colonial fort and both are shooting canons right over our heads, some splashing near the boats. This is the first room where the audio-animatronics are used to simulate human movement and behavior. From the battle scene, the boat enters the Caribbean town of Tortuga, a port friendly to pirates and not under royal control. We are given a glimpse into their lives. True to pirate nature, we witness them defying authority by dunking the mayor down a well, brides being auctioned off to the highest bidder,[9] men and women chasing each other around, and lots of drinking and merry-making. The tour continues through the Tortuga jail where some pirates are trying to bribe a dog for the keys. Some pirates drink too much and start shooting each other ignoring the nearby TNT, which causes a fire. Guests are spared from the fire by a long uphill water climb that takes us past one lucky pirate, Jack Sparrow, who we glimpsed throughout our Tortuga tour seeking a treasure map and key, and who finally found the treasure.

The boat returns to Lafitte's Landing and guests disembark, returning to civilization and New Orleans Square by walking along a garden then out a hotel-style doorway. So encompassing is this dark ride experience, which lasts about sixteen minutes, that it is easy for guests to be surprised when they exit to find that time is still daylight outside.

The shadow is an unconscious component to an individual's psychology, defined by Jung as the "'negative' side of the personality, the sum of all those unpleasant qualities we like to hide, together with the sufficiently developed functions and the contents of the personal unconscious."[10] The shadow appears throughout myth and literature as an archetypal figure, and it appears in real life as a collective projection onto people, places and things. The literary shadow figure is a personification of all the characteristics the hero does not possess or does not utilize. This character is presented to us as a nemesis or a rival, though not all nemeses or rivals are necessarily shadow figures, depending on the nature of the story.

In New Orleans Square, however, the shadow operates on a cultural level. The cultural shadow manifests in the tensions, sometimes simply projections, between disparate groups of people, culminating in war. This view was derived from Jung's observations during World War II, but modern America requires a more complex approach to the shadow.

Working with dark shadow imagery can potentially evoke images of the underworld or a similar underground otherworldly setting. It is fitting, then, that the two show buildings that house the New Orleans Square attractions are the only two in all of Disneyland that are underground and outside the berm. Both Pirates of the Caribbean and the Haunted Mansion include descents (the waterfalls and the elevator) early in the attraction to take guests down and out. The practical reason for this is that the attractions grew too complex to be housed in the small amount of available space, but those descents nonetheless help enhance the experience. Whereas a crossroads indicates a turning point, a descent is symbolically connected in mythology with a death and rebirth adventure. Having this adventure into the underworld coupled with cinematic kinesis gives the Pirates of the Caribbean the unique position of transforming a guest through the catharsis of comedy. That the pirates are allowed to roam free without punishment reminds us of people we encounter or recognize from real life. While the pirates may not be subject to punishment, they nonetheless experience a form of punishment in their actions: they set fire to the entire town. The only pirate to escape the blaze, and thus punishment, is a vigilante, recognizable from the film franchise, who willingly works with non-pirates to accomplish a common, albeit mercenary, goal.

Because Americans have perceived themselves in a cycle of perpetual crisis,[11] affinity for the ghosts and pirates reflects a shift in trust of the American leadership. No longer can Americans easily place the country's fate in the hands of a president or CEO, though sometimes a charismatic one comes along, seducing the population and either earning collective undying loyalty or proving disappointing in light of unheld promises. Now, the leadership of a mythic rogue into territories unknown proves more interesting, fascinating, reliable and reassuring than traditionally upheld leadership.[12] This shift became pronounced in the mid-century and is reflected in several of Disney's works. New Orleans Square reflects this ideological shift. The two attractions take us out of time and space into an underworld, and present us with fantasy characters of the counterculture, a manifestation of the cultural shadow on the home front that takes many different forms.

For example, in the Pirates of the Caribbean attraction and films, we are led away from established authority by the lure of the sea. It is in this respect that Disney's pirates fulfill their role with the American shadow. Historically, and within the literature of Robert Louis Stevenson and Disney, pirates represent "outlaws": there is no legal system, except for a Pirate's Code that holds pirates to a certain amount of self-governing honor that can control them. They sail the seas, well beyond the boundaries of any single country's/nation's/kingdom's jurisdiction, with the liberties to travel anywhere, restricted only by the temperament of the sea or warrants for their crimes.

As vehicles for the American shadow, Disney's pirates carry with them American ideology. Not only are they "outlaws," but they are subversive, defiant of authority, and represent the globalizing force of Manifest Destiny, taking America's perceived God-given duty to spread American Democracy to all corners of the world. For this reason, we can identify with them and are happy to project our desires for shadow imagery onto them despite their outlaw behaviors: "We pillage and plunder, rifle and loot. Drink up, me hearties, yo ho!"[13]

The Haunted Mansion: The Shadow in Caricature

In 1969, New Orleans Square's other attraction opened after nearly eight years of delay caused by conceptual and technological changes. Originally conceived as a Museum of the Weird, it was to be, like Pirates of the Caribbean, a walk-through, but as an original story developed, the Haunted Mansion evolved into an ambitious and complex attraction, on par with Pirates of the Caribbean.

The story revolves around two main arcs: the first is that of a haunted house filled with 999 happy haunts that are looking for their 1000th roommate among the guests. The other is the legend of Captain Gore of Bloodmore Manor and his new bride, Priscilla, which evolved into the mansion of late Master Gracey[14] and the "Black Widow Bride," Constance, who was added to the attraction in 2006.[15] The Captain Gore story is more prominent at the other Haunted Mansions; it was rewritten under the supervision of Walt Disney who found it too gruesome.

The Haunted Mansion grounds and queue line wind through a cemetery, leading to the porch of this antebellum mansion. Guests are ushered through the front door into the foyer, where the disembodied

Ghost Host welcomes "Foolish Mortals to the Haunted Mansion." Doors open and guests are herded into a room lined with portraits. The portraits on the walls stretch to reveal how some of the Mansion's happy haunts met their demise. The Stretching Room is actually an elevator, though the Ghost Host presents the question whether the walls are stretching or whether it is actually an illusion. The Ghost Host also remarks how there are no doors, so the challenge is to find a way out (his way was to hang himself from the ceiling). Doors in fact do open, revealing a corridor lined with paintings that, through tricks of illusion, flash from scenes of calm to scenes of terror. Two busts at the end of the hallway look as though they turn to follow the guest, watching as we enter the Doom Buggy loading area. The Doom Buggy is a car with its own sound system that runs on a constant track that never stops. A Doom Buggy can be programmed to pivot the guest at a set time to look at a point of interest. It is meant to protect the guest from the many "terrors" that lay ahead.

The tour begins in a dark corridor, featuring an endless hallway with a floating candelabrum, knocking doors, a ghost trying to escape a coffin and many chilling sounds and screams. The Doom Buggies then enter the séance room, where a woman in a crystal ball, named Madame Leota after an Imagineer who helped design the attraction, chants incantations to reveal some of the ghosts. After the séance room, the Ghost Host announces that the Mansion's "happy haunts have received [our] sympathetic vibrations" and that they have decided to have a party. Guests look down on a dinner party, with dancing and merriment, meeting some of the first audio-animatronic ghosts.[16] After the ballroom, the tour continues in the attic, where portraits and presents from Constance's weddings can be found, including a hint how she killed each of her five husbands. The Doom Buggies then descend into a graveyard, in which spirits dance and sing, tombstones quake and a caretaker shivers in fright.

As the tour nears the end, the Ghost Host returns, warning guests to watch for Hitchhiking Ghosts who may have snuck into the Doom Buggy during the tour. The hitchhiking ghost is revealed in a mirror just before guests disembark. Exiting guests then ascend an escalator to return to the realm of the living. Before leaving, Leota returns telling guests to "hurry back, be sure to bring your death certificate!"

4. New Orleans Square

A caricature is a style of portrait art that distorts, exaggerates, or even oversimplifies a feature of the future. This exaggerated feature plays upon a certain, easily recognizable trait of the figure in the name of humor or satire. Caricatures have been used for some kind of agenda, such as highlighting a political issue, simplifying it to visual symbols, or they can be used simply for entertainment, such as caricatures drawn by sketch artists at a fair or amusement park. Caricature is no stranger to Disney, used not only within their animated shorts and features, but also within their *True-Life Adventures* and other edutainment documentaries, and within Disneyland to emphasize the simulated environment.

Even New Orleans Square is itself a caricature of the Crescent City emphasized by the fact that the streets of the area intersect at Disneyland though they do not in real life; the voodoo lady casts a spell from the balcony; and this is the home of the Pirates and the Ghosts, the latter comfortably housed in a Garden District-style plantation house. While the Pirates are also full of caricature, the Ghosts are caricatures of death, seen by Disney as another potential for adventure, the next great adventure.

The Cold War and the atomic bomb in the mid-century revealed the possibility of the inevitability of death, taking it out of American control and put it into the hands of an enemy capable of destroying the country in a single attack. This helped create a fear of death that pathologizes the dying process. The country's mythos already shares elements with the Edenic garden and the very real quest for the Fountain of Youth. The fear of death promotes any action that could potentially prolong the inevitable—improved medical care, health related public programs, plastic surgery—sending the message that the goal of public health is not health for the sake of health, but to live longer. The fear of death witnesses epidemics like addiction and obesity with nervousness: these "diseases" accelerate the coming of death.

One of Disney's first *Silly Symphony* shorts, "The Skeleton Dance" (1929), recalls the Medieval *danse macabre*, or the dance of Death. The *danse* symbolism provided coping mechanisms for people constantly surrounded with death during phases of bubonic plague. Disney's "Skeleton Dance" is the dance of death, but in caricature. Some of the skeletons cannot keep their bones together and become musical instruments for the others. The "metaphysical evil" of death is turned into a joke.

Walt's Utopia

The Haunted Mansion claims to house "999 happy haunts," but "there is always room for one more." At the end of the attraction, guests are invited to return, as long as they bring their death certificate. The caricatures of ghosts, like the skeletons, represent "metaphysical evil," but are also turned into jokes: they "make possible the satisfaction of an instinct (whether lustful or hostile) in the face of an obstacle that stands in its way. They circumvent this obstacle and in a way draw pleasure from a source which the obstacle had made inaccessible."[17] There are three primary characteristics of jokes: one, playful aesthetic; two, they make connections between two otherwise unconnected ideas, such as metaphysical evil and good hospitality; three, jokes are deeply embedded in both psyche and identity. Jokes and caricatures that speak on a social level, such as those present in New Orleans Square, give voice to shadow issues, "that the wishes and desires of men have a right to make themselves acceptable alongside of exacting and ruthless morality."[18] By making light of a serious issue emanating from Cold War anxieties, Disney's ghosts offer a substitute for any traditional religious conception of the afterlife—one witnessed at every single Disney resort, not just in an esoteric theoretical realm. This caricature results in a Disneyfied shadow.

The Disneyfied shadow relies on humor to work its magic on us. As he described tragedy, Aristotle described a cathartic experience as an emotional group release experienced during a performance of a tragedy that leads us to sympathize and pity the main characters. Though the comedy portion of the *Poetics* is lost (assuming it ever existed), it stands to reason that a similar release could be experienced from a good comedy, only through laughter rather than through sorrow. In laughter, then, "the conditions are present under which a sum of psychical energy which has hitherto been used for [catharsis] is allowed free discharge."[19] The success of a joke relies on an audience to be complete, culminating in the audience reception. Neither the author nor audience will benefit from the joke if the audience does not understand or "get" it. Thus, to work on a cultural level, the humor must play to a common spectrum.

The Disney New Orleans Square dark rides find a common humor in shadow material, enhancing the joke so we can experience the cathartic release the shadow needs. The use of humor to induce us to love the shadow provides us an opportunity to play with shadow material without fear, or a state of apprehension focused on "isolated and recognizable dangers so that they may be judiciously appraised and realistically countered,"[20] and anxiety, or a state of tension "caused by a loss of mutual regulation and a consequent upset in libidinal and aggressive controls" which magnifies and causes "the illusion of an outer danger, without pointing to appropriate avenues of defense or mastery."[21] One of the benefits of the Disneyfied shadow is the removal of anything that could provoke these states, thus reinforcing a state of comfort and reassurance, as though Disney is responding to our "culture of fear" by providing a counter to it.

Disneyland emerged at a time during the early years of the Cold War when everyone needed an outlet. Laughter "arises if a quota of psychical energy which has earlier been used for the [catharsis] of particular psychical paths has become unusable, so that it can find free discharge."[22] While this implies nervous laughter, it has been the task of the Hollywood culture industry to provide humorous outlets of release, one of the few defenses against the full effects of the cultural shadow, which potentially could subjugate the entire culture.

Pirates and Ghosts Go to the Movies

These two New Orleans attractions take place underground in a mythic depth. According to the Disney experience, to get to the place of the cultural shadow, we must go underground to an underworld. As a literary trope, a descent into the underworld signifies a period of depression or darkness. As a metaphor for culture, this implies a voyage into the depths from which we return with a boon or some nugget of truth that brings us closer to wholeness and cultural unity. When we go into the depths at Disneyland, we are hopeful for the experience that is coming. Although Disney gives us an outlet, it does not permit us to bring anything back up. The shadow stays down there. We are nonetheless improved and enriched because of our journey, but not because we faced full on the fearful images to be found there. Instead, we laugh at the shadow.

New life and new shadow elements were breathed into the New Orleans Square attractions in the early 2000s when they were adapted into films, a reverse from other attractions in the park, many of which were inspired by Disney films and television shows. Borrowing from the different versions of the attractions around the world, Imagineering archives, and fan interpretation, movie plots were constructed that incorporated recognizable features into new plots and characters. The more successful of these two adaptations was *Pirates of the Caribbean: Curse of the Black Pearl*, which proved to be so successful that it launched an immensely popular film franchise composed of four films as of Summer 2011.

At the heart of this franchise's success is the character, Captain Jack Sparrow, played by Johnny Depp whose own popularity as an actor contributes to the popularity of this character. Jack is cunning and intelligent, though his completely mad demeanor hides this. His name evokes an archetypal everyman (Jack) who is springy, flighty, not-down-to-earth (Sparrow). His most common tool is a magical compass that shows the holder whatever they most desire, which is either his ship his preferred means of transportation,[23] or treasure, the end-goal of contemporary American nationalism. The only time that the compass does not lead him is when he is unsure of what he is seeking. This loss of direction can occur when the shadow is at the helm, so to speak, because it means that the unconscious has taken over, and it is not exactly interested in telling us where we are going.

However, the success of this pirate helps fuel the trend of loving the shadow. Pirates represent deeply embedded nightmarish figures. Historical pirates, such as Blackbeard, inspired horrific ghost stories. They do things that we would normally abhor, such as "pillage and plunder, rifle and loot"[24]; throughout the process they reveal something about ourselves buried in our individual shadows that endears them to us. Jack, a trickster figure, bridges between "historical evil" and mainstream culture, shadow unconsciousness and cultural consciousness. His mercenary defiance gives Americans a mythic example of how to cope with destabilizing doubt, because no matter the situation in which he finds himself, Jack can always find a way out. Such hero figures provide reassurance when leaders and CEOs fail.[25]

At the same time, *The Haunted Mansion* was a colossal flop. This film tried to remain too faithful to the attraction while constructing a ghostly love story around Master Gracey, the mansion's owner, and the likeness between his forbidden lover and mortal real estate agent, Sara Evers. The film fails in that too much of its humor relies on the delivery of its mortal characters, rather than on the humor inherent in the attraction's Happy Haunts. In fact, the main ghostly characters appear solid and corporeal for the majority of the film. The other problem is that its latent message is too didactic. The "curse" on Gracey Mansion that prevents the ghosts from moving on and traps them in the mortal realm came about when broken-hearted Master Gracey lost his lover to what he thought was suicide rather than marry him. He hanged himself. The mortal Evers family reveals that the Butler, in fact, killed Gracey's Elizabeth to prevent their marriage on grounds that it would have destroyed the house. Without a specific sense of time, and knowing that Elizabeth was an African American woman suggests that the Butler's intervention was to maintain a Louisiana status quo that barred mixed-race marriages.

A further didactic message in the film is the marked distinction between Heaven and Hell. Gracey and his ghosts are only permitted to enter Heaven when Gracey has been restored to his love. The Butler, however, is sent to a fiery Hell for his betrayal against his master. The use of Heaven and Hell in the film gives the story a specific Christian undertone not present anywhere in the attraction, and diminishes the shadow nature of the Haunted Mansion.

The potency of the shadow imagery in the two films reveals a cultural reaction to its relationship with its ideological shadow. *Pirates of the Caribbean* makes plain the ways in which defiance of authority can be an alternative to the culture in crisis. To see the pirates victor over the repressive authority provides a catharsis that *The Haunted Mansion*, released the same year, was unable to provide. *The Haunted Mansion* offers no catharsis; instead, it offers a string of clichés that take us through a highly formulaic story, which itself dispels anything other than passive participation in the film.

The Shadow of Doubt

There is an individual shadow and there is a collective or cultural shadow, which is "the sum of the [individual] shadows, and also ...

would be something which does not disturb the group itself and which is apparent only to outer groups."[26] In the modern world, especially, this group shadow has manifested in war that aims to destroy anything or anyone believed to pose a threat to a nation's existence,[27] including one's fellow compatriot, which can lead to civil war. The target of this perceived threat ranges from the land and people to patterns of culture and anything that defines a nation's cultural identity. From the perspective of those writing during the first half of the twentieth century, there is some truth to this in that those from the first half of the century could easily recognize the enemy in a nation or group and the threat posed (Hitler, Stalin, Franco, Mussolini, Nazis, and Communists).

However, the events that occurred during the war years, specifically the years between the end of World War I in 1916 through the end of World War II in 1946, upset a "textbook" relationship to the shadow in America: the Great Depression, the Holocaust, the atomic bomb, and the beginnings of the Cold War. These events revealed to a contemporary audience how cruel humans can be to one another. All of this lead to feelings of doubt, anxiety, paranoia/fear and distrust on the cultural level, such that "many were convinced that relief from anxiety required a sharp turn inward, away from the public realm of politics and economics, and toward the neurotic, troubled, fragmented, and 'rootless' self."[28] This, in turn, caused a shift not only in American myth, but also caused a realignment of the cultural shadow with an ideology resulting in an unclear recognition of the target for shadow projections, including anything or anyone that threatens our American-ness, even fellow Americans. An ideological shadow is not anchored, and this doubt destabilized the American mythos, and commentators began to decry the end of civilization.[29]

Among the naysayers, however, were those who "imagined, even proclaimed a revitalized culture."[30] Disney proclaimed an optimism for America, presenting a viable imagery that helped create a mode of dealing with the shadow that corresponds to an ideology by giving us caricatures of shadow material that are easy to consume. These shadow caricatures have become hyperreal, seeming more real to the larger culture than the actual shadow, meaning that the genuine shadow is still boiling underneath the surface, arising at any point a catastrophe shatters our hyperrealistic world of illusion.

4. New Orleans Square

The Cold War introduced a new aspect of shadow, one not so easily recognized in a single enemy. Communism is an ideology, an abstraction, one with no cultural borders and a seductive quality that inspires fear for an unknown enemy: the "Communist," truly a shadow, is an enemy we cannot see. The same kind of fear projected onto a "Communist" was redirected at the end of the Cold War. This new unseen enemy, the "terrorist," proves even more difficult to recognize because this enemy is not necessarily aligned with a particular ideology. Communism and terrorism are both projected onto others, but the projection ultimately loses its meaning and potency because it reflects an internal cultural fear. The initial response in the 1950s was to project the fear onto our former allies, suppress and/or blacklist, and to repress this fear by offering media that projected happiness and harmony. Those who were able fled these feelings by relocating into the pockets of perceived security found in suburbia. Media outlets, such as film, television or comic books, addressed Cold War fears through metaphor—alien invasion or superheroes, for instance—providing an indirect outlet for pent-up fears and tensions. Initially, this "sanitization" of society created a conservative, Neo-Victorian idyllic environment, attempting to reaffirm the utopian destiny of the American dream.

However, the immediate response to mid-century neo–Victorian repression was an increased number of counterculture movements in the 1960s. These movements re-introduced the shadow into mainstream discussion. To be counterculture means to operate, often consciously, against the dominant mode. The 1960s counterculture movements were in reaction to the buried abstract of the American cultural unconscious. Students actively protested the war and government while hippies among many other groups protested against a loss of *communitas* in mainstream America. Their legacy is still potent today.

In *From Walt to Woodstock*, Douglas Brode posits the thesis that Disney helped create counterculture by incorporating subversive themes throughout its films and cartoon shorts. More importantly, however, Disney reflected the growing counterculture movements by creating New Orleans Square in response, likely acting on instinct or an unconscious connection to the greater culture. The area is formed

Walt's Utopia

from a portion of Frontierland, the land of Manifest Destiny and wilderness to become the only area in Disneyland to directly address the shadow. The dominant figures of this land's two attractions are counterculture-like figures. The conceptions for both of these attractions were begun in the early 1960s; that they both opened in the latter half of the 1960s is symbolic of the era's need for a shadow space, one that could be engaged without harm to others, as was the case in protest rallies. This rise of the Counterculture coincided with a new wave of domestic events to rekindle the American doubt introduced during World War II: equal and Civil Rights, the Vietnam War, the assassination of the Kennedys and Martin Luther King. Unlike the shadow of the 1950s, this new wave could not be easily repressed.

Doubt is the point when a particular set of assumed beliefs are called into question. It can bring a healthy amount of skepticism to an event, such as an argument or discussion. Doubt enters into a mythic modality when it runs so deep that uncertainty and skepticism turn into distrust. America's ideological shadow is fuelled by doubt, because doubt, more than any historical event, jeopardizes the utopian illusion. As more and more doubt fills the culture, American idealism becomes a shadow itself, teetering on the balance between the two in favor of the cultural shadow. As such, shadow imagery is tasked with becoming the vehicle that carries American mythos.

Understanding America's shadow lies in the assumption of a cultural crisis, which is manifested within the layers of society. This mythos has been perpetrated within the American experience for over a century and perhaps can be considered the cause of the events surrounding the Cold War and the collective disillusionment of recent generations. During the Progressive movement of the early twentieth century, Progressives perceived potential crisis, then fabricated the historicity of this crisis in order to emphasize the might and power of a strong leader. This leader, Progressives hoped, would lead society away from crisis and into balance and stability, two social dreams that could never become reality under the progressive mindset. Without crisis, the belief would have nothing to adhere to. This perception of constant crisis was fueled by the actual crises of the mid-century, resulting in a willingness of the people to submit a little of their freedoms to be brought out of the crisis.

Club 33

Tucked into a back corner of New Orleans Square is the mysterious entrance to Club 33, Disneyland's elite club. Envisioned by Walt to be an exclusive entitlement to select investors, special guests and dignitaries, although opened after his death in 1967, Club 33 has grown its own mythology throughout the years filled with tales of conspiracy and intrigue developed by an excluded population of guests who stare longingly at the ornate door that will not open for them. I haven't visited Club 33, and I have only seen videos of its interior on YouTube. Perhaps someday I will add my name to the waitlist and eagerly await my opportunity to enter the mysterious door.

Located above the Blue Bayou Restaurant that shares its footprint with the Pirates of the Caribbean, Club 33 boasts a membership fee of $11,000 and a lengthy wait list. The Club features a lounge, restaurant, and a bar with views over New Orleans Square and the Rivers of America. The Club initially featured a room called the Trophy Room, full of Walt memorabilia and audio-animatronics serving as a tribute to the park's visionary, but a recent 2014 renovation removed the Trophy Room in favor of an expanded kitchen. The same renovation also closed one of New Orleans Square's public courtyards (in my opinion, one of the most charming corners of the park) to make a waiting area for the restaurant.

The inclusion of Club 33 was a new kind of corporate gesture for the park. Rather than the usual corporate sponsorship that can be seen throughout the park, Club 33 was intended as a zone to cater to the Very Important People Disney wanted to seduce for future partnerships, and also to give them a private place within the park to do the things Very Important People do. The idea was inspired by the VIP Lounges Walt visited at the New York World's Fair.[31]

It's only natural that a place like Club 33 would be the topic of speculation by guests. Any exclusive organization sparks the imagination. One such example is the Freemasons, a group that has inspired conspiracy theories for decades. It makes sense that Club 33 would join the level of Freemasonry, given that Walt Disney was himself elevated to the status of a mythic figure. Club 33, in many ways, is like the innermost sanctum of Walt Disney worshippers.

Walt's Utopia

One of the standing claims circling around the Internet is that Club 33 was so named because Walt Disney was a 33rd degree Freemason, as though this is an indicator that Walt was in fact on an Illuminati mission to take over the world. There is no evidence in any Walt Disney biography I've come across that Walt Disney ever joined the Freemasons. As a child, he was a member of the Order of DeMolay, an organization modeled after the Freemasons and aimed at young men. Like the Boy Scouts, DeMolays are tutored in the behaviors and skills needed to prepare them for manhood. Had he actually been a Freemason, this information would have come to light by now. One's membership as a Freemason is not a secret, though perhaps it's not boasted as loudly as people would like. Furthermore, the 33rd degree is reserved as an honorary degree for those who have made significant contributions to their Lodge or community. One does not simply keep such an honor secret, but Walt Disney would have well deserved this honor if it were true.

But it's not. One indicator is the use of Masonic symbolism within the artist's work. A Mason often finds ways to incorporate their esoteric knowledge and symbolism into their work as Easter Eggs to fellow Masons. A keen eye knows what sort of images to look for.[32] There are two obvious issues with this. One is that the nature of symbolism is that we can ascribe any meaning to it that we want to. For example, this is what makes the game of finding Hidden Mickeys around the park so entertaining. The Hidden Mickeys are the Easter Eggs that we're intended to find throughout the park. Some of them look like accidents (who really is going to arrange three rocks in the corner of a pathway that way on purpose?), while others are clearly intended, such as the Mickey-shaped Haunted Mansion place setting during the Ball Room Scene. Similarly, people have claimed that the coral palace of King Triton in *The Little Mermaid* is phallic, or that the dust in one scene of *The Lion King* swirls to spell "sex," indicating subliminal messaging intended to corrupt the innocence of children. While I can accept that coral growth is conspicuously phallic shaped, I have yet to see "sex." And I've looked. One may argue that it's no longer there because the film was edited for release, but I was using a first generation VHS with the frame-by-frame feature on the VCR. The other problem is that knowing what symbols to look for. There are many books that claim to "reveal the secrets of _____." There are several videos on YouTube about Disney's secrets, one of which finds "666" in the loops of the Walt Disney signature logo. The claim believes itself to be legitimate, because Walt Disney was a Freemason, except that the claim is based on a false understanding that equates Freemasons with Satanism.

All of this is a manifestation of the cultural shadow. Whenever something is unusual, different, and unknown, we have a tendency to prejudge it as wrong, which can then lead to assumptions of evil. American history is fraught with prejudice of all sorts, from the obvious racial and gender issues that have defined major aspects of American history to the relatively innocuous prejudices against people who dress, eat, and define their leisure time differently. Even Disney seeped a little populist prejudice into the film canon, suggesting that the wealthy are the "bad guys," giving priority to the relatively poor and simplistic characters. Similarly, though American culture boasts a preference for the "rags-to-riches" Horatio Algier-esque story, there is often a prejudice that emerges against someone who has actually achieved the "riches." It is this prejudice that makes it easy to label Walt Disney as "Hollywood's Dark Prince," to see Disneyland as a money drain, and to prompt viewers to find random phalluses in Disney cartoons. This expression of the shadow occurs completely on an unconscious level. It would be too simple to say that it's motivated by jealousy, because the feeling of jealousy is motivated by the shadow.

Club 33 activates the shadow in Disneyland, because it represents the very kind of wealth that Mickey Mouse taught guests to abhor. Because it is an exclusive club in a place that publically welcomes inclusion—after all, Disneyland is a place where young and young-at-heart can play together—it tickles the shadow. And because Disney is Disney, it naturally invites analysis into the shadow that looks at ways in which corporate artifacts negate the illusion of innocence and family fare that are the cornerstones of the company's model.

5

Frontierland
The Myths of Frontier and Destiny

"Frontierland. It is here that we experience the story of our country's past. The color, romance and drama of Frontier America as it developed from wilderness trails to roads, riverboats and civilization. A tribute to the faith, courage and ingenuity of our hearty pioneers who blazed the trails and made this progress possible."—Walt Disney, "Dateline Disneyland"

"Frontierland celebrates the American pioneer spirit. It has always been the perfect embodiment of the wonder of—and quest to discover—the unknown, whether it be by land, water, or rail. It's also a time of endless summers and lazy rivers. Stay awhile, and you'll see why so many folks choose to call Frontierland 'home.'"—The Imagineers, The Imagineering Field Guide to Disneyland

The American Frontier captured in Frontierland stretches from the banks of the Mississippi to the deserts of the Four Corner states and the formulaic Frontier Town. It is no accident that Frontierland is situated to the west of the Plaza Hub, rooting it in its symbolic space in the park and connecting Disneyland metaphorically with the larger spectrum of American myth, which includes the progress of Tomorrow directly across the Hub.[1] Additionally, Frontierland has access routes to Fantasyland and Adventureland, and shares riverbanks with New Orleans Square weaving New Orleans into the frontier myth. This suggests the degree of adventure that conquering the West required and how the tales and legends of the West have been woven into America's own fairy tale repertoire.

5. Frontierland

More than any other Disney realm, Frontierland serves as a museum to a cultural memory that, even in 1955, was beginning to fade. By the time of the construction of Disneyland, the West had been mapped and most parts of it had ownership claims. What had once been a vast expanse of untamed nature became civilized and attractive to new generations. One particular spot in the Old West, Los Angeles, became home to America's "Dream Factory"—Hollywood—and lured dreamers from all parts of the world who wanted to be a part of the film industry. This industry kept the memory of the West alive and thriving until Neal Armstrong and John Glenn walked on the moon and changed our relationship to uncharted territory. Suddenly, a new frontier was in need of civilizing.

The imagery of Frontierland is so potent that its name is equated with the West. For most people, Frontierland evokes images of a West derived from popular culture.[2] What is being evoked here is the spirit of the West. Disney's version is more closely related to American popular culture than history, simplifying the Westward experience into the iconic imagery of the heroes of early America.[3] This imagery is conveyed through mythic space and time, giving it a sense of presence and progress helping to keep the frontier spirit alive and well. Rather than criticize Disney for trivializing America's past, cultural historian Richard Francaviglia suggests that Frontierland, indeed all of Disneyland, must be read as metaphorical maps of the imagination that combine representations from reality into a sustainable storyline.[4] This helps to provide grounding in the past as we move through the progress of post-modernism and post-industrialism.

Nonetheless, valid concerns can be made about Disney's romantic portrayal of the past and its relationship to the imagination. Each land in Disneyland can be read as its own complete macrocosm or it can be read as a component of the larger Disneyland microcosm. The American relationship to the West is consciously captured in Frontierland, but the complexity of this relationship comes through a read of the entire park. Disney's romanticized version celebrates the land that defines America without all of the skirmishes between settlers and local tribes and the dirty reality of America's natural landscape. Frontierland reinforces the themes Walt Disney sought to convey through his productions: love of nature and the value of hard work. To emphasize the natural, Disney resorts to the unnatural, creating a hyperrealistic environment in which everything works and functions properly. This speaks to a "new, more radical perception of nature," that has become the preference of Americans blurring fantasy to create a new reality.[5] In other words, we develop a preference for the Disneyfied version of the historical past, because it plays into an idealized fantasy of how we should remember the past. The Spirit of America associated with Manifest Destiny transformed from a geographic spirit to one linked to an ideology, defining America's national character.[6] Disneyland offers an opportunity to explore the Frontier.

Furthermore, Disneyfying the past rewrites it "in order to reshape audience's view of the present."[7] By reshaping the past, Disney's unapologetic patriotism and exceptionalism reinforces America's purpose suggesting that by following the model of America's frontierspeople, modern Americans could once again achieve greatness through hard work and community.[8]

The West played a key role in the development of America, but the portrayal of the West in cinema, television and at Disneyland helped reinforce the Western spirit into an ideology for the modern America. The dominant themes of the New West as portrayed by Disney include:

1. The Old West as a mythic past, which is one of the few distinctly American myths, emphasizing the heroes as key components to the creation of the country.
2. The Old West as Cold War Myth.
3. The Old West as the penultimate frontier and the significance of turning to outer space as the final frontier.

At various times in the history of Frontierland, it has reflected one or more of these themes. With its recent emphasis on thrills and pirates, Frontierland resonates more with themes of mythic past and penultimate frontier, though the latter has defined the area's direction since the 1970s.

Due to the intersection between Hollywood, American myth, and Disney, a brief exploration into the place of Hollywood is helpful for understanding America's mythos, especially when considering the West and the Western movie genre.

5. Frontierland

Film scholar Douglas Brode uses the term "Dream West" to describe the theme of the Frontier in Hollywood Westerns.[9] This is a potent term to use, because it separates the reality of the Old West from the Hollywood version, which concentrates on the mythic West. The reality of the Old West is that it was difficult to settle: the landscape was harsh in some areas and Native Americans were not easily willing to let go of their claim to the land; yet, Westerns form a key component of American mythos, surpassing even the legends of pilgrims and founding fathers. Westerns reflect what it took to make America a great land "from sea to shining sea," not just the crossing and establishment of the colonies, significant for establishing and exerting America's independence from her European parents. The American mythos is firmly rooted in our relationship to place and we have defined ourselves by the majesty of the terrain. Western films act as reminders for the work it took to claim the land and, more importantly, what the land looked like before we settled it while it was still the wild terrain. This plays into American nostalgia and collective memory. For this reason, in part, we trust cowboy figures (Reagan/Bush/Bush) to protect us, even if their knowledge and application of the law is shaky at best.

Hollywood is at the core of modern myth-making, although the "media amplify and redefine myth: they do not create it. Television, film, and printed matter detect new values in the environment, then send them back to the audience as the final test of operative success."[10] Nonetheless, Hollywood is a myth machine that detects a trend and then gives it shape. The trend can be something intentional, such as the recent popularity of vampire romance, or it can be something unexpected, such as the overnight popularity of Mickey Mouse and Davy Crockett, that is made apparent through the audience response. Beginning in the 1930s, these Hollywood trends have been linked to consumerism, one that stretches beyond an afternoon at the movies. Merchandise brought characters from the screen to the home.

All of this was made possible by the new spare time found in technological innovation and New Deal employment regulations. Rather than call it a "myth-machine," Steven Watts and others describe Hollywood's role as the "culture industry": "The 'culture industry' swiftly came to dominate the dispersal of entertainment and information in postwar America. Large corporations mass-produced cultural commodities by industrial techniques and then marketed, advertised, and sold them to an enormous national audience."[11] The trajectory of the culture industry begins with the trend. The trend is then given shape in the form of some entertaining media, such as a book or film. Other media are then employed to encourage consumption. The end result is a doubled or tripled myth, with many outlets for experience that strengthen the myth's role in culture, which can change at any given time as society has proven fickle when it comes to how it consumes a myth.[12]

The establishment of Disneyland is an example of media synergy. Walt had an idea and developed it. He gained sponsorship and funding, which included a weekly television show that would periodically update viewers on the park's construction progress. Following the opening of the park, merchandise doubles as souvenirs and as convenient advertising of the park that can travel across the world. The practice branched into the outer consumer spectrum as acquisition of park memories no longer relies on park attendance, in part thanks to the online Disney Store, no doubt furthering the scheme of easy advertising.

It is no accident that Hollywood was established in California, the coastal land of prosperity. Early film producers moved west for cheap land and consistent weather; however, the choice of locations situates Hollywood deep within the Manifest Destiny myth. As the wilderness disappeared under the hand of civilization, it was replaced by the Dream Factory. Through cinema, the ideals of Manifest Destiny took many forms: westerns, cops and robbers, slapstick comedy, swashbuckling, musicals and follies (after sound), suspense/thriller/horror/*film noir*, fantasy, and cartoons. The Disney studio recognized Hollywood's dream connection, and made it their primary focus. Disney provides the tools to make "dreams come true," and offers Disneyland as the real-life place where it happens, situated down the interstate highway from the Hollywood studios in Burbank. In the mythology of Los Angeles, "life, liberty, and the pursuit of happiness" reside on the surface of the city; this also attracts people to the area with hopes of "making it big." The American credo is linked with success, which is measured in terms of money, the key facilitator in America's consumptive behavior.

In the meantime, however, Hollywood has set events in motion to ensure that we continue to consume the trends it produces for us. One way it does this is through sequels, which introduce new stories and merchandise opportunities for a popular franchise. Roger Ebert, film critic, wrote an editorial for *Newsweek* about the film line-up for the 2011 summer season, noted for its action blockbusters. This line-up included a record twenty-seven sequels, many of which overshadow fresh, original stories.[13] That sequels continue to make money, which is again America's measure of success, is a testament to the potency of these mythic trends, some of which have been well-established since the 1940s (the Marvel franchise) or were surprises no one expected to sell (*Pirates of the Caribbean*) or have a built-in fan base that emerged from smart mixture of media (*Harry Potter*). These sequels also reflect a lack of imagination in Hollywood as a result of the "hollow idols of this city that carry the projections of heroes and gods," themselves having lost their meaning in a city that over-stimulates visitors and residents in simulacra: "So many long to find the real gold of meaning, deep relationship, and soul, but instead are left with a worthless mirage."[14]

Frontierland Key Attractions

- Nature's Wonderland (closed)
- Big Thunder Mountain Railroad
- Indian Village (closed)
- Tom Sawyer Island/Pirate's Lair on Tom Sawyer Island
- Rivers of America

Walt Disney's plan for Frontierland, as he announced in the land's dedication speech, was to capture "the treasure of our native folklore, the songs, tales and legends of the men who built the land."[15] The memory that built Frontierland has little foundation in history, but it is inextricably tied with the significance of the place to the memory, creating a "mental map of the natural experience."[16] As is described below, the West as a place has shaped an essential piece of American mythos and identity, situated at the core of what being "American" means. In the 1950s, Walt Disney emphasized this point not only through Frontierland, but also on the "Frontierland" segment of the *Disneyland* television show, the *True-Life Adventures* series of nature films, and, to an extent, in the United States pavilion of the 1958 World's Fair in Brussels with the Disney-produced *The USA in Circarama*, a film projected in 360 degrees highlighting the splendor and majesty of the United States landscape.[17] This latter attraction helped convey a Disneyfied romantic view of the United States to the entire world.

Nature's Wonderland and Manifest Destiny

Two geological landmarks form the core of Frontierland: The Rivers of America and Nature's Wonderland. At the opening of Disneyland, Nature's Wonderland was an unnamed barren landscape that recreated a small Frontier mining town, named Rainbow Ridge, and the Painted Desert. This area featured a daily shoot-out and a revue at the Golden Horseshoe Saloon, and showcased three modes of frontier transportation to give guests a chance to experience the conquering of the West from the settlers' point of view. Added in 1960 during the transformation from barren landscape into Nature's Wonderland, inspired, like Adventureland, by the *True-Life Adventures* films, was the Rainbow Caverns Mine Train that took guests on a tour through the desert and through the Rainbow Caverns.

The Western wilderness is the wild, untamed land of the American imagination, stretching from the Mississippi River to the promising lush lands of the Pacific coast. Having divorced themselves from Great Britain, the exemplars of imperialism, early Americans established this country with a heart for exploration and nationalism. The vast lands to the West offered promise for individual freedom, ownership, and a new life. The lands of the West were advertised to potential prospectors and settlers as a place where one could play out America's inalienable rights entitling us to life, liberty, and the pursuit of happiness. This is at the heart of the American Dream, and its promises for opportunity for all classes, creeds, and, at least after the Civil War, colors.

The reality of this land, however, is that it is harsh and unforgiving. The wild of the Western frontier is ingrained into American consciousness, playing a key role in how Americans define themselves and the country, such that we take our mission to cultivate the wasteland for granted as a function of human nature, becoming myth. It is a function of such myths "in any society, that they can—and do—by their juxta-

5. Frontierland

position of images and metaphors and ideals make logic out of the rationally illogical. They provide, thereby, a tension which seems necessary to human thought and necessary, too, to maintain dynamic human societies."[18] The myth of Westward Expansion became the symbol for the search for all frontiers,[19] some of which might be physical wastelands to conquer, but they could also be imaginal and metaphorical. Westward Expansion helped bridge the gap between the two oceans, a gap made all the less significant as improvements in transportation (especially the construction of the Transcontinental Railroad) made the journey west shorter and safer, opening the door to the modern era.

However, Americans were not content once we conquered the land of the West. Instead, we needed to find new frontiers to cultivate, eagerly seeking new territories to contain and to construct the utopian Eden we believed must exist. The birth of the film industry in the early 1900s was one such frontier, a wilderness of the imagination, which filled the minds of many Americans with images of heroes and faraway places. The World Wars offered another opportunity to cultivate a new frontier, this one economic and ideological, as the idealism of Westward expansion found new audiences in new parts of the world. As the globalized world continues shrinking, we retreat more and more into the imagination, which, one could argue, is a wilderness in danger of disappearing as we deplete the resources of its offering. The same argument is made with regards to the planet's physical resources.[20]

As America's relationship to the Western wilderness has changed, so has its portrayal in stories and myths. Throughout the 1950s, western films portrayed a hero struggling against nature personified by Native Americans, which represents the struggle between civilization and wilderness. Wilderness, in turn, "represented isolation and violence, and the hero's quest was thus for peace and community. These things are defined as progress and are much desired today."[21] This was seen in Disneyland in Nature's Wonderland, which combined civilizing modes of transportation with homage for the beauty of the West. Although initially a romanticized Disney image of the struggle of humanity versus nature, the meaning of Nature's Wonderland eventually gave way to the idea of the wild as an escape from the civilized world, a view of the wilderness that dates back to the mid-eighteenth century Romantics, notably Henry David Thoreau and his *Walden*.

111

Walt's Utopia

To understand America's relationship with the West, our relationship to Manifest Destiny needs to be explored before discussing how we have conquered and tamed the West.

"Manifest Destiny" is the phrase for the widely held belief in the nineteenth century that Americans were entitled to all of the land from the Pacific to the Atlantic.[22] Though the term was not coined until the mid–1800s, the ideas behind it fueled Westward Expansion from the country's early history, and helped justify such events as the Louisiana Purchase in 1803 and the Mexican-American War that yielded Texas and the Southwest region.[23] The Founding Fathers promoted the ideals of westward expansion as fundamental to the nation's mission of freedom, independence, and nationalism. Without Manifest Destiny, it was believed that America could not fulfill her destiny to become a great nation; in short, "independence, nationalism, and expansion are *mutually* causative, as well as the logical and inevitable results of each other, in American myth."[24]

With this destiny made manifest, it became not only the mission of settlers, pioneers, and frontiersmen to lay claim on savage areas for America, but to take with them the ideals of Democracy, civilization, education and government. This mission quickly became myth, creating and dominating the American perspective of an entitlement to the West. Like the untamed wilderness, the tenets of democracy could not be contained, thus its spread is symbolically linked to the taming of the wilderness. By spreading democracy, Americans could generate freedom: "freedom from outside oppression and interference; freedom to expand, move, and find happiness; freedom to determine a common course, common ways, and common purposes, and to follow them."[25]

As Walt Disney notes in the Frontierland dedication speech, this area of the park is dedicated to the memory of the men and women who played their part in establishing this nation. His romantic view of the frontier celebrates Manifest Destiny, while overlooking the difficulties westward expansion entailed. Sure, there was recognition in the daily shoot-outs in Rainbow Ridge of conflicts inspired by the quest for land, but Disneyland overlooks the conflicts with Native Americans and other nations who also claimed the land. In his analysis of Walt Disney World, Steve Fjellman labels this whitewashing of history "Distory,"[26] and numerous Disney critics have likewise remarked upon Disney's imperialism of the minorities and disenfranchised. Such discussion is valid, though it overlooks the similar trend in mid-century media. If the reemergence of the Frontier Mythos during the 1950s was to reinforce the national identity during the Cold War, a time of doubt and instability, then the use of "Distory" is not intended to distort the view of history, but to utilize a mythic imaging—that relies on a historical connection—to reach as many people as possible. As any study of Disney should emphasize, the corporation is a business of entertainment. The use of caricature and stereotype is rarely out of accordance with the caricatures and stereotypes of the era. Indeed, some may argue[27] that these are far more sympathetic than in other media. As an example, early Disneyland celebrated Native American culture, in contrast to the pervading theme in Westerns of the "savage" opponent.

In the modern era, we have no direct connection to the concept of wilderness and the mission of Manifest Destiny, having ensconced ourselves in cities, suburbs, and behind computer screens, but this does not mean that its myth is any less potent. Notably, the "myths which shaped American perceptions of the wilderness have been transformed over the past two centuries[....] Wilderness today is a symbol of, and provides an unconscious ritual for, the American mission: It is a metaphorical stage for a historical pageant, no longer the real world."[28] This "metaphorical stage" plays a pageant of memory, kept alive in cinema and Disneyland. The transformation from physical to metaphorical, additionally, plays out in American consumption behaviors. Indeed, the myth of consumption is a constituent to the myth of Manifest Destiny. Westward expansion was not only about entitlement in claiming territory and spreading democracy, it was also about consuming the West, its resources and the idea of freedom. Following World War II, consumption and democracy are conceptually bonded together. Within America, this coincided with the new prosperity the country experienced following the War that allowed for increased leisure time and financial resources for enjoying it. Across the world, American consumption is linked with Democracy and having the right and freedom to choose a means of consumption. Americans and their corporations have responded both domestically and abroad by designing new avenues of consumption, in some cases borrowing the Disney business model.

Furthermore, the Cold War marked a paradigm shift for American myth. This is the first period when Manifest Destiny first reaches global proportions in response to the new globalism introduced by the World Wars. Because of the nuclear threats the Cold War posed, this period was justified as a continuance of war following World War II,[29] but this war heightened fears and anxieties that "produced a climate of idealized coercion—reflected in the pervasive ideal of 'loyalty'—the culture perversely claimed 'freedom' as its dearest possession."[30] Hollywood and the birth of television present mythic stories that reflect an increased unconscious awareness that the constant fear during the Cold War was a fear more of losing our "Americanness" (individuality, idealism, and freedom) than it was of fighting the Soviets. Communism posed a threat to our culture's way of life.

During the 1950s, arguably the peak period of Westerns, motifs of the Old West were used to reinforce American ideals. This decade also believed that the enemy of the Cold War was the Soviet Union, thus traditional "white hat" versus "black hat" High Noon duals helped reinforce the fight of good against evil (or, in this case, the two super powers). As the fifties melted into the sixties and beyond, the shift is captured in cinema by means of a change in the role of a cowboy, now more an anti-hero, and the internal struggle with himself or a trauma (much like returning Vietnam veterans). This eventually gave way to the space Western that projected Manifest Destiny onto Outer Space. This, in turn, shift coincides with the realization that the real threat is Communism, an ideology as opposed to a specific group of people, the fear of which ultimately led to the failed Vietnam War and opens the door for the present fear of terrorism.

As the United States was obsessed with protecting itself from Communism, "the word 'frontier' also signified the boundary between two political systems," thus turning Frontierland into "a Cold War statement about the irrepressible spirit of America in overcoming the hostile frontier of that part of the world behind the Iron Curtain where individual aspirations were crushed."[31] The Cold War proved to be a mythic source for Disney, inspiring stories that celebrate America and all that she offers. Outwardly, Walt Disney was a staunch anti–Communist, testifying in front of the House Un-American Committee as a friendly witness in 1947.[32] Through its pictures, however, Disney conveys a pacifist agenda, promoting peace between the United States and the Soviets. Disney's themes supported themes of freedom and cooperative unity. As Cold War films, these movies suggest reconciliation among Americans and the Reds, while acknowledging that at some times, such reconciliation might not be possible.[33] This gives a new dimension to Frontierland. As a Cold War land, it is not just about the vast expanse of psychic freedom, but a social commentary about human freedom. Disney thus becomes a mediator and advocate for the *Pax Americana*, or the notion of relative world peace under the blanket of American democracy.

As the Disney studio moved through the 1940s and 1950s, Walt Disney recognized the studio's position as a role model and educator. He coined the term, "edutainment" to describe the films he produced. Rather than produce straight educational productions, which he found boring and uninteresting, Walt sought to make his educational films entertaining by coupling the content with an interesting story line, characters, and a style that disguised the educational nature. These edutainment films, notably historical pieces such as Davy Crockett or the *True-Life Adventures*, are filled with drama, conflict, adventure, and romance, most of which is added for the Disney affect. These films emphasize Walt's romanticized American values of "loyalty, honor, and the nobility of the American past,"[34] making his voice a perfect reinforcer of Cold War American values, defined by Middle America with a nostalgia for the Victorian Era. The Cold War era "romanticized the power that American wielding over other non–Western peoples over the environment."[35] Frontierland is thus exemplary of the Frontier, but its relationship to technology and audio-animatronic control over the environment is a metaphor for America's new endeavor at a globalized, Americanized world. While Disney's version of the past is oversimplified and idealized, Frontierland's themes of "unity, community and reconciliation"[36] make it a fitting foil to Cold War fear and paranoid tensions.

Big Thunder Mountain Railroad: Cultivating the West

By the 1970s, however, Nature's Wonderland proved to be too bland for teenagers, who were being lured to other Southern California theme parks with the promise of thrilling kinetic roller coasters.[37] Imagineers responded by designing Disneyland's first thrill ride, a ride that revolves around thrill of the ride as opposed to the experience of the story, Big Thunder Mountain Railroad. Nature's Wonderland was completely uprooted, though some elements of the landscape and audio-animatronics were retained for ambiance. The design for Big Thunder was inspired by Utah's Bryce Canyon National Park and the mesas from Monument Valley.[38]

Big Thunder Mountain Railroad makes a noticeable departure from Walt Disney's original conception that envisioned Disneyland as a safe environment for adults and children to play together. Though the guests of the 1950s were eager for the family-friendly escape Disneyland provides, the guests of the 1970s were seasoned with the more heroic images that were broadcast during the 1960s of counterculture and civil rights protests and the Vietnam War, the first war to have full-television coverage. Additionally, the 1970s saw a rise in independent cinema, which had more ability to show horrific, uncensored stories than the faltering studio system. As such, the guests of the 1970s required "something more kinky,"[39] a trend that continues to influence imagineering projects today. As information becomes more cluttered and a key constituent of contemporary American anxiety, the type of escape needs to become more and more thrilling to sufficiently drown out the pressures associated with these anxieties. Disney's hyperreality is the escape from the real world hyperreality that was initially designed as the escape from Cold War anxieties.

To cultivate the historical West, two key steps had to first happen: one, the competition needed to be eliminated and two, the infrastructure needed to be built in order to support the settlements. This mission was further enhanced by Protestant ideals that equated the mission of Manifest Destiny with fulfilling God's mission:

> It is true that the usefulness of a calling, and thus its favor in the sight of God, is measured primarily in moral terms, and thus in terms of the importance of goods produced in it for the community. But a further, and, above all, in practice the most important, criterion is found in private profitableness. For if that God, whose hand the [Protestant] sees in all the occurrences of life, shows one of His elect a chance to profit, he must do it with a purpose. Hence the faithful Christian must follow the call by taking advantage of the opportunity.[40]

5. Frontierland

Thus, those moving West had an obligation to bring "the soul's food," education and religion, with them.[41] This Protestant work ethic further helped bring rationalization to the West, by systemizing economic conveyances, a necessary convenience to accommodate the distance between outposts and settlements.[42]

This also included "saving" the Indian. Native Americans were perceived as "savage" and "uncivilized," especially in their resistance to relinquish control of the land to American settlers. Wholesale destruction of native populations was secondary to the hope that one could "improve" them. Nonetheless, wholesale destruction took place in the course of guerrilla battles for the land, through which American settlers proved to have the better technology. Native Americans, if they could not be improved, were then seen as barriers to progress.

Native Americans were celebrated at Disneyland in the now-closed Indian Village, where performers from different tribes staged pow-wows. At a time when Native Americans were portrayed on screen as villains, or helpful albeit "simple-minded" sidekicks, Disney instead chose to showcase them as contributors to how the West was shaped. One might argue that this portrayal was nonetheless a colonial caricature of Native Americans—after all, the Indian Village did not distinguish or take into account tribes and tribal politics, and it was located on the fringe of Frontierland as though like a reservation. Within the context of mid-century entertainment, I believe the inclusion of Indian Village *at all* is of significant note as Walt Disney's Frontierland was meant to give a simulation of the founding and cultivation of the West through modernized and mythologized experience. This land was closed and converted to Critter Country.

As civilization progresses, so does our destruction of nature. The economy of westward expansion demonstrates that progress leads to destruction of the wilderness, and that preserving wilderness hinders the growth of progress. Progress understood here in the context of Manifest Destiny is a blanket term for the West's consumption of the wilderness and her resources. It was further assumed that humans were capable of understanding the wilderness and the limits of her offerings, and thus could reasonably manage them accordingly. Because of our higher capacity to reason, it was assumed that we could be trusted with the seemingly endless plethora of resources, and our duty under Manifest

Destiny was to tame and civilize the wilderness. This reflects our entitlement over nature. Nature is a tool; it is useful in the furthering of civilization, and in its usefulness lays its only value. Even areas that were not useful in resources were useful as outposts to those areas that were.

The West was further shaped by the formation of regional identities. The further from Washington the settlement, the more essential self-government became. The earliest fragmentation of American identity occurred in the distinction between East and West.[43] The East is recognized as the region of the establishment, which, in contrast to the West, appears cultured, organized, and is generally more powerful.[44] Migration to new parts further encouraged a fragmentation of loyalties, as people began to identify with their land and local communities.[45] As regional identities became more significant, so did American nationalism for the sake of preserving the nation. Through media and education, American virtues were transmitted across regions, thus ensuring that those travelling from one region to another would encounter common beliefs and behaviors, no matter how radically different the new region.

The heroes who settled the West evolved from explorers and settlers, but the most heralded today is that of the cowboy. While historical cowboys were ranchers in the southwest, borrowing from the Mexican cattle-ranching tradition, the cowboy in popular culture is one who embodies the specific politic of the rugged frontier individualist. The cowboy often fights the heroic fight, siding with the cause he/she feels is the most just. Disney's heroic figure, Davy Crockett, though technically not a cowboy, reinforces Disney's view of American individualism, teaching "us to question all authority and, when (if) finding it invalid, to strike out against those who would repress youthful freedoms, even if this necessitated employing violence as a last resort."[46] Crockett follows his own rules, as do many popular culture cowboys, sometimes making them up if the situation calls for it, such as grinning down an enemy rather than directly engaging in combat. These cowboys, the rugged individualists, embody the spirit of Manifest Destiny and take the future of America into their own hands, rather than wait for authority figures to come through in a time of need. Cowboys and other western heroes also "stood for the myth of the healing power of the new land. These mythic heroes were quite conscious of their func-

5. Frontierland

tion as God's agents appointed to civilize the west."[47] This healing power, characteristic of the New West, was seen as a "rebirth of humanity," one free from the threat of savagery.[48]

The heroism of the cowboy represents the ability to conquer fear, providing the courage to engage a new frontier. In Westerns, the cowboy is seemingly fearless; Davy Crockett is fearless. This is a constituent behavior along with individualism and loneliness in the ability to conquer and tame the wilderness. At least, the heroic cowboy has to convince those watching the film that he is fearless. If he can convince the audience, he can convince his opponent.

Disney took the image of the lonely cowboy in a different direction than Hollywood westerns. Underlying the vast expanse of Frontierland, or of Crockett's journeys, is the idea that the lonely cowboy is actually incomplete in his loneliness, whereas other studio cowboys are identified by and embrace loneliness. Disney's incompleteness comes from the cowboy's lack of family or community connection. This theme is so prevailing throughout the entire of the Disney corpus that it has earned the title as the "Disney Doctrine": "a notion that the nuclear family, with its attendant rituals of marriage, parenthood, emotional and spiritual instruction, and consumption, was the centerpiece of the American way of life."[49] As a post-war theme, the Disney Doctrine suits the Baby Boom and the restructuring of the American family, which would change again after Walt's death and is arguably undergoing another change in response to recent economic tensions. Under the Disney Doctrine, the hero or protagonist never works alone, but with a community of others, often close friends working together when blood family is absent, to achieve the goal. For example, before Davy Crockett left for Congress in the *Disneyland* serial, he learned that his wife had died and his children were in the care of their aunt. Because Davy Crockett found himself separated from his family, the Disney Doctrine suggests, he had to die at the Alamo, never mind the Alamo was already part of his historical narrative. The way that Disney reconstructs Crockett's story, the emptiness of his loneliness lead him to San Antonio even knowing that he was taking up a lost cause. The settlers to the West, in constructing their regional identities, demonstrated an early form of the Disney Doctrine, forming "family" beyond the boundaries of the biological nuclear family.

119

Cultivating the West also requires a fair amount of subversion. The individualism that helped shaped America was not only borne out of necessity from the isolation the vast expanse of space offered, but it also came from the Founding Fathers and their contemporaries exerting independence from Britain during the Revolution. As a collective, Americans favored individuals and their right to "life, liberty, and the pursuit of happiness," itself a metaphorical frontier that spans as far as the imagination. Subversiveness is at the core of this individualism, because in order to maintain it, someone needs, at some point, to stand up to authority. Those who were willing to move west and embrace its challenges did so against many popular opinions. After the railroads connected east to west, moving west became a feverish desire by many, helping build the nation's boundaries and population after the Civil War. The law of the west was likewise subversive and indicative of American individualism. Conflicts were solved by a local body, often a sheriff, who was the one person in the community willing to take up the badge.

As the expanse of the western wilderness disappears under the tools of progress—urban and suburban development, interstate highways, pollution and resource depletion—Americans react with more and more extreme adventures to return to nature, sometimes without proper preparation or consideration. Big Thunder Mountain Railroad embodies this thrill-seeking spirit of adventure: the thrill of returning to nature, to escape from our urban realities while maintaining some perceived control over the experience.

Davy Crockett and Frontierland

All of the above is exemplified by the *Davy Crockett* serial that originally aired on the "Frontierland" segment of the *Disneyland* television show and was later re-edited into a film. Because of the significance of the Davy Crockett craze to Disney's Frontierland themeing, the show merits a brief review. *The Davy Crockett Adventures* were originally broadcast beginning in December 1954 and ending in February 1955, one installment per month. There are three episodes in the trilogy: "Davy Crockett, Indian Fighter," "Davy Crockett goes to Congress," and

5. Frontierland

"Davy Crockett at the Alamo." Each installment addresses a different theme relevant to the heroism of the character. When we first meet Crockett, he is a settler who volunteers for the American army against the Creek Nation to make settlements safe for "red and white" alike. His goal is never to force the Native Americans off their land, but to find a way for both groups to co-exist. He believes in the treaties between the two nations, and upholds them with liberal nobility. Crockett is the mediator between two groups, and this can be read in two ways. On one hand, Crockett as mediator represents the bridge between civilization and nature, following the interpretation of the Native Americas as Nature, but Crockett is also mediator between the red and the white, or the Communists and the Americans. "Red men" was common parlance to describe Native Americans, and overtly Crockett's statement is a call for frontier cooperation. The "reds" also referred to the Communists, derived from the use of red in Communist propaganda (especially in China). Crockett is then turned into a Cold War mythic hero trying to find a balance between the tensions inherent in this era. His message of peace places Disney far ahead of the historical events surrounding *détente*, but provides us with the mythic groundwork to make *détente* possible. Crockett's mediation, on the other hand, is an embrace of diversity also long before integration made successful progress in American culture. Crockett reminds us that the land, the heart of America, is the issue because it is the common cause shared by all who call this nation their home. It is not worth fighting and dying over when there is a much better alternative: sharing.

The next time we meet Crockett in "Davy Crockett Goes to Congress," he is pulled into politics as Tennessee's representative and becomes a political champion for the Western settlers and Native Americans, advocating for peace. Being an honest man, he does not fully recognize the games that politicians play, and is caught off guard when he finds out that he was sent on a "Goodwill Tour" so Congress could try to pass the "Indian Bill" without his involvement. This bill, being pushed by then-president Andrew Jackson, would grant government entitlement to Manifest Destiny and give force to Westward Expansion by permitting the wholesale subjugation of Native Americans. Crockett, himself a settler, does not have any opposition to the idea of moving West, but he is opposed to the idea of moving West if it is going to harm those who already live there. He makes a comment early in this episode before he goes to Washington that the country is getting "mighty civilized," and he says this with sorrow in his voice. In this one line, Crockett acknowledges the future of America, the one that Walt Disney inherited, of a fully civilized country spanning, from sea to shining sea, getting ever smaller with the Eisenhower interstate system. In the mid-century, Crockett's concern about the civilizing of America echoes a nostalgia felt by the country at a time when it was struggling with its own identity. What makes America great, Crockett reinforces, is the land not the people who live on it, speaking to an American national identity defined by regionalism and, to an extent, tribalism. One could argue that this also paved the way for the calls for equality and diversity in the '60s and '70s.

After his disillusionment with Congress, he heads to Texas in "Davy Crockett at the Alamo." Settlers had moved there as part of the Westward expansion, but Mexican president Santa Ana sought to reclaim the land for Mexico. Gaining Texas would not be as easy as the Louisiana Purchase, and the only way to do so quickly appeared to be to fight for it. Yet, oddly enough, no one really wanted to fight for it except the people who were already there. The Alamo is a mission in San Antonio, and it held out against Santa Ana for an impressive amount of time, especially considering that the Texans were outnumbered and lacking sufficient supplies. The Alamo was, however, a diversion. The real power of the war for Texas Independence was General Sam Houston, and he needed time to build up an army. So Crockett and team stalled Santa Ana's army in what is recognized as a major turning point in this war, and a major component in the state's mythic identity. Having received the Disney treatment, Davy Crockett is remembered as a true American hero, which makes his martyrdom at the Alamo more potent, as though Disney is trying to say that, indeed, the land is worth defending in war if all other peace negotiations fail. In this third installment, the Mexican army replaces the Native Americans. Nature, thus, takes the guise of the civilized America to maintain a stance that wilderness is not easily tamed. The serial ends at the Alamo with Crockett's death, not with the Battle of San Jacinto, where Houston's troops conquered Santa Ana's army and won Texas for the United States, cementing Davy Crockett as a Frontierland hero.[50]

5. Frontierland

During the opening broadcast of the Disneyland park, Crockett is resurrected. Fess Parker, actor of Davy Crockett, represents this hero in the opening parade and the dedication of Frontierland. This establishes Disneyland as a liminal space, where the historicity of time has little meaning. Interestingly, for all of Crockett's pro-peace statements on the television show, his opening day performance at Disneyland involves him singing praises to his gun, Betsy.

Rivers of America: The Next Frontier

The Rivers of America mirror the water of the Mermaid Lagoon in Tomorrowland, forming a Western waterway that accounts for roughly thirteen percent of the original park.[51] The Rivers, inspired by the Mississippi and Missouri rivers, are actually more of a large lake that encircles the island at its center. They connect the Frontier with New Orleans Square and Critter Country, connecting the stereotypes of the West from the Mississippi River to the Pacific Ocean. This play on guests' geographic memory unites us in our memory of the West: New Orleans and the Mississippi ports, Critter Country and the Great Plains, Big Thunder Mountain and plains/desert, many of which were only remembered in film and television.

The Rivers showcase three aquatic transport attractions: two historical steam ships, the *Mark Twain* and *Columbia*, the Tom Sawyer River Rafts that ferry guests to Tom Sawyer's Island, and the Davy Crockett Canoes. If Main Street's and Tomorrowland's emphasis are on ground transportation, then Frontierland's is on water transportation emphasizing a pervading American belief that the waters of the West possessed healing qualities. As historian Richard Francaviglia remarks, "It is thus not surprising that American culture, ever in search of renewal in the (westward) move into the interior, would cast the rivers as entryways and passageways to both opportunity and adventure,"[52] a belief to which Walt Disney likewise subscribed, evidenced by the design of the Rivers of America as conduits to adventure.

The Ships The *Mark Twain* Riverboat is a large paddleboat modeled after the nineteenth century sternwheelers characteristic of the Mississippi River that inspired the writings of Mark Twain.[53] It is visible from the Plaza Hub and its docks sit directly opposite the Frontierland entrance gate. To get to the dock, guests have to pass through Frontierland's main street, and be drawn deep into the wild frontier.⁵⁴ It sails along a hidden track in the Rivers of America, circling Tom Sawyer Island, taking a leisurely tour of the Rivers. This ship pays tribute to the iconic paddleboats of the Mississippi River as vessels that embark the journey from east to west. It also pays tribute to author Mark Twain, whose comic realism not only entertains readers, but it provides a snapshot of America after the Civil War, an industrialized nation that was still exploring and understanding the riches of the West. Twain's writings provide for Frontierland what Walt Disney's memories provide for Main Street, U.S.A.—an idealized yet realistic expectation for the cultural memory of America's past.

The *Columbia* shares the track with the *Mark Twain*. Stylistically it resembles a Revolutionary Era windjammer pirate ship that celebrates the age of sailing and exploration. It is modeled after the original *Columbia*, which was the first American ship to circumnavigate the globe in 1790.⁵⁵ The inclusion of the *Columbia* on the Rivers helps connect the nineteenth century Wild West with the neighboring eighteenth century New Orleans. To further connect the ship to New Orleans, Disney claims that it depicts Jean Lafitte, a Gulf Coast pirate of the early nineteenth century who used New Orleans as his homeport.⁵⁶ If the *Mark Twain* ties the Rivers of America to the Frontier, the inclusion of the *Columbia* transcends the notion of the Frontier as contained solely in the West. As the first American ship to circumnavigate the globe, it was the first to explore the possibility of an Americanized globe, centuries before it was actually achieved. The "frontier" of American expansionism necessarily extends beyond the West, which is simply the proving ground for the mission behind Manifest Destiny and the spread of Democracy.

Tom Sawyer Island/Pirate's Lair Tom Sawyer Island at the center of the Rivers of America is a self-contained play-world. It has no shops, rides, or any set time schedule. The only rule is that guests have to be off the island, which can only be gotten to and from by raft, by sunset. It is designed to be a play space in which imaginations can run wild; Disney simply provided the themed environment, but minimal other structure. The Island is loosely based off of Jackson's Island, an island in the Mississippi River described by Mark Twain as a place explored by Tom Sawyer, Huck Finn, and their friend Joe Harper,[57] in the spirit of Mark Twain's novels, even though the island is not a storied location as many other Disneyland attractions are. Guests make up their own games and stories, pretending "to be characters from their favorite stories, or act out plot elements, or imagine that their play is taking place in the settings described in the stories."[58]

In 2007, the island was refurbished into a pirate theme to tie it together with the popular *Pirates of the Caribbean* films. Renamed Pirate's Lair on Tom Sawyer Island, the redo is meant to keep the island's original spirit while making it look as though it was taken over by pirates. New features maintain the play and exploration aspects while adding hidden treasure, a sunken pirate ship and ghostly apparitions.[59] Furthermore, "visitors to the redesigned version of Tom Sawyer Island may not be inclined to pretend that they are Tom or Huck, but by pretending to be pirates, they are doing exactly what Tom and Huck do while visiting Jackson Island."[60] These changes, again, link the frontier spirit with the New Orleans port, giving better symbiosis to the area while further emphasizing the idea that the Mississippi River is the boundary between the East and West, with New Orleans the starting point for the great adventure to conquer the country, and subsequently, the American imagination.

By the twentieth century, America's relationship to the West was changing as wilderness was replaced with cities, sprawling metropolises of chaotic "civilization." All of the promises for opportunity and freedom originally associated with the West were transferred onto the cities.[61] Though much of the wilderness has disappeared or been depleted, it is nevertheless is a potent metaphor for the modern city, in which one may or may not have any communal ties or room for growth and transformation. From within this cultivated wilderness, a new frontier has emerged, one of ideas and technology, fueled by human ingenuity rather than earth's resources helping the goals of Manifest Destiny to spread to global proportions at exponential rates. Disneyland's Tomorrowland captures the possibilities of this new wilderness, but Frontierland remains the living memory of the West that was.

By the time of Walt Disney's death in 1966, the United States was already exploring the possibility of travel into outer space, moving it from science fiction into scientific fact. The Tomorrowland segment of the *Disneyland* television show explored, over three episodes, how a space launch and trip to the moon could actually happen, with a guest presentation from a prominent rocket scientist, Dr. Werner von Braun.

With the success of *Star Trek*, television's first space western, came the realization that there was no more West, only the frontier romanticized by cinema. Outer space supplanted the Old West as the frontier wilderness, except that this wilderness is not easily explored by current technology. So much of space is currently still viewed from afar and admired from earth. Nonetheless, our longing to make progress in space encourages technological advancements. Space gives us a "real" wilderness full of potential, just as the American West did 200 years ago. Science fiction and Hollywood have already prepared us for the eventuality, even projecting the same restorative characteristics into space—restorative of humanity after we destroy earth—that was once projected onto the West.

The Cold War officially ended in 1990 following negotiations made in the aftermath in the toppling of the Berlin Wall; yet, the same fear remains active. Rather than call it Communism, it is now called Terrorism; and just as we "fought" a "Cold War," America currently "fights" a "War on Terror." Terror is just as much an ideological fear as communism. For this reason, Frontierland and all of its Cold War pro–American idealism remains as valid and viable now as it ever did.

6

Fantasyland
The Myth of Utopia, Part 1: Fairy Tales and Happily Ever Afters

"Here's a world of imagination, hopes and dreams. In this timeless land of enchantment, the age of chivalry, magic, and make-believe are reborn and fairy tales come true. Fantasyland is dedicated to the young and the young at heart, to those who believe that when you wish upon a star, your dreams do come true."—Walt Disney, "Dateline Disneyland"

If the western half of the park (Frontierland, New Orleans Square, Adventureland) represents the past, and the eastern half of the park (Tomorrowland) represents the future, and Main Street, U.S.A., represents the present, Fantasyland forms the northern point of the line Main Street begins, bisecting the park. Though set in a fairy tale past and firmly rooted in fantasy, the Magic Kingdom that Fantasyland constructs reflects America's dreams of a utopian happily ever after, while Main Street, U.S.A. to the south presents a fantasy of a utopian reality, a model repeated in various hyperrealistic consumerist enterprises.

Fantasyland Key Dark Ride Attractions

- Snow White Scary Adventures
- Peter Pan Flight
- Mr. Toad's Wild Ride
- Alice in Wonderland
- Pinocchio's Daring Jouney

127

Fantasyland is the most storied area of Disneyland. Not only is every single attraction inspired by Disney films, but every ride tells a story, unlike other areas of the park that combine Disney's stories with America's history or showcases possibilities for America's future. The films that inspire Fantasyland's key attractions are themselves adaptations from fairy tales that are used by Disney to promote a message of optimism, hope, new beginnings, and American values, such that the Disney brand is still equated with these themes.

So far, we have explored the culture of doubt and anxiety, and how Disney presents Disneyland as a place of reassurance and escape. Through the totality of a themed environment, the events of the present are shut out of the park. It is not possible to keep the effects of the present out of the park, and these are handled through the stories and the architecture to promote and reinforce the greatness of American heroism. The stories in Fantasyland serve as reminders of the possibility for a "happily ever after" for Americans, using a fairy tale heroism to suggest a new utopian image, one achieved by the exploration and conquest the new frontiers of space, progress, and information technology. This utopia can exist in Main Street, Disney suggests, with some "faith, trust and Pixie dust," and by bringing the wonders of tomorrow to the realm of today. Fantasyland slays the past to prepare the present for tomorrow. Though the heroism of the Spirit of Adventure and the wonders of the frontier remind guests of what it means to be American, Fantasyland and Tomorrowland, with their respective romances of utopia and progress, suggest what it means to be a post-war American struggling with Cold War or terrorism by creating a new mythology of a globalized community sharing in the Nature's Wonderland that is represented in the attractions of these lands.

The Dark Rides: Disney and Fairy Tales

The "dark rides" are a collection of storybook rides that transport the guest on themed vehicles through the events of a Disney story. They take place entirely encased in a show building lit only by lights highlighting relevant story elements, hence the description "dark." These rides in Fantasyland are short, typically one to three minutes long.[1] Given the short duration of the attraction, the Disney Imagineers have the added task of condensing a feature-length film into a couple minutes, allowing them only enough time to capture the recognizable highlights, and to do so in a way that the guest can drink in as many story details as possible within a few seconds. All of the dark rides require a degree of familiarity with the film story, or at least the ability to recognize and identify the figures so as to be able to concentrate on the story.

There are five dark rides in Fantasyland: Snow White's Scary Adventures, Peter Pan Flight, Mr. Toad's Wild Ride, all three of which opened in 1955; Alice in Wonderland, which opened in 1958; and Pinocchio's Daring Journey, added during the 1983 renovation of Fantasyland that altered the landscape from 1955's circus-like atmosphere to that of a Bavarian town in accordance with the animation style of the films, and the German-inspiration of Sleeping Beauty Castle and the nearby Matterhorn Bobsleds. None of the attractions is a straight retelling of the film or the original fairy tale. In fact, they share a common kinesis-as-participation, but otherwise differ in their approach to retelling their respective stories.[2] Some of the rides, specifically Alice, Pinocchio, and Peter Pan, attempt to recreate a tour through the film version of the story, while the others, Toad and Snow White, revise the story toward a thrilling end goal. A common feature to all dark rides is that they attempt to retell the story with the guest in the role of the main character. Some are more successful than others at accomplishing this. For instance, there is no doubt of the perspective in Mr. Toad's Wild Ride, whereas Snow White's Scary Adventures appears to be more the wicked Queen's story rather than that of Snow White. Similarly, all of the attraction plot lines differ greatly from their film version. This is in large part due to the limitations of the medium. While it would be possible to re-create the films in a three-dimensional environment that vehicles move guests through, it would not be conducive to the amusement aspect of the Disneyland experience. Guests want to ride as many attractions as possible during their visit. So the condensation of the narrative is necessary.

All five of the Fantasyland dark rides share the common theme of the hero embracing his or her individuality to defeat a villain and how this leads toward a utopian happily ever after. They all are set in a fantasy "other world" to reinforce that, although none of these stories are American (three English, one German, one Italian), their messages and values have a universal appeal. Disney uses this universality to adapt these stories to reflect American values and mores. By taking these stories out of their cultural context,[3] Disney draws attention to the messages they hope to convey.

Fairy tales have been key components of the modern era's literary and mythic experience, especially in the "culture industry" headlined by Hollywood, contrary to the long-standing assumption that they are stories written/told for children. These stories are shared with children from a young age, but continue to fascinate into adulthood. The fairy tale tradition parallels that of mythology, telling archetypal stories that communicate the culture's beliefs and behaviors. While both myths and fairy tales are rooted in the culture that birthed the story, the connection between myth and its origin is much stronger than it is for fairy tales, which are able to transcend time and place through the potency of their symbolism and lack of cultural benchmarks or indicators. However, a shift occurred in the eighteenth century that began to root fairy tales to their culture of origin. There were two contributing factors to this shift. One was the collection of fairy tales by the Brothers Grimm, Andrew Lang, Charles Perrault, and several others, who put into print what had previously been an oral story form, creating a concretized version that is difficult to transcend. The other factor is the birth of the fairy tale novel. During the Enlightenment, fairy tales shifted from parlor entertainment to child entertainment, or to the nursery, as J. R. R. Tolkien observes in an oft-quoted essay about fairy tales, where they were treated like old furniture that no one cares about.[4] Writers noticed an opportunity to write novels for children, creating fairy tales that are longer, culturally concrete, but just as fantastical as fairy tales of old. Thus, there are essentially two genres of fairy tale: the traditional, which bears closer resemblance to the tales that inspired the Grimm project, and literary, which resemble a novel and have a definite author. Disney pulls from both categories.

There are many different versions of traditional fairy tales, some of which can trace a lineage all the way back to ancient mythologies. Characteristics of these stories include: a setting that is both out of time and out of place, marked by phrases such as "Once upon a time" and "in a kingdom far, far away"; characters who are either identified by an attribute of their personality or profession, such as "Belle" or "the Miller," or by a common name, such as "John" or "Jack"; and finally, a formulaic story that involves three tasks of some kind leading the characters to a more or less happy ending. These stories are intentionally left abstract in order to highlight their archetypal nature, meaning that fairy tales are universal to the human experience and can be transmitted across time and culture without a loss of meaning.[5] Thus, fairy tales speak a universal language. Each telling of a traditional fairy tale is inevitably tweaked according to the situation of the storyteller, which is why different versions of the same basic story may exist.[6] Through fairy tales, and likewise myths, a society's history could be conveyed in a way that was accessible to future generations, especially children.[7] Because of their simplified nature, values and mores could be transmitted without the weight of an esoteric meaning. The simplicity of "once upon a time" in "a kingdom far, far away" is always given ordinary treatment, as though one could walk out the front door and enter this world.[8] However, once these fairy tales are given any hint of definite and specific cultural flavorings, then the stories cease to be fairy tales and enter into the realm of myth, legend, and saga.[9]

More so than myths, fairy tales fulfill a psychological quest through the facility of their ingestion and digestion. They provide images for life's road bumps, and mechanisms for coping with them; they help listeners and readers develop character.[10] Since the Enlightenment, and more so since the adaptation of fairy tales by Hollywood, fairy tales have fulfilled roles traditionally ascribed to myth. Snow White's Scary Adventures is the only Fantasyland dark ride based on a traditional fairy tale.

Snow White and the Seven Dwarfs was Disney's, and the world's, first feature-length animated feature. The film is based on the version of the fairy tale collected by the Grimm Brothers. The film version follows almost the same plot as the Grimm tale, with the noticeable difference that it focuses on Snow White, rather than on the Queen, and her relationship to the dwarfs: Snow White is portrayed as a servant to the Queen rather than her stepdaughter; she faces only one (as opposed to three) trials from the Queen in her merchant woman disguise; and after the Queen is defeated and Snow White is encased in the glass coffin to sleep her poisoned sleep, she is rescued by the Prince, whom she met at the beginning of the film, with love's first kiss, rather than the chance bump in the road. And they go off to live happily ever after.

Walt and the Disney Company have noted that many of the changes made to the story were due to budget limitations and the Hollywood formula for good entertainment. One notable change was to include names for each of the seven dwarfs to give them their own personality. Walt borrowed so much money to make this film, which most of his contemporaries believed was destined to fail believing no one would want to sit through a feature-length cartoon, that the project was nicknamed "Disney's Folly." It went on to become one of the highest grossing films of 1938. It was so successful that it gained recognition for the Disney Studio as a viable Hollywood entity, not just the home of Mickey Mouse and friends.

Ken Anderson, who had served as art director for the Snow White film, designed the ride version. Given a limited amount of time and money, not unlike when he was making the film, Anderson's initial design involved "vehicles run[ning] on a swerving track through a labyrinth constructed mainly of flat plywood cutouts."[11] In describing the rudimentary nature of the original ride, Anderson said, "You didn't need a lot of animation because you were moving. You were going so darn fast that what you did was supply the movement for the characters."[12]

The ride's original premise was that the guests riding through the woods did so from the perspective of Snow White, so she is decidedly absent from the ride. Though moving on a track, the story design gave guests the illusion of participation by posting signs that offered choices in which way to go. The choices taken, inevitably the wrong ones, heightened the drama of the attraction story.

Snow White's Adventure, later renamed Snow White's Scary Adventures during the 1983 Fantasyland remodel, holds the honor of being the most frightening ride in all of Disneyland. Because of the scary nature of the ride, Disney Imagineers softened the story while also emphasizing the scary themes of the ride to give guests, adult and children alike, adequate warning of the nature of the ride. This is why it is now titled Snow White's *Scary* Adventures (emphasis added). The new ride boasts technological advancements, and the inclusion of Snow White in the opening scene.

In contrast to traditional fairy tales, the literary fairy tale emerged or came into prominence during the mid– to late–1800s, and is a story in the form of a short novel mostly aimed for children, though the moralistic message within these stories is just as applicable to adults. The earliest literary fairy tales were in fact aimed at adults to "reinforce the mores and values of French civilité," but they allowed a lot of room for interpretation.[13] The shift of emphasis to children was initiated during the end of the eighteenth century because these stories were perceived as having a connection to the lower classes, and thus were seen as an expression of social vulgarity.

These stories are not abstract, having named characters and a specific setting. Some of these stories begin in a known place, such as London, from which the lead character or characters depart to visit a fantasy "other world," such as Neverland, Wonderland, or an unnamed location. These qualify as fairy tales under J. R. R. Tolkien's postulate that the key elements of a fairy tale include a setting in this other world, which he calls the Faërie, and that they contain magic. As he notes, an "essential power of Faërie is thus the power of making immediately effective by the will of the visions of 'fantasy.'"[14] Although these stories have a definite cultural flavor, they are separated from myth in that they contain no divine influence.

The writing medium allows this sort of fairy tale to enter into depths of meaning traditionally carried by myth while still maintaining the fantastic wonder associated with traditional fairy tales. The author of a literary fairy tale provides the story as a dialogue with the beliefs and values of a culture. Indeed, nineteenth-century literary tales aimed at children provided guidelines on how to behave and the consequences of disobedience. Beginning in the mid-twentieth century, literary fairy tales began addressing heavier subjects that were once addressed by myth: good versus evil, death, why the world is the way it is. In other words, literary fairy tales, including the spatial texts of Disneyland, provided by the nature of their depth the cathartic experience had from engaging with myth. Traditional fairy tales provide a level of catharsis, one that is too often confused with entertainment and this mode of transmission is easily ignored, downplayed as infantile.[15] The symbolism of a literary tale has a definite cultural context, often Victorian, which creates a contrast to the fantastical, liberating other world that helps the main character or characters realize his/her/their own heroism, making these stories of interest for Disney as it is reinforcing America's own heroism.

The remaining four Fantasyland dark rides are inspired by literary fairy tales. Despite the German theme of this area, three of these dark rides are English, and one Italian.

Peter Pan Flight is the favorite attraction of many guests.[16] The story on which the attraction is based, J. M. Barre's *Peter Pan*, is likewise held to high esteem. Barre's story tells of the three Darling children, Wendy, Michael and John, and their adventures with Peter Pan in Neverland. Disney adapted this book to film in 1953. Though boasted as the first time Barre's vision is brought to life, Disney nonetheless simplified the plot because of time limitations. Retained is the wonder the Darling children experience while learning to fly and arriving at Neverland, Tinker Bell's jealousy and banishment, Tiger Lily's rescue, the kidnapping and final battle with Captain Hook. Downplayed is Wendy's role as a mother. Captain Hook and his pirates are turned into sympathetic loveable characters in the similar manner as the Pirates of the Caribbean.

The attraction, Peter Pan Flight, places guests into a pirate ship and takes us on a tour of Disney's film, recreating the wonder the Darling children experienced as they flew around Neverland. The ride begins in the Darling nursery, though we quickly leave it to fly over the rooftops of London, which get progressively smaller as we get closer to Neverland. After a brief tour of Neverland, we rescue Tiger Lily, then the Darling children from Hook, and just before we sail home, we laugh at Hook's predicament as he tries not to get eaten by the ticking crocodile. We wave goodbye to the mermaids as we return to the loading platform. The story is essentially a recap of the movie elements, which were still fresh in the memories of the park guests when Disneyland opened. The unique element of this ride compared to the other dark rides is that the pirate ship ride vehicle is suspended from an overhead track, emulating the sensation of flying.[17]

Mr. Toad's Wild Ride and the 1949 short film on which it is based, *The Adventures of Ichabod and Mr. Toad*,[18] are based on the Kenneth

Grahame novel *The Wind in the Willows*. The novel is a romanticization of the English country side versus a fascination with the intersection between human progress and the animal kingdom, each represented by an animal protagonist: Mr. Mole for the former and Mr. Toad for the latter. Mole's plot is a poem full of animal friends, teas, and ruminations on the natural flow. Toad's story, however, is about the danger of disobedience. Toad is always remorseful in the face of punishment, but will quickly change his tune once the danger has passed.

Disney's short film removes Mole and Rat's romantic song to nature and focuses only on Toad's adventures. In this film, Mole, Rat, and their mutual friend MacBadger function as Toad's caretakers. MacBadger manages Toad's dwindling estate while Mole and Rat chase him around. Of Toad's adventures in the novel, the film concentrates on one episode, that of the Motor Car, in which Toad trades his home for a stolen car, is convicted, sent to jail, escapes, and has to reclaim Toad Hall in order to have a happily ever after.

Toad's obsession with transportation reflects Walt Disney's own fascination for various modes of transportation, likely a key inspiration for the changes made to the novel's ending, and Toad's obsession for the "poop-poop!" of the motorcar is at the core of Disneyland attraction. In replicas of Toad's motorcar, guests are taken on his wild ride, beginning in Toad Hall and into the streets of London, barely dodging policemen and passers-by. We cause a major car accident on shipping docks, and continue driving into a courtroom, where the judge pronounces us guilty. We continue driving, as though to avoid the sentence, and drive right into a train. In the book and film, the train serves as a means of Toad's escape from jail. However, in the attraction, we emerge from the car crash—in Hell. A hot, fiery Hell presided over by the same judge that condemned us in the role of the Devil. This is the only attraction in Disneyland to deal with imagery of Hell or to propose such a serious punishment for our actions. Only after passing through Hell are we allowed to return to the loading area and the fantasy of Disneyland, as though waking from a dream. The plot of the attraction bears no connection to the original story or its animated adaptation, and it is the only attraction in Disneyland to both veer so far from the original or to encounter such a denouement.

Lost in the Disney version of *The Wind in the Willows* is the story of Mr. Mole, an underground creature who comes to the surface to the river to live. He is leaving the depths and coming into the light. Another character known for his underground habitat is Mr. Badger, who is the recognized voice of wisdom for the animal's river community. Also lost in the Disney version is the extent that Toad's adventures cannot be confined to the riverbanks and regularly cross over from the animal realm to the human. The two worlds are already combined, emphasizing Disney's goal that a civilization and nature can harmoniously coexist in a convergence culture. In Grahame's novel, Toad's behavior is seen as insensible, encouraging his friends to stage an intervention. In Disney's film, his friends try to keep him from bankruptcy. Made in 1949 on the brink of America's new post-war prosperity, *The Adventures of Mr. Toad* serves as a warning against financial irresponsibility, similar to those actions that initiated the Great Depression.

America's new wealth is represented through the emphasis on movement and transportation in the three versions of Toad's story, which parallels the heart of Walt Disney's own fascinations. The film and attraction both incorporate turn-of-the-century imagery, which allows the story to build up to the interest in motorcars as the ultimate mode of personal transportation. Indeed, as America moves into the 1950s, there is a boom in transportation to accommodate urban and suburban growth and as a result of the end of war rationing. Americans quickly came to identify themselves by their cars. Toad reflects this fascination as though anticipating America's relationship to cars. The attraction, then, serves as a warning against reckless behavior, reminding guests that jail is not the worst punishment, but, rather, death and with it a trip to Hell.

Of the Fantasyland stories, Alice in Wonderland is different in that it is based on not a single story, but on two. Disney's *Alice in Wonderland* is a composite of Lewis Carroll's two Alice stories: *Alice's Adventures in Wonderland* and *Through the Looking Glass*. Alice's adventures are episodic, which posed a problem for Disney's artists. To make the film work, Alice's adventure needed continuity, so the film gives her the mission of chasing the White Rabbit then finding her way home, meeting along the way a few of Carroll's iconic characters, such as Tweedle-Dee and Tweedle-Dum, the Cheshire Cat, the Mad Hatter and the March Hare, and, of course, the Queen of Hearts.

6. Fantasyland: The Myth of Utopia, Part 1

Like Carroll's original stories, the attraction Alice in Wonderland is episodic. Guests are transported on caterpillar-shaped vehicles down the rabbit hole and on a tour of Wonderland: we receive directions from Tweedle-Dee and Tweedle-Dum, share in the White Rabbit's panic over being late, sing with the flowers, meet the caterpillar, get lost in Tulgey Wood, follow directions from the Cheshire Cat, and get thoroughly lost before we stumble into the Queen's land. We paint the roses red, stand before the deck of guards, play croquet with the Queen, upset the Queen and trigger her temper. We dodge the guards and burst out into the open air of Disneyland, gliding down to the floor and the finale of our own unbirthday party with explosive gift.

The Alice in Wonderland attraction opened in Disneyland in 1958, three years after Fantasyland initially opened. It was immediately unique in that it shares a show building with Mr. Toad's Wild Ride, forcing part of it to take place on the second level of the building. For this reason, a gentile glide returns the caterpillar vehicle to ground level, but unique to Alice, this glide is outside the attraction in the open air as though the Disneyland ride area is in fact just another madcap vision from Carroll's original stories.

The last story to join the Fantasyland dark ride family was Pinocchio, based on the 1940 film adaptation of Carlo Collodi's stories of the same name. This attraction was added as a part of the 1983 Fantasyland redo in the space that used to house the Mickey Mouse Club theater, where the original television shows were filmed.

Collodi's original *Pinocchio* stories were features in serial form in a children's weekly publication, and were later compiled into a book. Like Alice, Pinocchio's adventures are also episodic, placing emphasis on the punishment of bad behavior. Collodi's Pinocchio is a rebellious marionette, and is marked as such before Geppetto carves him. He is made from magic wood, presumably the same wood that made the other marionettes in the story because they all act independently of the Puppet Master. Pinocchio is consciously defiant, to the point of actively hurting Geppetto, his "father." When he is not attacking Geppetto him, Pinocchio's misbehavior is so deeply ingrained in his *composition* that he is only capable of making poor decisions. A Talking Cricket appears to set him straight, but whom he winds up ignoring until the very end of his adventures.

So that Pinocchio's story can function as a behavioral teaching tool—in the vein of nineteenth century perceptions of fairy tales as tools for children—he often self-reflects on his bad behavior and learns from his mistakes. For example, when he is freed from the tree in which the bandits hung him, he reflects on how he would not have even met the bandits had he followed his father's wishes, gone to school, and not been blinded by the prospects of easy money. When the donkey curse is lifted, he reflects on how he would not have become a donkey had he stayed in school; in fact, the fairy was about to make him a real boy. Pinocchio, however, for all of his ability to self-reflect, is incapable of stopping himself from getting into trouble.

Disney's version shifts the focus away from Pinocchio's malevolence and stresses the importance of listening to one's conscience, a cricket, with emphasis that all good boys must be brave, truthful, and unselfish in order for their dreams to come true. The Disneyland attraction likewise stresses what happens when one fails to listen to one's conscience. The results of "going the wrong way" lead us right into the mouth of the whale. Based on the plot of the film, the Pinocchio attraction highlights the results of bad decisions, as opposed to the bad behaviors punished in the novel. The attraction narrative seems less like first-hand experience of the story, as with the other dark rides, and more as though the guests are actually flies-on-the-wall for Pinocchio's story. Unlike the other dark rides, Pinocchio appears frequently throughout the ride. As the 2000 souvenir book describes, we "*follow little Pinocchio and his faithful conscience Jiminy Cricket....*"[19] Of the other dark rides, this one offers one technological achievement. It is the first use of hologram technology in a Disneyland attraction, which adds an air of magic to the attraction.

Pinocchio enters this journey as a half-boy. He can talk and do things, but he is still made of wood. He cannot necessarily feel and his ties to life are superficial at best. They are his marionette strings, though he does not have any literal ones. These strings bind him to the cosmos, because he otherwise should not exist. Moreover, the marionette strings represent ties to "the old ways" and stand as hindrances to growth. They cannot be simply cut, figuratively, because that would result in being cut off from life. These bonds have to be transcended in order for Pinocchio to become a boy, an apt metaphor for America and her identity crisis after the War. The doubt that has seeped into the culture since the War binds cultural progress, preventing growth as a nation.

Cultural Context

Most analyses of fairy tales do not take into consideration cultural influence, in large part because that influence is not perceived as relevant to the understanding of the tale. In the case of traditional tales, this is true; however, literary tales are flavored heavily with latent cultural themes. Regardless of the time of the reading, having an understanding of other myths or stories from the time help facilitate a deeper understanding of the story. No matter how abstract the story may be, culture and society play an important role in determining how the characters behave and interact with each other; for example, context helps explain why is it so important that an anonymous prince must rescue the princess ("Sleeping Beauty" or "Snow-White") or why Pinocchio's antics are perceived as so disobedient. From our modern perspective, some of the actions of the characters seem rather obvious, but this is due to the fact that we have been raised on these stories, shaped and molded by them. Because they were written down and printed, we have access to the same version children were reading 150 years ago. For this reason, the new versions provided by storytellers such as Walt Disney help shape new understandings of the fairy tales, helping to prevent them from growing stagnant in their meaning, a danger resulting from the concretizing of traditional tales to print, which is one of the dominant complaints about Disney's version.

Cultural context is important for understanding any mythological system. For all of the universality of archetypes, the guises they take are informed by the culture of a specific time and place. Taking an archetypal image out of its time or place devalues its meaning. An ancient Greek archetype of a hero, for example, is full of the archetypal meaning of the hero, but it is a fundamentally Greek hero with Greek concerns.[20] It is possible to retell an archetype's story, but all but the base elements must be changed to suit its new context.

In working with fairy tales, Walt Disney and the Disney Corporation have translated these archetypal modalities into versions more palatable for the post–World War II American culture, adults and children alike, and the tools they provide us with, from merchandising to theme parks, help to further enhance our imaginative experience of these stories. Many fairy tales experienced a long trajectory of retellings before being written down, some even tracing their lineage back to ancient myths and legends. The result of written collections of fairy tales is they now have a "definite" version, the go-to version of any given story. While the Brothers Grimm meant well, their efforts have "Grimmified" fairy tales, capturing the imagery into a single collection, and they were not alone in this endeavor. Other fairy tale collectors caught and trapped the imagination by the printed word. Disney's films and their connected theme park attractions are simply contributions to this long history of fairy tale versions, with two notable exceptions. First, Disney's medium is primarily film or other visual media, which requires a fair amount of translation and license to turn the word into the screen. Second, with the exception of very few stories, Disney was working with European tales and translating them to suit the American culture. Walt Disney's goal with his studio was never to draw a line of distinction between adults and children, so the translation is further meant to reflect American family values while reinforcing utopian ideals. Each of Fantasyland's stories do this: Their film version is very specific to the environment of its release; each of the dark rides further retells the story to reflect other pressing cultural concerns, namely the Cold War.

7

Fantasyland

The Myth of Utopia,
Part 2: Disneyfication, Disneyization
and Globalization

"Fantasyland is a gateway to the world of make-believe. Faraway kingdoms and adventures in imaginary realms lie around every corner. You can live out your daydreams and look into the windows of your childhood. It's a place where you can dream like a child no matter your age."—The Imagineers, The Imagineering Field Guide to Disneyland

Walt Disney and the Disney Corporation have come under the scrutiny of many critics for the "Disneyfied" versions of beloved fairy tales, often recognized as a process that takes a familiar story and sanitizes it down to something considered more palatable for children. At the same time, however, Walt Disney and the Disney Studio translated these stories into a version palatable for the American culture, adults and children alike, and have provided us with tools to further enhance our imaginative experience of these stories, from merchandising to the theme parks.

"Disneyfication" is a term that emerged after the 1960s to describe the process of translation from fairy tale into film.[1] Critics of this process are quick to comment upon the degree to which the Disney process sanitizes the story by taking out aspects that are considered inappropriate for children, thus trivializing the imagination by creating a concrete image that is more easily evoked than the original characters. In a 1959 interview, Walt Disney describes the company's approach to fairy tales:

141

Walt's Utopia

All the world's great fairytales, it must be remembered, are essentially morality tales, opposing good and bad, virtue and villainy, in dramatic terms easily understood and approved by children. Without such clash of good and evil and the prevalence of goodness—of good people—fairytales like *Snow White, Cinderella, Pinocchio, Sleeping Beauty* long since would have died because they would have no meaning. [...] But in our movie versions of these venerable morality plays—read to youngsters by parents of many, many generations over several centuries—we have tried to keep all the elements in proper balance of entertainment. We have often eliminated or greatly modified the "horrific" material in the classic fairytale literature. [...] We don't pussyfoot with evil; we deal with it forthrightly.[2]

Here, Walt reveals a belief that the Disneyfication process does not sanitize or trivialize the stories, but emphasizes the morality play as the key component of all fairy tales. Thus, Disney villains are designed in stark contrast to the good characters to emphasize their villainy, communicating to viewers the advantage of being good and unselfish that one is less likely to die unhappy and hated by the people of the land. It is my contention that Disney's films (and by extension their theme park attractions) are simply contributions to a long history of fairy tale versions, with two notable exceptions: the first is that Disney's medium is primarily film and other visual media, which requires a fair amount of translation and license to turn the word into the screen, and the other is that, with the exception of very few stories, Disney was working with European tales and translating them to suit the American culture. Walt Disney's goal with his studio was never to draw a line of demarcation between adults and children, so it is erroneous to conclude that Disney's movies are solely for children.

Further criticism of Disneyfication is that Disney versions are transmitted through the magic of cinema, television, and video technology across generations, promoting a single version of a fairy tale while preventing the development and growth of the imagination. This literalized version is made into a commodity by the "culture industry." A commodified fairy tale, then, is one "designed to reinforce [one's] consumerist status rather than to address them as individuals."[3] This encourages consumerist behaviors in conjunction with the fairy tale's release. Indeed, product merchandising has been one of Disney's specialties since Mickey Mouse was licensed in the 1930s, and merchandising is a crucial component of Disney annual profits.[4]

The latent result of a commodified fairy tale is ideological. The "mass-produced fairytale" provides a "sense of familiarity achieved through the outward material and ideological sameness."[5] While using imagery of fantasy, fairy tales, especially as retold by Disney, paint a utopian world: one in which everyone lives happily ever after, where only the bad guys (villains) die, and true love rules the land. Because there is no death (villains excepted), these stories suggest only a cycle of new beginnings, never endings. Disney reinforces this throughout Disneyland, especially in the Fantasyland dark rides. Peter Pan brings the Darling children home, but the presence of the mermaids, mythological creatures known for pulling men into the depths, before the final door of the attraction opens suggest that the story is not over, and that if we stay on the boat we can return to Neverland. Pinocchio's story ends with dancing and festivities celebrating his new life as a human boy. Alice throws us an unbirthday party before we leave, a metaphorical new birth that can occur at any time of the year. And then there is Snow White that takes us from the Witch's plunge into the storybook reminding us that they lived happily ever after. A new life, a happy one, borne from the villain's death. Even Toad's story could be argued to reinforce the utopian sense of beginning. He/we have chosen an eternal life of playing with motorcars, and thus have chosen freedom and adventure—two things near and dear to the American spirit—and were sent to Hell for this, but Hell is essentially the Other World but only achieved after death. The horrors associated with it are linked closely with the dominant ideology of the culture.

Fantasyland Key Attractions

- Sleeping Beauty Castle
- Matterhorn Bobsleds
- it's a small world

Sleeping Beauty Castle and Disneyfication

Let's look a little closer at one such Disneyfied fairy tale: *Sleeping Beauty*.

Sleeping Beauty Castle is the "wienie" of Fantasyland, or the thing that draws the guests to the place; it is also the "wienie" of Disneyland. The castle was the central figure of the original design plans of the park and was named after Sleeping Beauty in hope of promoting the upcoming *Sleeping Beauty* film, based on both the fairy tale by Charles Perrault and the ballet by Pytor Ilyich Tchaikovsky. At the time of its construction, the film was still in the early stages of production (it was not released until 1959), so inspiration for the design was taken from a conglomerate of European Castles, notably Bavaria's Neuschwanstein Castle.[6] It is built to the same forced perspective as the rest of the park.

Sleeping Beauty Castle became not only one of the most recognizable features of the park, but also of the Disney Company as it was used for many years as the logo of Disney features: first, in the opening credits for the Disneyland television series, then in the beginning of films and in other points of advertising.[7] Imagineer John Hench described the castle as not only a Disney logo, but as a symbol of the public unconscious:

> We carry these so-called myths, and they're part aspiration, part dream, and it's something we share, on a fundamental basis, of course, with every living person. The castle was a strong point, and I suppose it actually has something to do with the relationship with mountains, too—with a high point in the landscape. It's a place of safety. I think the medieval churches also played up that same kind of feeling. It was a large architectural statement and it said something to people about a rallying point, a safe place, a protector.[8]

To downplay the intimidation that can be experienced from tall structures, the Imagineers toned down the size of the castle to enhance its reassuring architecture. Indeed, Sleeping Beauty Castle is the smallest of all other Disney theme park castles.[9]

In Perrault's fairy tale, a celebration is held for the newborn princess. An old fairy arrives uninvited and curses the princess to prick her finger on a spindle on her sixteenth birthday and die. Although efforts are made to avoid this event, fate cannot be undone. Instead of dying, a fairy blessing puts her and the entire kingdom to sleep for 100 years, at which time she is married to the prince who awoke the kingdom.

The film adaptation follows the original story with minor changes. Instead of seven good fairies, Disney has three good fairies who keep the princess hidden, raising her in ignorance of her true identity to protect her from Maleficent's evil curse. Princess Aurora is betrothed to the son of her father's friend, so the story is modified for him to awaken her with love's first kiss after defeating Maleficent within a few days of her birthday. The film ends with their celebratory dance and they live happily ever after.

The castle was opened in 1957 as a walk-through attraction, featuring dioramas portraying scenes from the forthcoming film. As a walk-through attraction, guests do not ride a vehicle and can take the time to stare at the artwork. In the early 1960s, it was modified when guests complained about scenes in the attraction that were not in the film. It was re-opened in the 1970s with statues rather than painted scenes, but closed in 2001 when the scenes became outdated. In the 2008 re-opening of the attraction, the art was updated to feature graphics that gave dimension and movement to the characters, combining the Pepper's Ghost illusion with digital technology. It now most closely follows the film story.

The release of the film made the attraction essentially useless as it was meant to advertise an unreleased film, so Imagineers were tasked with keeping its relevance fresh. The present incarnation pays homage to the original attraction "plussed" to incorporate new technology. It is necessarily a walk-through because of space limitations, but it still enchants because it allows the guests inside the castle, giving it life as an icon, not just a building dominating the landscape.

As a product of the mid- to late–1950s, *Sleeping Beauty* addresses the emergent new Baby Boomer teenager. This demographic differs from its predecessors in that the Boomer teenager had a new relationship to leisure and consumption. As such, this teenager had to find new ways to exert his or her independence. Princess Aurora has lived in isolation her entire life in an attempt to avoid Maleficent's spell. Her only friends other than the fairies that raise her are the forest animals. Thus, when she meets Prince Phillip by chance in the woods, she is frightened, but quickly drawn in by his charm. She tries to maintain a respectful distance, but dances with him anyway. When the three fairies tell her that she cannot be with him because she is a princess and already engaged, she protests. Unable to fully exert her independence, she goes along with the fairies to the castle. She is clearly depressed, determined not to enjoy herself in an act of protest. Prince Phillip, meanwhile, informs his father that he has met the woman he is going to marry and will not be around that evening to welcome Princess Aurora. He is better equipped to exert his independence in keeping with society's attitudes toward men and women in the 1950s.

The attraction does not fully reflect this subtle change to the story. It, rather, is an elaborate marketing piece. It was produced simultaneously with the film, drawing from concepts and storyboards. Books outside the dioramas offer a brief synopsis of the story and the dioramas preview the level of art that is present in the film. The walk-through gives us just enough information to recognize the story and characters, but not enough to form sympathies. In the first couple years of the castle walk-through, guests were handed a souvenir gift book further whetting the appetite for the coming movie. In short, the walk-through fulfilled the same role as a movie trailer, but because of the kinetic aspect of the tour, it formed a more intimate connection between guest and film. Needless to say, *Sleeping Beauty* was a hit success.

That the castle would become one of the corporation's most iconic symbols in a country designed in opposition to traditional symbols of a king reflects how potent Disney's fantasy world is to America's utopian fantasies. The castle, depicted in the film as a glowing building situated on a hill, reflects hope of a strong leadership to bring the people out of the dark times it was and is facing. However, that the king, symbolic of leadership, is decidedly absent from the castle (he is asleep) not only reinforces the American desire to not be ruled by a king but also the hope for the next generation to restore optimism and hope to a land that is plagued. The prince, who represents the next generation of leadership, rescues the princess, not the king. In fact, a common feature among Disney heroes is that he or she "is a rebellious teenager who will not follow parental orders, eventually proving himself right rather than merely arrogant."[10] In this, we see Disney's subversive message of defiance to the children that would eventually grow into players in the counterculture movement in the 1960s, that when the leadership fails, or falls asleep, it is up to the youth to restore and revitalize the utopian image of the land, in which their people can live happily ever after.[11]

All of this has led to what is called "the culture industry," or the commodification of art, stories, and other creative outlets, for the purposes of corporate profit.[12] This is achieved by playing on the culture's "desire for pleasure and happiness":

> In order to maximize profit, the culture industry has to instill standard expectations in audiences so that they think they are getting what they want, and that by getting what they supposedly want, they can become like the stars with whom they identify. When accused of "dumbing down" their programs and products, corporate representatives in the culture industry are fond of announcing that they are conceding to the wishes of the public and are only as guilty as their audiences. Of course, they never mention that they seek to control these audiences through their own polls and conditioning processes. The culture industry is indeed "totalitarian" ... in its intention to totally take over markets and dominate demands and wishes.[13]

The concern shared by many Disney critics, is that the commodification both forces the same kind of story onto audiences and conditions them to expect it, achieved through the rigorous marketing practices of Disney and the other players in the Industry. From the corporate standpoint, however, the Industry has no real way to garner audience response other than to review revenues from product channels. Ticket sales and polls are flawed systems of survey. Ticket sales do not reflect whether or not the product is liked, and polls are only able to survey a select group, one that may or may not be representative of the entire population. However, the purchase of product tie-ins, even if these products are trashed after a couple months, offers a more immediate response to the product. People buy toys, clothes, and other accessories to feel a part of a story that was particularly inspiring.

On the other hand, the audience perspective is one driven by consumption, made possible by the "equalizing nature of television" and "the rise of the new television-raised middle class with a shared cultural experience" that made commercialized, corporate consumption possible for the first time in history.[14] The culture of consumption creates a linkage between individual world and icons that are perceived as archetypes. Thus, in order to be a good citizen or parent, one must consume the merchandize that connects one to the story. Not only does this create easy advertising for the company, but it also creates a hunger for more of these items to evoke the warm feelings the memory of the story generates.

Disneyization and Utopianism

Scholars have considered the Disneyization of America as both a harmful practice to society by sanitizing the culture to paint illusions, and as an unavoidable factor of contemporary society. However, what is not considered is whether the inherent nostalgia of Disneyfication is hindering the transition of American myth by encouraging Americans to idolize a previous way of life that prevents forward thinking. Over the past decade, the culture only seems collectively interested in change if it manifests catastrophically—natural disasters, the housing market economic fall-out—meanwhile Americans have spent the last decade fighting a war to protect a nostalgic, utopian, Disneyfied America, whether the purpose of the war is recognized as one against terrorism, which is the official claim in the media; oil, the fuel of American freedom; or Christianity, whose protestant values inform America's attitudes toward work and child-rearing. Those who have protested the war, either vocally or privately, seem better prepared for the transition, likely raised on the same liberal, counterculture values that awoke the mythic language of transition in the 1960s. Those still supporting the war maintain the attitude that the country is falling down a rabbit hole and charge the leadership to fix the problem without raising taxes. These polarities reflect those of Disneyization between the entertaining, themed environment and its backstage (shadow) area. The new mythology can only function in the culture if the boundary between these two worlds can be made more transparent.

The real fear of Disneyfication rests with the perceived transformation of the individual from engaged participant who is likely going to learn something, to passive consumer, which is precisely what philosopher Umberto Eco believes occurs at Disneyland: "An allegory of the consumer society, a place of absolute iconism, Disneyland is also a piece of total passivity. Its visitors must agree to behave like its robots. Access to each attraction is regulated by a maze of metal railings that discourages an individual initiative. [...] If the visitor pays this price, he can have not only the 'real thing' by the abundance of the reconstructed truth."[15] The perceived truth that is being consumed is the utopian dream, a place such as Disneyland where "people can perceive themselves as members of one united community that shares norms and values, and cherishes the same concept of happiness."[16] America was founded on utopian ideals of an egalitarian society with balance between work and leisure and no persecution.[17] Although initially discovered on accident and pursued for its wealth of resources, America ultimately attracted colonists who were seeking a utopia and freedom from oppression. This utopianism also promoted the tenets of Manifest Destiny so as to maintain control of the West that American settlers were already calling home. With the anxieties of the early twentieth century, America's utopianism was breaking under the pressures of the age, described in previous chapters.

The relationship between Disney's fairy tales and America's utopianism is that Disney's romantization of America's past showed that the dream was still possible. America's history is

> the most romantic of all histories. It began in myth and has developed through centuries of fairy stories. Whatever the time is in America it is always, at every moment, the mad and wayward hour when the prince is finding the little foot that alone fits into the slipper of glass. [...] Ours is a story mad with the impossible, it is by chaos out of dream, it began as a dream and it has continued as dream down to the last headlines you read in a newspaper.[18]

The American mindset has always attempted to maintain this dream and to construct a utopian world outside the images and metaphors of fairy tale, prompting psychologist C. G. Jung to comment that Americans have the most complicated psychology, one linked to a Heroic Ideal, the land, and American concepts of success.[19] Utopianism in an age of Cold War and globalism, however, is not so easy to maintain, which is why its maintenance relies more on simulacra than on American ideals. By constructing Disneyland and bringing to life two-dimensional stories from the screen, Disney brought to life the utopia from one of its own fairy tales, the *Disneyland* television show, compiled for television from an amalgamation of all of Disney's other productions. Disneyland is thus America's meta-utopia that has inspired the hyperrealistic America that has been constructed since 1955, including the other Disney theme parks.

A Disneyized utopia is actually a reenactment of a romantic America, which in turn is the expectation and projection of Americans of what utopia should be. It stands to reason that if the American dream has failed to live up to expectations, those that were shattered by the Great Depression, then America's failed utopianism has helped create the culture of consumption. For, as the body craves the nutrients it is lacking, so does the cultural psyche for the dream it is missing. Hyper-reality feeds us with simulations of the dream, satiating our cravings temporarily, but the hunger, the addiction to the simulation, grows with each "hit." But rather than shatter the American Dream, Disney tries to inject new life into it by reminding us of American heroic ideals. For although the dream of utopia of America's past may have failed in the past century, there is no reason why a new one cannot emerge.

In late 2010, the Disney Corporation announced that it would no longer make fairy tale films, believing that they have exhausted the genre. Perhaps the Disney Corporation is again picking up a shift within culture, one that is so complex that it is leaving the more simplistic stories provided by fairy tales behind. When Disneyfying fairy tales to make them into films, Disney made them into stories of their time and culture. That Disney has placed a lot of trust in Pixar, its computer animation subsidiary, suggests the direction the Industry's relationship to fairy tales is heading. The culture is primed to receive new myths that incorporate fairy tale elements and restore our relationship to magic. In other words, the medium is changing to adapt to the complexities of the cultural unconscious, while still maintaining the hopeful happy endings of fairy tales.

Meanwhile, American culture is undergoing a major shift. The Left wants us to make peace and end the war already, while the Right is on a moralistic crusade to return to the values of a golden past. Technology makes it easier for us to ignore each other. Films push for a savior hero to rescue us from the impending apocalypse, while television programs remind us that our lives suck a lot less than those of the reality show contestants. There is a tension underneath the surface, a great force threatening to unleash. Contemporary mythic fairy tales offer coping tools. It is no longer a simple Disney formula to get from "once upon a time" to "happily ever after." It is trial, error, and working with one's friends to vanquish the villain who cannot be easily toppled off a mountain. Today's villain is pure evil, such that they may not have any humanity left. And while we still fear as a culture of losing our individuality, our fear of losing our humanity is increasingly the greater concern.

7. Fantasyland: The Myth of Utopia, Part 2

And then, *Frozen* happened, surprising even Disney with its popularity. The film's message of sisterhood as the truest love, struck a nerve with audiences, as did the anthem, "Let It Go," a song about release and liberation. The success of *Frozen* reveals that the fairy tale medium still resonates with American audiences, and the salvation from an ice kingdom suggests a renewed interest in pursuing an American utopia.

All of the fairy tales in the Disney canon have been modified to fit an American sensibility, and lend themselves to social interpretation. For instance, *Snow White and the Seven Dwarfs* was made during the 1930s, when the Great Depression was in full force over the country and the world. In a cultural reading of the fairy tale film, Snow White becomes a metaphor for Lady Liberty, thus representing American culture. She is working a job (servant to the queen), and while we know she wishes for something better, we are not necessarily given any reason to think that she used to be a princess. She makes a wish on the wishing well for a prince to come take her away. That wish is a metaphor for the American Dream, often seen as the easy road to success. So the queen seeks to have her killed in a sudden change reflective of the Crash of 1929. Snow White's life as she knew it is over forever. She flees into the forest and settles in the dwarfs' cottage, a makeshift Hoovertown. The Seven Dwarfs seem to own their mine, evoking a memory of the California Gold Rush. Together, with Snow White's skills as a housekeeper and the Dwarfs mining, they pool their resources and are able to live in relative happiness. But the queen is not done. She represents the Great Depression and the apple reinforces the upset to the stability of one's world. The apple is typically interpreted as the apple of Eden, but in this reading it is more appropriate to compare it to the apple of discord. Just when Snow White is finding happiness in her new life, the Depression comes and shakes it up again, planting discord not only for Snow White, but for her newly found friends and the entire balance of the forest, just as the Great Depression threatened to destroy American stability because of the culture's self-definition on grounds of economy. The Prince, then, represents the New Deal hope of Franklin D. Roosevelt. From his rescue of Snow White, we are lead to believe that America will again live happily ever after. The film offered an optimistic end for the Depression in an escapist fashion.

Walt's Utopia

Snow White's Scary Adventures, the Disneyland attraction, retranslates this message into a Cold War story. This version is more appropriate to the social shift that occurred in the mid–1950s, suggesting that the happiness and prosperity prior to the Great Depression (the merry-making in the Cottage) was forever upset by the Depression (the apple), World War II (the darkness of the forest), and finally the looming fear of Cold War destruction of America (the topple from the mountain). While the ride suggests a grim, uncertain future, Disney nonetheless offers the optimistic reminder that we will live happily ever after. This final message helps secure the relevance of the fairy tale in today's climate. No matter the life experience of the guest riding through the attraction, he or she will always perceive the ride experience through his or her own frame of reference. Arguably, Disney's optimism that "they will live happily ever after" is a vital message to counter negative news and world events.

In another example, Disney's version of *Pinocchio* was released in 1940 as a follow-up to the surprisingly successful *Snow White and the Seven Dwarfs*. America was still in the Depression and Europe was at war. Tensions at the Walt Disney Studio were nearing a breaking point—the famous animator's strike would take place in 1941, forever changing Walt's business model—and the United States government was asking Walt Disney to take a goodwill tour to South America.

Disney's *Pinocchio* is representative of a young boy of the era. Geppetto is affected by the Depression. He does not "have" a lot, but he is an artist, as evidenced by the number of cuckoo clocks and music boxes on his shelves, and he is extremely happy. His only sadness is when he loses Pinocchio. It was difficult to be a child during the Depression. Walt uses Pinocchio as an idealized vision. Geppetto has no family, and creates Pinocchio out of a dream for a family, with no expectation of Pinocchio coming to life. But, as a good father, he is entirely devoted to the boy.

The recurring theme is that a boy should be "brave, truthful and unselfish" and always listen to his conscience. If a boy fails to listen to his conscience, he is likely going to get into trouble, and if he does listen, then he should reflect a model citizen. But what happens if he listens to his conscience and it leads him to a task counter to society's norms? Then he gets swallowed by a whale. Disney's whale, named

152

7. Fantasyland: The Myth of Utopia, Part 2

Monstro, more resembles Melville's Moby-Dick, than he does Collodi's asthmatic whale: a vindictive, unsympathetic, all-consuming monster of the ocean. Pinocchio's conscience, Jiminy Cricket, persists in telling Pinocchio to go into the whale and to be brave. In the book, Pinocchio's greatest problem in fleeing the whale is getting too tired while carrying Geppetto; in Disney's film, the whale actively chases them and Pinocchio dies. His Christ–like resurrection foreshadows the coming re-awakening of America, inspired in part by our involvement in the war that required bravery, honesty by the politicians, and massive amounts of unselfishness on the part of the home front in support of the war effort.

The main theme of Collodi's tale is that a boy should be obedient to his parents. All of Pinocchio's punishments stem from his conscious disobedience. Disney's theme, however, stresses the good behavior of boys, suggesting a value akin to Boy Scouts behaving as model citizens. Pinocchio learns not to lie when he watches his nose grow, and learns to be unselfish in Stromboli's cage, and he demonstrates bravery in his determination to rescue Geppetto from the whale.

Finally, both *Alice in Wonderland* and *Peter Pan* were introduced to the world via television, the first Disney films to do so. In fact, Walt Disney was one of the first Hollywood producers to embrace television as a potential extension of the entertainment industry. The two television specials he aired served as practice-runs for what eventually became the *Disneyland* television show. Television emerged during an interesting confluence of events in America. Though developed in the earlier half of the century, it became a commodity that found a home in an increasing number of households following World War II. This nascent medium was able to transport people to other worlds from the comfort of their own home. It was able to bring visual images of events that previously had been left to the imagination. It was a novel new form that created *communitas* through shared images. Since 1950, almost all of the nation's great events have unfolded before our eyes on television.

At the same time, however, the entertainment industry was battling censorship. Following the Dionysian Roaring 1920s, the subdued 1930s, in large part due to great affect by the Depression, instilled a Production Code of guidelines so films could reflect the moral values of America's middle class. This was partially due to the realization that Hollywood celebrities were being followed as idols, and the belief that they had a responsibility to uphold social values because of their public presence. Throughout the 1930s and 1940s, as European directors and actors immigrated to Hollywood, reports were brought over of the German and Russian propaganda films that were defining the behaviors of entire groups of people. Following World War II and the realization of the severity of these propaganda machines, the Code got stricter, and the same guidelines were extended to television.

Alice in Wonderland and *Peter Pan* were not themselves homages to the wonders of television, but they are both episodic narratives, like a radio or television serial, that reflect a post–War utopian Other World and an escape from the stresses of the Cold War. Both novels emerged from Victorian England, known in the modern world for possessing a repressed, homogenized sensibility. This same sensibility was attractive to a Production Code-driven American society. The values spoke nicely to the values that the newly established mid-century suburban (white) culture sought to project all over the country.

Throughout the Cold War and more recently the "War on Terror," stories of Wonderland and Neverland are constantly being remade and retold. These places offer escapism into an imaginary utopia, the same kind of other world at the other side of the television screen. The Cold War forced Americans to define their values: to exemplify what it means to be "American," not only on the changing face of the home front but also in the international community, taking into account that the American face was now a dominant one in the world market.

Both *Alice in Wonderland* and *Peter Pan* were recent films when Disneyland was designed, so the pressure was stronger to stay to the films as closely as possible when constructing the attraction. Rather than offer any great ideological reminder, the Pan and Alice attractions instead help us escape. Through the window of the nursery or the rabbit hole—both metaphors for the boundary imposed by the television screen—we are taken into episodes of these other worlds. Each room of these attractions is its own episode in the larger adventure of the main character, the guest. Yet, because of our cultural relationship to television, we can embrace the lack of an over-arching narrative.

Bringing Us Closer Together: *it's a small world and Global Community*

it's a small world is the only Fantasyland attraction with no connection to a Disney film. The attraction is a result of a joint commission by Pepsi and UNICEF for the 1964–1965 World's Fair designed to depict the children of the world. Initially, all of the children were to sing their respective national anthems. Realizing that this resulted in a cacophony of noise, Walt Disney asked the Sherman Brothers to write what became the wildly familiar tune, "It's a Small World." All of the children sing this tune, some in their native language, to send the message that humanity may be different on the outside, but the experience is fundamentally the same, thus, "it's a small world after all." The attraction, as well as the others Disney designed for the fair including Great Moments with Mr. Lincoln, made use of the then-new audio-animatronic technology. At the end of the World's Fair, Small World returned to Disneyland to give it a permanent home in Fantasyland.

To move guests through the attraction, they sail on boats. It is billed as the "happiest cruise that ever sailed 'round the world."[20] Each country is represented mostly through the dress and dance of the children, but also through the scenery that evokes a sensibility of the native culture. The unique style of the design combines color and geometry to emphasize the similarities of the people of the world while also celebrating their diversity.

Following World War II, the world got smaller. New technologies introduced during the two world wars made contact with distant cultures more immediate. Film, photo, radio, and tele-communication technology spread to new corners, making trans-continental communication a little easier. As most countries were rebuilding and restructuring, America stood out as a beacon of solidarity, which gave the country the added responsibility for addressing the global community.

The it's a small world [sic] attraction is Disney's testament to the shrinking planet. Guests sail from "country" to "country" watching happy children dance, all to the soundtrack of a song that communicates the attraction's message:

It's a world of laughter, a world of tears.
It's a world of hopes and a world of fears.
There's so much that we share that it's time we're aware:
It's a small world after all!
—

There is just one moon and one golden sun,
And a smile means friendship to everyone.
Though the mountains divide and the oceans are wide,
It's a small world after all![21]

Most American children know this song even if they have never been to Disney Parks. It is taught in grade school along with many other iconic tunes, such as "This Land Is Your Land," or "America the Beautiful." Also, the tune is very catchy and it can become deeply embedded in one's memory, repeating over and over just like it does in the attraction. Now with international Disney Parks, children from other countries now have the opportunity to learn this song.

Douglas Brode in *From Walt to Woodstock* argues for Disney's subversive messages throughout the films Walt produced. These subversive messages, he contends, helped create the counterculture movement of the late 1960s that still informs some of the current American ideologies. Brode points out that it's a small world gave the American culture a concept of multiculturalism long before the term was coined and celebrated. For, although the ride emphasizes all of the cultural differences among the children, they are united in singing the same songs. "Disney delights in diversity," Brode writes, "yet his key point is that what draws us all together in a human community most ultimately and always be seen as primary."[22] As the Cold War threatened to tear us apart through invisible fears, it's a small world reminded us to come together.

While not the direct result of it's a small world, the world has become even smaller through corporate globalism and social networking, the latter operating on an individual level, making it possible to chat—live!—with people in other parts of the world. Recent uprisings in the Middle East were made known to world news because of social media; families are reunited after natural disasters through social media. Outlets such as Facebook become people's primary mode of communication, such that offices and professors use them as a tool for communicating with their younger employees and students.

7. Fantasyland: The Myth of Utopia, Part 2

At the end of the first hour of the television documentary *The Power of Myth*, Joseph Campbell calls for a new myth of the society of the planet.[23] Each generation is becoming more and more primed for this myth, and this harkens back to *it's a small world*, which helped start the conversation; today's social media actually makes it possible. Globalization is not just the American corporate imposition onto other countries, but in order to truly achieve a society of the planet, globalization has to include a fusion of disparate myths. For example, one of Disney's current projects is to open a Disneyland Magic Kingdom in Shanghai, China. When Disney constructed Tokyo Disneyland, the Japanese financiers asked for an identical replica of Disneyland. Disney made the assumption that the same formula would work in Paris, which proved to be a financial mistake. So in developing the Chinese parks (Hong Kong and Shanghai), Disney has taken Chinese mythos into account. What is happening in the construction of the Shanghai park is a true example of globalization: a fusion of American and Chinese mythologies.

What *it's a small world* fails to consider is the shadow: the reality of the egos of those in power. Each country/nation/political power would rather not compromise their autonomy and power. This is perceived as giving in to the other party. This ideology has been at the core of civilization for millennia. However, for the first time in the history of humanity, the myth of a truly globalized world has been formulated and developed for over fifty years. It would be difficult for the now internationally opened doors of communication to close, so this new global myth needs to help us redefine civilization and humanity.

8

Tomorrowland
The Myth of the Spirit of Progress

"Ever since the bow and arrow, mankind has both worried and been fascinated by the flow and march of science. Today, with the recent discovery of tremendous natural forces and their harnessing to man's use, man is still anxious yet still hopeful."—Walt Disney, *"The Disneyland Story"*

"A visitor into the world of wondrous ideas, signifying man's achievement. A step into the future, with predictions of constructive things to come. Tomorrow offers new frontiers in science, adventure, and ideals—the atomic age, the challenge of outer space, and the hope for a peaceful and united world."—Walt Disney, *"Dateline Disneyland"*

"Tomorrowland is your glimpse into the Future. Or at least the Future we'd like to believe it will be. Catch a passing rocket ship to the next galaxy over or grab a bite to eat with your favorite alien friends. It's your best chance to have tomorrow's fun ... today!"—The Imagineers, The Imagineering Field Guide to Disneyland

When Disneyland was initially conceived, it included not only a treatment of the past, recent past and fantasy, but also posited a world of tomorrow. Tomorrowland was originally intended as a platform to experiment with and showcase new technologies for the future, including innovations in public transportation, household conveniences, and travels to outer space. However, technological innovation went into hyperdrive in the Cold War years, and trying to keep Disneyland's Tomorrow far enough advanced ahead of the future became increasingly difficult and the premise for Tomorrowland had to be reconsidered.

158

Tomorrowland Key Attractions

- Autopia
- Alweg Monorail
- WEDWay People Mover (closed)
- Star Tours/New Star Tours
- Space Mountain
- Buzz Lightyear Astro Blasters
- Finding Nemo Submarine Voyage

In its original design, Tomorrowland's setting was 1986, chosen because it was the next return for Halley's Comet. Imagineers soon realized that 1986 quickly became outdated; Walt Disney acknowledged this problem when he said, "tomorrow is a heck of a thing to keep up with."[1] In 1967, a New Tomorrowland opened, giving the area its first dramatic update themed as "a shiny 'World on the Move,'"[2] filled with new modes of mass transportation. As the decades creeped by, however, the exciting new transportation began to look dated, prompting another update in the late 1990s. This time, however, the Imagineers gave up on creating a new future altogether, and instead designed a "retro-future,"[3] giving up on predicting the future. Instead, Disney turned to romanticizing the future as imagined by the past.[4] This newer New Tomorrowland exemplifies "technostalgia" or "the nostalgic appreciation of earlier forms of technology for what they conveyed about our lost connections with time and place."[5] This nostalgia has lead to the resurrection of previously dead attractions, such as the Submarine Voyage and *Captain EO*; the revitalization of older attractions, such as Star Tours; and the rumored resurrection of still-dead attractions, such as the WEDway People Mover. Tomorrowland increasingly becomes firmly rooted in its own past, especially as technology seeks new limits and people hunger for simplicity, escape from reality, and freedom from hyperreality.

Tomorrowland on the Move: The Spirit of Progress

Modern Americans approach the power of and place trust in science and progress with near religiosity. Science promises "ultimate truth and everyday, secular, natural life—a promise religion had fulfilled in the dark past, but did no longer, for many Americans."[6] Science, it is believed, could describe the past and present, predict the future, tell the truth, and solve our problems. Even if science does not immediately provide answers, the assumption is made that with enough reason, dedication, pervasive curiosity, and Pixie Dust, science will someday provide the answers if only we ask the right questions. Thus, the fascination is with the process of scientific inquiry, with the expectation that it will eventually yield answers; the answers are the product of tomorrow. In the late nineteenth century, the myth of science fused with the myth of progress[7]:

> In an industrial society devoted to the production of goods for individual consumers to use, Americans believe the purpose of those goods, the reason for consumption, to be the acquisition of "absolute personal freedom, mobility, privacy." Progress is measured by the degree of individual independence available. And in contemporary America, the consumer is the engine of progress.[8]

The two myths were fused into one, creating an environment in which science became a consumable product, and each new innovation is seen as a step forward in the development and evolution of science. This relationship shifted with World War II, when scientific progress revealed the capacity of mass destruction, and this was met with the fear and anxiety of the Cold War, unanchoring American values and initiating an "ongoing disintegration of the idea of progress in the American mind," expressed with the popular culture of the mid-century.[9]

Disney refused to cater to these fears and continued to advocate for the creative power of technology. This optimism is reflected in the Spirit of Progress, who is personified in the Donald Duck edutainment cartoon, *Donald and the Wheel*. In this cartoon, the Spirits of Progress, Senior and Junior, try to convince a caveman Donald through their catchy song about progress that he should invent the wheel, even explaining how and why. Donald walks away from the divine message, thinking the idea of a round wheel—his cart uses square wheels—is absurd. Though faceless, the junior Spirit of Progress is clearly a young man, wearing a short tunic, long curly hair, frolicking and dancing in contrast to Senior's long robe, rotund appearance, and deep, soothing

8. Tomorrowland

voice. The youthful vitality of Progress communicates the newness of youth, that Progress never ages and is constantly in flux as the needs of an age mold and alter the ebb and flow of progressive development. His father, Progress Senior, is present to keep Junior from getting too crazy in his ideas, because, as Donald demonstrates, not everyone shares Junior's enthusiasm for change and innovation. For purposes of this discussion, I will concentrate on the youthful image of Progress, because this character not only reflects American perceptions of progress, but also a playful childishness that is similarly characteristic within Disney products and among Disney fans. Progress taps into the sense of play and wonder of children, and invites adults similarly to play by the same rules. This playfulness toward progress comes through the Tomorrowland transportation attractions.

One example of playfulness in Tomorrowland is the attraction Autopia. Autopia was designed as a way to allow kids the fun and pleasure of driving their own car before they are allowed to do so by law, itself a rite of passage toward adulthood. Disney violates the sanctity of this ritual by placing kids of the right height behind the wheel of a car. These cars were described in the 1956 souvenir book as "Disney's cars of the future,"[10] but their design and reliance on gasoline hardly qualifies these cars as "futuristic." Nevertheless, the Autopia cars are among the park's historically most popular attractions, an irony considering that "most guests hope to fight their way through freeway traffic just to get to Disneyland."[11] Transportation is seen as an extension of the American Manifest Destiny as improvements in technology make moving from one place to another easier. However, the shadow side of this freedom of movement is the limitations of resources, especially fuel, that make transportation possible. The myth of freedom includes a fundamentalist grip on our perceived entitlement to move, which has slowed the national adoption of fuel-efficient, eco-friendly alternatives to fuel-based automobiles and public transportation. The myth of freedom linked with transportation emerges in the 1970s as the fuel crisis, labor strikes, and the state of highway infrastructure restructured motorized freedom.[12] In recent years, despite improved highways and fuel-efficient vehicles, gas prices have cut into the ability to freely drive, but has not been able to crush the perception of the American highway as the road to freedom, a myth reinforced by Lightning McQueen's own journey in the Pixar film *Cars*. Autopia helps maintain the connection between the myth of freedom and transportation, but for all of the attraction's popularity, Disney's emphasis is really on public transportation. To get cars off the road, Walt explains in a promotional video for EPCOT, makes the roads safer for pedestrians at home, thus encouraging play and safety for children, and in the civic center, taking on anxious component out of consuming.

Walt Disney was fascinated with the idea of public transportation and hoped that the attractions in Tomorrowland would prompt a social move to incorporate some of Tomorrowland's innovations into the greater public, a hope reflected in the original concept for EPCOT. One such innovation, for instance, was the Monorail.

Disney's Monorail was the first American use of a single-rail elevated train designed by the German company, Alweg. The Alweg Monorail is capable of moving people quietly and with clean energy. The one in Disneyland connects the park with the Disneyland Hotel and the outreaches of the Resort, and the station in Downtown Disney serves as a secondary entrance to Disneyland. Walt's hope was that major cities would adopt the Monorail, and while some did, such as Seattle, most did not, notably Los Angeles. This lack of interest in the train reflects a post-war social shift in America that favored and continues to favor the individual empowerment the car provides and the freedom and speed of the highway that the train has yet to provide (though the technology is slowly being imported from foreign countries). Furthermore, trains are associated with the past, romanticizing an era when a rural setting could help a person to withdraw from the hustle and bustle of society and "he could recover his animal and natural self,"[13] but this withdrawal could not compete with the freedom and empowerment of the open road. Cities that boomed in the post-war years, such as Los Angeles, define themselves by their car culture, and the suburbs of these cities reinforce the car culture with little to no transportation alternatives.

In another attempt to solve urban transportation problems, the WEDway People Mover was designed as a short-range transportation alternative, especially useful in urban centers, again, as suggested in Walt's original design for EPCOT. The People Mover moves at a gentle pace, but is a continuously moving train. It is fast enough to not be a boring ride, but slow enough for guests to hop on and off without the train stopping, similar to the Omnimover used in the Haunted Mansion's Doom Buggies. Because it continuously moves, the People Mover could reduce people traffic and congestion in train stations.

In the renovation of the late 1990s, the People Mover closed and was replaced by the Rocket Rods, which were a little more high-speed, resembling more a gentle rollercoaster than a transportation alternative. But constant breakdowns and disappointing guest response led to the closure of the attraction. The tracks still hang over Tomorrowland, as a reminder of a defunct past, casting a shadow on the shiny promises of Tomorrow.

Tomorrowland and Rejuveniles in Outer Space— "To Infinity and Beyond!"[14]

The Spirit of Progress invites examination from two different angles: the childlike angle that invites both play and nostalgia, and the other angle that considers the shadow of Progress, which is Doubt. On the personal level, Progress encourages play, because playful experimentation forms the core of innovation and development characteristic of progress. With this emphasis on play, the potentials of Progress are limitless. As Walt Disney once said, Disneyland would never be finished as long as there is imagination in the world,[15] thus invoking the Spirit of Progress to carry the life of Disneyland and its guests and employees (from cast members to Imagineers).

The Tomorrowland segment of the *Disneyland* television show not only demonstrated technological innovation, especially with nuclear power in "Our Friend the Atom," but it also theorized about sending man to the moon in a series of three episodes: "Man in Space," "Man and the Moon," and "Mars and Beyond." As such, outer space has always had a home in Tomorrowland. "Old" Tomorrowland included attractions that simulated flying to the Moon/Mars or riding on a flying saucer, but the current Tomorrowland attempts to actually take us into space.

Star Tours was the first attraction built in partnership with George Lucas.[16] As Disney struggled to update Tomorrowland, they had to turn outside their own repertoire because the few instances of science fiction films by Disney, such as *Tron* and *The Black Hole*, were not popular enough to merit their own attractions. The *Star Wars* trilogy, on the other hand, had proven to be immensely popular. At the time, because of Disney's inventiveness in attraction design and demonstrated experience in themeing, a partnership between Disney and Lucas to bring *Star Wars* to life seemed natural.

In the story of Star Tours, guests are the passengers on a quick tour that doesn't go as planned, because the novice pilot loses his way, dropping the tour into the familiar battle scene from *Star Wars*. The attraction is innovative for combining realistic visuals, which utilize visual technology and a big-screen in a precursor to IMAX, with simulated flight movement built into the seats enhancing the movement of the movie with movement in the seats. The ride is so intense that cast members check seat belts with the same vigor as a roller coaster.[17]

In 2011, Disneyland opened Star Tours II, which updates the ride, digital and visual technology, and the story to include tours to other planets in Lucas's universe. To add excitement to the attraction, the tour is chosen at random, leaving guests with no clue where they are about to go.

To lure teens into their new theme parks, other Southern California parks began building new and exciting roller coasts in the 1970s. Disney responded with Big Thunder Mountain Railroad in Frontierland and Space Mountain. Space Mountain is a roller coaster ride through outer space, but the innovation is not an attempt to simulate the actual space environment with zero gravity but, rather, that it is an indoor roller coaster, with simulated starlight as the only light. The darkness gives the coaster the illusion of going faster, and brings excitement to the turns and dips because they are unseen and unexpected.[18]

The Spirit of Progress, especially in the form of Junior, resonates with the archetypal figure known as the eternal child, an inspiring figure associated with the search or the adventure for inspiration, innovation, risk, and creative playfulness that may extend into adulthood and beyond the physical boundaries of childhood. Childhood, thus, like nature, represents innocence and naiveté. On the other hand, social commentator Neil Postman defines childhood as a social construct necessitated by advancements in print technology beginning with the Renaissance:

8. Tomorrowland

From print onward, adulthood had to be earned. It became a symbolic, not a biological, achievement. From print onward, the young would have to *become* adults, and they would have to do it by learning to read, by entering the world of typography. And in order to accomplish that they would require education. Therefore, European civilization reinvented schools. And by so doing, it made childhood a necessity.[19]

In his opinion, this concept of "child" is disappearing as a result of the growing adult-child demographic, unique to the modern world only in sophistication of technology, similarities with the adult-to-child relationship that characterized the Middle Ages when child mortality was high.[20] On an individual level, the childlike identity is seen as a potentially dangerous problem because the adult-child finds interaction with the "grown-up" world difficult, because they do not prioritize according to society's expectations. As psychologist Erich Fromm notes, they do not believe in time: "People comfort themselves, not only because they do not really do something but also for not making any preparation for what they have to do, because for such things there is plenty of time and therefore no need to hurry. [...] The older such people get, the more they cling to the illusion that *one day* they will do it."[21] The concern occurs when the numbers of these individuals pose a significant demographic in the larger society.

A cultural conflict arises between the desire to nurture the creativity of adult-children and the need for maturity and rationality to run the society. Rather than seeing this as a negative conflict, Christopher Noxon describes the lives of adult-children, whom he calls "rejuveniles," as some of the potentially happiest adults. Noxon defines the rejuvenile as one who enjoys the toys and games of childhood with a concept of independence and responsibility: "rejuveniles generally take pride in controlling their own destinies. They can move comfortably in the world of practical realities, but they also enjoy reaching back into childhood without being treated like a baby or being stripped of the ability to make their own decisions. *They've grown up enough to finally appreciate the pleasures of being a kid.*"[22] Noxon identifies Walt as the classic example. He constructed an imaginative world that gave a vocabulary to the modern generations of rejuveniles, who, in turn, extend their enthusiasm to their own children such that modern children have increasing fewer and fewer "traditional" adult role models. Rejuveniles rely on play for their sources of conflict and happiness.

Sociologist Johan Huizinga describes play as an instinct, "a function of living, but is not susceptible of exact definition either logically, biologically, or aesthetically."[23] One aspect of play allows children to absorb behaviors they will need as adults. Another aspect is connected with ritual and the pretending associated with liminality. Modern play is associated with leisure, a luxury unique to the modern era. Following the Renaissance, modern play was associated with childhood as the outlet for the creativity and imagination, crucial to the development of children, but something relegated to childhood. Adults slowly accepted play as a part of adult life over the last century typically in the form of some sort of hobby, such as Walt Disney's hobby of playing with model trains for stress relief. But this evolved into more "childish" aspects of play, such as adult softball leagues and frequent trips to Disneyland.[24]

The emphasis for a successful Spirit of Progress, then, is play, which is a crucial aspect of progress, and is why our Spirit of Progress is playful when he explains to Donald Duck the possibilities for his wheel. Play invites the imagination to make new connections between ideas and things that differ from their initial intended use. It is progress-through-play that thinks of technological innovations, because Progress's childlike laziness invents appliances to make its chores easier. Progress's childlike optimism invents social networking tools to bring people of the global community together, and Progress' childlike dreams put humanity on the moon and devises methods to go to "Infinity and Beyond!" At the same time, it is Progress's childlike sense of boredom that will tear down the institutions of culture, because it perceives that they no longer serve a function, and it is Progress's childlike temper that devises means of eradicating entire sections of populations because they would not play the game according to Progress's rules.

Through play, one satiates an individual need for spontaneity as a foil for one's structured life. But this is seen as a problem, for play stands in the way of responsibility, because if one is busy playing, then, it is perceived, one is not successfully contributing to society. Play is counter to the Protestant Work Ethic that has defined American culture; "it is this opposition to work which gives play a number of connotations. One of these is 'mere fun'—whether it is hard to do or not."[25] As such, play places progress on a path of constant movement, because Progress cannot envision, like the adult-child, contributing to today, but perceives tomorrow as the goal point of opportunity. The past century has witnessed a technological boom imagined by the Spirit of Progress, making the toys and tools that can be used today to make a better tomorrow: the automobile broadens one's home radius and increases the possibility for better success and wealth; the television broadens one's perspective of news and entertainment, bringing the visual media capitalized by cinema into the comfort and security of one's home; video games stimulate the mind and personal computers function as all of the above. This constructed world of hyperreality, though entertaining, is not sustainable, even for the rejuvenile, because technology is too fleeting. Consider how quickly the American culture was changed by the introduction of the Internet into the home in contrast to the decades it took for Gutenberg's printing innovation to spread information across Europe.

Pixar Comes to Tomorrowland

Pixar was founded as one of the first computer-based (CGI) animation companies. They partnered with Disney to enhance animated features of the early 1990s, such as *Beauty and the Beast* and *The Lion King*, creating new breakthroughs in animation. In the mid–1990s, Disney distributed Pixar's first, fully–CGI film, *Toy Story*. Following a shaky relationship, Disney formally acquired Pixar in the mid–2000s, continuing to support Pixar's ingenuity in story and animation while embracing the Pixar characters as part of the Disney family. Pixar-based attractions have found home in other Disney theme parks, and the two in Tomorrowland are the only two within Disneyland: the Buzz Lightyear Astro Blasters and the Finding Nemo Submarine Voyage.

Buzz Lightyear is one of the heroes of Pixar's *Toy Story* films. He is a Space Ranger who battles the evil villain Zurg to save and protect all life in the universe. The Astro Blasters transforms each guest into one of Buzz's Space Rangers who help Buzz defeat Zurg by blasting targets throughout the ride with laser guns. The ride vehicles utilize Omn-imover technology, with a string of constantly moving two-seater cars. Each car has a joystick to swivel it around, and each Space Ranger has his/her own gun. The attraction is filled with targets, some moving and others stationary worth fewer points, and guests point and shoot their laser gun at these targets for points that are calculated individually in the car's panel. Statistics at the end of the game ranks both players to see who wins, and compares the scores with the overall scores of the day.

Walt Disney boasted in 1959 that he had one of the largest, active, peacetime submarine fleets in the world when the Submarine Voyage attraction opened at Disneyland. The submarines in the fleet sailed guests around a mermaid lagoon then through a waterfall that masked the entrance to the show building that housed an exploration of Disney's undersea world. In the late 1990s, as New New Tomorrowland was reopening, the Submarine Voyage was closed. In 2007, the Submarine Voyage re-opened with not only a technological upgrade replacing the diesel engines with electric, but with investiture that themed the attraction around Pixar's film, *Finding Nemo*, in which a little clownfish named Nemo is captured by a diver prompting his reluctant father to go on a quest through the seas near Australia to find him. In this attraction, guests are led on a tour of Nemo's ocean by Nemo and his friends.

When 1986 Came and Went: Turning Tomorrow into Yesterday's Memory

The original Tomorrowland was set in 1986—the year of Halley's Comet—but when 1986 came, it was quickly observed that the future of Disney's vision, which included flying saucers and efficient mass-transit, was either not present or only in planning stages. In response, Disney Imagineers revisioned Tomorrowland as a nostalgic look at what the future might have looked like if the present was in fact 100 years in the past. Thus, in a redesign of Tomorrowland, they turned toward science fiction and away from science fact. This led to the closing of such attractions as Mission to Mars[26] because they were too factual, and the opening of others like Space Mountain imitating flying through space, and Star Tours placing guests right in the middle of one of the most popular science fiction franchises.

Though a non–Disney film, *Star Wars* demonstrates the fusion of classic mythic themes—it was written following Joseph Campbell's formula of the hero journey described in *Hero with a Thousand Faces*— with the new myth of technology increasingly dominating American mythos. *Star Wars*, like Tomorrowland, makes an unexpected suggestion, and one easily overlooked by the Spirit of Progress: that the older technology (the Millennium Falcon) will inevitably prove superior to the newer (the Death Star). This is also the case in Pixar's *Wall-E*, though *Wall-E* has yet to find a home in Tomorrowland. This nostalgia for older technology is reflected in the revival of the 1986 3-D Jim Henson/George Lucas film *Captain EO* starring Michael Jackson. The nostalgia for science fiction was the attraction's draw, more so than the attraction *EO* replaced, *Honey, I Shrunk the Audience*, which is based on the *Honey, I Shrunk the Kids* films and suggests a new technology capable of altering the size of a person. By the same token, Star Tours was recently updated to include trips to other worlds of George Lucas' galaxy, and not just to throw space tourists, the guests, into the middle of *Star Wars'* epic Death Star battle.

This technostalgia is the same that idealizes the utopian possibilities of Main Street, U.S.A. The New Tomorrowland suggests that progress, when not balanced with time, nature, or even accountability, becomes fatiguing. Fatigue loosens the meaning of new innovations, creates feelings of ennui in the face of Progress' excitement. Technology of the past was always "built better" compared to today's technology that "isn't made like it used to be." It is also remembered as simpler, with fewer buttons, controls or commands, and more intuitive such that "even an ape could do it."

Nostalgia for older technology implies a need for Progress to slow down, especially in the aftermath of the bomb:

> The bomb became for Americans the prime symbol of their ambivalence about war (which could bring both progress and destruction), about science (which could harness the forces of the universe and unleash them), and about power itself, which was terrifyingly beautiful to watch, awesomely furious and destructive, and ultimately able to shake, change, and destroy the world and humanity.[27]

169

Through this nostalgic Tomorrowland, Disney no longer sought to endorse the possibilities of the future, but rather the "abstract, even nationalist, concepts of 'American-ness,' community, and discipline that are under debate in the twenty-first century."[28] However, this "American-ness" is one that is defined by the same popular history Disney uses to construct its utopian vision, "produced in periods when the country appears threatened by uncontrollable outside ideologies ... [resorting] to the reinforcement of a common narrative of American history, which they see as resulting in a common American character."[29] This common American character, prior to television, shared the goals of Manifest Destiny.

The Spirit of Progress teamed with the Spirit of Adventure made Manifest Destiny possible, but a new mythology is trying to emerge that views Progress and Adventure as catalysts for mythic imbalance and suggests that they need to be placed in conjunction with a balancing agent, one that has yet not been introduced in the Disney theme parks. Outside the theme parks, Disney has approached the question of restoring a dystopian world: *Wall-E*, with the restoration of life on Earth; *Epic Mickey*, in which Mickey sprays either paint or thinner on a dystopian Disneyland world to free Wasteland from the shades of the Blot; Ridley Pearson's *Kingdom Keepers* young adult book series, in which five kids work together to try to save the Disney universe from the Overtakers, or the Disney villains; and *Once Upon a Time*, a television series in which one woman has the mission of restoring the memories to cursed fairy tale characters. Within the park, Disney still places emphasis on memory. To never forget the past, Disney suggests, is now more important than living for Tomorrow under the Spirit of Progress, even if the Past is constructed from utopian fantasies.

Beyond the Shadow of Doubt

In his commentaries on modern civilization, psychologist C. G. Jung makes an observation that articulates how and why Doubt became the shadow of the Spirit of Progress, and indeed of American culture:

All divine powers in creation are gradually being placed in man's hands. Through nuclear fission something tremendous has happened, tremen-

dous power has been given to man. [...] the forces that hold the fabric of
the world together have got into the hands of man, so that he even has
the idea of making an artificial sun [with the atomic bomb]. God's powers
have passed into our hands, our fallible human hands.[30]

Progress led to the creation of the atomic bomb, the end of the War,
and the subsequent arms race that defined the Cold War, bringing with
it a fear that destabilized American mythic/material culture under the
burden of potential destruction. As we have seen, this fear and doubt
lead to the creation of a simulated America and the shift of "frontier"
from American's Manifest Destiny to metaphorical realms of the imagination and outer space.[31]

Two of the dominant criticisms voiced by doubt for Progress are
directed at the benefits of technology and its role as a homogenizing
mechanism, criticisms Disney attempts to satiate by promoting both
positively within its parks.

Technology: Friend or Foe? As has already been discussed,
World War II brought to light the awesome capabilities of technology
used for destruction. Cold War fears stemmed not from the actuality
of technological progress, but from the potential use of it against Americans. Tomorrow was always perceived as much more violent than yesterday,[32] so it was up to those today to figure out a solution. Although
most of this hope was placed in the hands of politicians, Disney
responded by using the media of television and the theme park to
demonstrate that technology, science, and progress were not themselves dangerous. Disney, however, did not use the media to make a
didactic statement that the people who used technology irresponsibly
were the danger; rather, Disney cited those who would stifle science as
the danger, celebrating "the ways in which humankind's expanding control of nature improved its quality of life."[33] Technology helps humanity
to both control nature and to access untapped natural resources. Disney
equates the Spirit of Progress with freedom in a way new to the Manifest Destiny myth. The "new frontier" of the modern world could no
longer be defined by place, because of the new globalism World War
II introduced. Thus, it had to be defined by the products of ideas, themselves too fleeting to be the basis for cultural definition.

Technology, then, is perceived by Disney as a friend, not something
to be feared as the atomic bomb suggests. Walt believed that technology

171

has always been a source of both anxiety and hope for humanity.[34] By showcasing positive uses of technology, Disney restores American hope in progress; however, these same positive purposes have been used to create entirely new problems in technology. At the click of a mouse, an American can chat with someone else in the world reflecting Disney's utopian globalism, but that same click of a mouse can hack into another computer system and download all of its information. Walt Disney in the 1960s could not have foreshadowed this new information technology warfare; this problem is outside the confines of present analysis. Thus, Disneyland's reassurance can buffer against anxieties and fears of the destructive nature of technology, but not against the anxieties associated with information technology.

Homogeneity: The American Way   The War invited Americans to celebrate their similarities, to unify under a national banner and reaffirm their Americanness. Television was a tool for homogenizing America, creating a "culture of the whole" or a "set of ideas about what *ought* to be; it was also a description of the encroaching social reality. The day-to-day experience of most Americans was with an increasingly uniform culture."[35] This perception of homogeneity is expressed in the "generic child," the same child that would grow up to become the first generation rejuvenile. The "generic child" is not identified by unique factors, such as race, gender, or class, and all "generic children" are entitled to the same treatment and resources. These children were viewed not as America's future, but as future consumers and were thus taught these behaviors from an early age.[36] Furthermore, the "generic child" is the homunculus of American culture "produced by and eventually reproducing a mass culture of which Disney products were but one element...."[37] Media was recognized as a key source for communicating to and molding children's consumptive behaviors, and Disney was one of the first studios in the 1950s to produce programming and products aimed specifically at children, many of whom grew into adulthood maintaining brand loyalty and sharing Disney with their own children.

The homogenization of culture sought to unify America through an organization of ideas and collective culture.[38] The collective culture connects all humanity with a common psychology, an attractive concept in the post-war America that sought reassurance. The collective

8. Tomorrowland

psyche opens the culture to a collection of archetypes and myths, but in order for these myths to work, Americans need to first be directed toward their mythos, heritage, and history. Thus, television proved helpful in communicating these ideals, because it "demands participation and involvement in depth of the whole being. It will not work as a background. It engages you."[39] Television serves as the voice of the simulated collective unconscious of hyperrealistic America, and Disney a successful director among many to reinforce a homogenized culture of the whole.

The immediate backlash appeared in the years following Walt Disney's death with efforts such as *Sesame Street* to speak to the diverse aspects of specific groups.[40] When Walt Disney produced the *Mickey Mouse Club*, Annette Funicello was the only regular cast member with any ethnicity, and *Sesame Street* responded with a cast full of ethnic representations, a snapshot of the New York neighborhoods that inspired the show. Diversity became a cause for celebration that remains a dominant force in American schools. Disney's "generic child" continues to emphasize that children are children, no matter what life they were born into; it's our similarities that we should celebrate, not our differences—"It's a Small World, After All."

Epilogue
After Walt:
Critter Country
and Mickey's Toontown

"Take a homespun tour through the nooks and crannies of the forests where all of your favorite friends are found. You'll splash down into a briar patch and go chasing adventures with that silly ol' bear. Come to Critter Country to find your laughing place."—The Imagineers, The Imagineering Field Guide to Disneyland

"Mickey's Toontown is your chance to meet the characters where they live. You'll be 'drawn' into an animated world and become a Toon for a day. Be sure to visit Mickey's house and take a spin with Roger Rabbit. Just don't forget to 'Squash' and 'Stretch' on your way in!"—The Imagineers, The Imagineering Field Guide to Disneyland

Walt Disney died unexpectedly in 1966, leaving an influential gap within the company and the country. The Haunted Mansion and the Pirates of the Caribbean were under construction, but not yet opened. The company was experiencing a new wave of success, riding on the tails of *Mary Poppins* (1964) and participation in the 1964–1965 New York World's Fair that showcased new technologies, including audio-animatronics, designed in service to conveying the message of a unified World in Motion. Before he died, it was apparent that Walt's utopia hadn't been achieved. The area surrounding Disneyland had been filled with hotels and attractions capitalizing on Disneyland's popularity, but not operating in a Disney manner. In the years and months leading

Epilogue

up to his death, Walt and a few trusted colleagues enacted their Reedy Creek plan, buying as much Florida real estate in secret as possible, eventually amassing as much land as two Manhattans. The goal was to build an east coast theme park, but to retain control over the surrounding area. Less than two months before he died, Walt filmed *EPCOT*, a short explanatory film to send to investors to raise funds and support for this renewed utopian vision. Sadly, Walt died before EPCOT could become a reality, and his vision has never been fully realized. His utopian dream, however, continues to resonate throughout American culture.

Walt's death coincided with a turning point in American culture. The Summer of Love head yet to occur; Robert Kennedy and Martin Luther King, Jr., were still alive; and Woodstock was not yet a dream. The Baby Boomers who grew up watching *Disneyland*, *Mickey Mouse Club*, and *Davy Crockett* were entering college or the military, and carrying Walt's populist optimism with them, expecting to find a unified America in sex and race, and fighting for it when they found out that it didn't yet exist. These young adults sought cultural meaning that brought their Disney idealism into accord with the reality of mid-century America.

The Cold War era in America's history is a turning point in the country's mythos, revealing a hunger that Disney attempts to satiate with its theme parks and all of its merchandising, marketing, and entertaining ventures. Because the Disney brand is equated with family entertainment, it provides reassurance from the stressors of the culture, and the theme parks provide escape. The culture has become one of hyperreality and consumption. Hyperreality reinforces the American utopian dream, while consumption indicates a craving for the simulacra of reassurance. The argument can be made that clearly the hyperreality is unsatisfying if the consumption continues; however, this analysis assumes these two factors to be part of the same problem: that American myth is in a period of transition. Key factors of this transitory myth are the new developments in technology that depersonalize warfare and the globalization of the world that is slowly attempting to unify the world's mythologies, both made apparent during World War II and processed during the Cold War.

The American generations following the Cold War at present

Walt's Utopia

know of no world without technology (computers, nuclear weapons) or a connection with other cultures through social media. Events of the last few years revealed use of these tools to encourage a conversation in social change (Arab Summer, Occupy) but concern is nonetheless raised for the ability of these younger Americans to judge the positive use of technology or even to survive without it if something happens to the computer servers. This latter concern has been expressed in cinema and television through motifs of apocalypse, super heroes, and the undead (vampires and zombies, representing primitivist fantasies), each worth of its own exploration.

Cultural shadow, however, cannot be overlooked, ignored, or optimistically ideologized away, and brings disillusionment. America has needed Walt Disney—Uncle Walt—more than ever. Throughout the 1970s, 1980s, and 1990s, the Disney company had to rewrite its corporate narrative without Walt. This is never an easy task, as Walt's narrative was strongly integrated to the company's identity. Meanwhile, the company had to continue to respond to and be relevant to the mythic needs of the American consumers, producing cultural artifacts that could continue to excite meaning among the foggy clouds of disillusionment.

Despite concerns for buy-out and take-over, the company built new theme parks to reach new audiences taking the Disney mythos to a global level. Walt Disney World opened in Florida in 1971 in tribute to Walt, Tokyo Disneyland in 1983 at the request of Tokyo investors, EuroDisney (now Disneyland Paris) opened in 1992 to the chagrin of the French, and most recently, Hong Kong Disneyland opened in 2005.[1]

CEO Bob Iger announced in 2011 plans to step down as CEO of Disney. This marks a transition phase for the Disney Company. Much Disney scholarship has concentrated on the growth of the corporation under Walt Disney and the synergistic, sometimes controversial, enhancement of the corporation under Michael Eisner. On the surface, Iger's Disney appears to be a fusion of Walt's and Eisner's Disneys. Iger's era reveals a phase of mythic transition for the American people who need increasingly complex stories to nurture the hunger for direction and sense of the surrounding world. During his era, he placed an emphasis on a memory filled with nostalgia for Walt's America, but the intended abandonment of fairy tales, announced in 2010 in favor of the Marvel and Star Wars franchises suggests a preparation for what is to come. If Disney uses stories to respond to the needs of the American culture, then the reliance on superheroes and science fiction suggests the recognition of a dystopian cultural shift. That Disney is recognizing its role as mythmaker and acquiring these outlets reveals that even Disney is aware that Walt's utopian vision is perhaps an optimistic view of the past that cannot and will not be made manifest at this time. After nearly 60 years of trying to bring Walt's dream alive, is Disney giving up? On February 5, 2015, Disney announced the promotion of Tom Staggs to Chief Operating Officer, which positions him as the successor to Iger once his contract expires in 2018. Iger said of Tom during his announcement:

> "Tom is an incredibly experienced, talented and versatile executive who has led Parks and Resorts during a time of unprecedented growth and expansion, including the construction of Shanghai Disney Resort. His proven ability to lead a business as well as his successful tenure as Disney's former CFO make him an ideal Chief Operating Officer, expanding his portfolio into all the company's businesses."[2]

Only time will tell what a new CEO will mean for Disney's understanding of its own mythos and the ways in which Disney will continue to influence America's perception both here at home and around the world.

The original Disneyland too has faced major changes. Walt had once said that Disneyland would never be complete as long as there was imagination in the world. Updates are constantly being performed on the parks adding new and revitalizing old attractions. Since the attractions are the language of the parks' mythology, looking at these updates either reveals the myth in transition or enhances nostalgia for the past. The park had to keep up with the changing nature of audience demand. The American audiences wanted and continue to want a fusion of nostalgia for Walt's Disneyland and an updated experience that includes thrilling rides and new product lines. The characters from *Star Wars* and *Frozen* dance alongside familiar classic characters like Mickey and Snow White, testing their permanence within the Disney canon.

Changing the map of Disneyland is a slow process. Attractions may come and go, but the organization of the park remains constant.

Since 1970, only two new lands have been added: Critter Country and Mickey's Toontown.

Critter Country and Mickey's Toontown both stand as testaments to American post-identity culture, which emerged during the late–1960s and 1970s, and came to prominence during the 1980s. Post-identity culture promotes, manifestly, the perception that all people are equal, that the activism that brought people together is no longer needed. However, in practice, post-identity culture carries with it the latent discrimination from a perceived status quo defined by mid-century white America. The two primary forms of post-identity culture are post-feminism and post-racism. The latter is the focus of this chapter.

Critter Country Key Attractions

- Country Bear Jamboree (closed)
- The Many Adventures of Winnie the Pooh
- Splash Mountain

Critter Country

One of the long-standing complaints against the Disney corporation is its lack of diversity. True, there are numerous examples of diversity represented in recent offerings, but not so much in early Disney projects, in keeping with cultural norms of the times. Disney was criticized for casting Annette Funicello, of Italian heritage, in 1954 for the Mickey Mouse Club, while some of the studio's other more subversive attempts at cultural diversity went unnoticed. Douglas Brode suggests that Disney's subversive approach to diversity helped prime Baby Boomer children for the paradigm shift of the late–1960s, promoting a world of quasi-equality and diversity acceptance.[3]

Frontierland was one of the few displays of diversity in Disneyland,[4] and one such example was the Indian Village, located in a corner of Frontierland, where local tribal representatives would gather to pow-wow, or dance. Though marred in stereotype (not all Native American tribes lived in teepees, for instance), the area was nonetheless intended to showcase and educate guests on Native American customs and traditions. But this, too, fell under controversy because the area inadvertently promoted a colonial view of Native Americans that ignored tribal differences. Its endearing quality was that it diverged from the rest of Hollywood that portrayed Native Americans as savage enemies of the White Man.

One of the difficult questions for Americans to answer is, "What is an American?" The nature of our identity lies within contradiction. As Sheldon Hackney, director of the National Endowment for the Humanities during the Clinton administration, reported in 1997:

> Most Americans with whom I have talked so far think that it is not, but they also believe that there is an American culture—"conventional ways of believing and behaving"—that is shared across regional, religious, ethnic, and racial lines. The problem is that for almost every trait one can cite as being characteristically American, there is its opposite as well. One can construct a veritable Yin and Yang of American culture.[5]

This helps, in part, to explain how and why the role of Native Americans within the American mythos has been so tenuous. Americans pride themselves for being "E pluribus unum" (Out of many, one), but fail to understand how this can be accomplished. Prior to the pluralistic paradigm shift of the late 1960s, "one" out of many was governed predominantly by British and/or Western European cultural constructs. While this was thought acceptable for maintaining a status quo, it allowed little to no room for social mobility among the "minority" races. The struggle of Native Americans during the 1960s and 1970s to, among other things, reclaim their tribal identity from the stereotypes of Hollywood, became symbolic of the Civil Rights Movement.[6] Though often portrayed in Westerns as a war-mongering "savage" people, they came to represent the struggle against the hegemonic White Man's culture.

To avoid becoming a political entity in the battle for pluralism, Disney decided to sacrifice a diverse Frontierland in favor of removing any perceived conflict and examples of non–Anglo races from its park. The result is a Disneyland that can be described as a "whitewashed Potemkin village."[7] The Indian Village was closed in 1971, but rather than allow the land to remain unused, the Imagineers replaced the tribal dancers with audio-animatronic singing bears.

The racial politics of the whitewashing of Frontierland merit further

179

discussion. It is widely known that Westward expansion was bloody. Native Americans were widely perceived as inconveniences. One aspect of Manifest Destiny, especially to the early pioneers, was to cultivate or Christianize these "savages." But because culture clash is often violent, many Native Americans were lost to acts of violence/war and disease, and later to neglect after they were herded onto reservations. To include Native Americans in Frontierland is to recognize their involvement in Westward Expansion and thus the Frontier myth, without acknowledging the colonial acts that destroyed tribal cultures. This aspect of "whitewashing," of hiding the negative, reinforces the notion of Disneyland as a utopian space and alters our perception of history. Conflict does not occur within a utopia, and all groups who call such a place home are welcome to cohabitate in peace. Thus, the White Man (the cowboys of Frontierland) are allowed their daily shootouts in their constructed village while the Native Americans are allowed to stay in their personal habitats, away from the hustle and bustle of White Man's "progress."

The period of post-settlement as the Frontier "closed,"[8] however, saw the Native Americans residing on reservations that were earmarked by the Federal Government as land for them to maintain and manage without American influence. For our purposes, they were effectively erased from the mythos. So removed, they are no longer part of the American identity. In keeping with the interpretation of Bear Country as a land of post-settlement white hegemony, Native Americans no longer played a key role in the ambiance of Frontierland, and the purpose of such an attraction is diminished as the United States emerges from the turmoil that accompanied the mid-century, post-war cultural identity reformation.

Bear Country, now Critter Country, was designed to house the Country Bear Jamboree, a widely successful attraction at Walt Disney World.[9] The area was re-themed into a different kind of rustic style than Frontierland. Rather than borrow its inspiration from the United States' Southwest desert (specifically Utah and surrounding land), Bear Country was inspired by the 19th century Pacific Northwest, with exposed wood structures blended with the planted forestry.[10] This area was meant also contrast the movement of the West. It represented the place of settlement as opposed to the exodus of expansion. Indeed,

Epilogue

unlike other lands in Disneyland (except for Mickey's Toontown, constructed later), Bear Country had one entrance, and because the main attraction was a show, it was observed as more calming than other areas of the park. This has since changed, but for our purposes, we will concentrate on this early incarnation of the area.

So what do the bears have to do with anything? The teddy bear becomes an American phenomenon in the early 1900s in tribute to Theodore Roosevelt, then a world explorer who embodied the Frontier mythos on a global stage, making the bear a symbol of the post-colonial spirit of the West.[11] The Country Bears, then, following this thinking, are the replacements for the Native Americans—from colonial to post-colonial, equally "savage." The songs they sing are familiar old-timey tunes. They reflect an America more confident in herself than that of 1955. Each of the bears can be further analyzed as stereotypes of popular American personalities, devoid of any sub-cultural indicators. The self-doubt that informed the revival of the Frontier Myth following World War II gave way to the imperfect acceptance of a multi-faced America. One could argue that the reemergence of the Western in the aftermath of 9/11 reveals a culture once again filled with doubt about its identity.

A. A. Milne's collection of Winnie-the-Pooh stories, told across two books—*Winnie-the-Pooh* (1926) and *The House on Pooh Corner* (1928)—and a series of poems, was borne from the stories he would tell his son, Christopher Robin, about his toys. In each of the stories, Pooh would have an adventure with one of his friends in the Hundred Acre Wood. The kinds of adventures Pooh and friends would have involved trying to find a solution for a problem that was often self-induced. In all of these stories, Christopher Robin is the voice of reason, the conscience, of all the toys.

The Victorian-style children's novel was particularly attractive to mid-century audiences. These novels were written in an Other World setting with the sole intention of teaching children how to behave, even if the desired behavior is the directed imagination. Alice teaches us how to avoid allowing curiosity to dictate the adventure, and Wendy teaches us to value growing up. Christopher Robin is not a Victorian character in the strictest sense—*Winnie-The-Pooh* was published in 1926, 25 years after the end of the Victorian Era. Milne's characters, just like their Victorian cohort, help reinforce the unspoken caste system that inhabits the British class hierarchy. Each character has his or her own place, and the role of the hero—who broke the restrictive mold to explore another character status—is to reinforce society's boundaries. Christopher Robin is the reinforcer of the Hundred Acre Wood. He is called upon to resolve problems and settle disputes. As the products of his imagination, it is logical that his toys would turn to him in times of need.

This style of children's novel helped model the potential outcomes for post-identity culture to thrive. Because uncharacteristic behavior was discouraged among Victorian and neo–Victorian heroes, the same could be easily assumed of the readers of these books, young and old. Inclusion of novels such as *Winnie-the-Pooh* in the Disney canon helped mainstream their messages at a time of massive cultural upheaval in the United States. Unlike other Victorian novels, such as *Alice in Wonderland* and *Peter Pan,* or even the fairy tales converted into first-wave Disney features, *Winnie-the-Pooh* was released as a film in 1977, before the mass propaganda of Reagan's utopian America, but during a reactionary response period following the Civil Rights movement. Post-identity culture during this window was an attempt by the "mainstream" culture to restore balance and the expected status quo.

The Many Adventures of Winnie the Pooh (1977) is a package film bringing together three previously released Disney Pooh featurettes: *Winnie the Pooh and the Honey Tree* (1966), *Winnie the Pooh and the Blustery Day* (1968), and *Winnie the Pooh and Tigger Too* (1974). The segments were sewn together and framed by a storyteller reading an animated storybook through which Pooh navigates along with the narrative. The film does not attempt to retell all of Milne's Pooh stories, but rather chooses highlights that, when told together, create a comprehensive, cohesive image of the Hundred Acre Woods as a collective utopian community in which all of the toys get along, even if they annoy each other from time to time.

Each of the characters has an attribute that is both his or her identifying characteristic and the trait that becomes the central focus of their interactions. Pooh, we are reminded, has Very Little Brain, whereas Eeyore is always Gloomy. Tigger bounces too often, and Owl frequently uses (and misuses) long words. In the Disney versions of

Epilogue

the Pooh stories, it is how the characters learn to accept each other and to overlook their obvious faults that brings them together as friends and family. For instance, when Pooh visits Rabbit in the short segment "Winnie the Pooh and the Honey Tree," he eats too much and gets stuck in Rabbit's front door. Rabbit, though inconvenienced and annoyed that his friend ate all of his food, has to learn to accept Pooh's friendship and his genuine sincerity. Similarly, when Tigger arrives, everyone has to learn to accept his bouncy nature, because bouncing is what tiggers do best.

During the 1990s, Disney's Pooh surged in popularity to become one of the company's most profitable product lines. Realizing this, Disney responded with additional films, television shows, and a wide array of consumer goods. In keeping with the company's synergistic approach to its products, Winnie the Pooh needed a concrete presence in the theme parks. A ride had originally been planned around the release of the film in the late 1970s, but was delayed to allow for other projects. Proposals for a Winnie the Pooh attraction included placing it where Mr. Toad's Wild Ride is housed in Fantasyland or placing it in Mickey's Toontown where Roger Rabbit's Car-Toon Spin is located. Ultimately, the attraction was developed and opened in Walt Disney World's Magic Kingdom in 1999. Its success encouraged Imagineers to move forward with a West Coast companion. The problem with this plan, however, was that Disneyland has little space for expansion and the only way to introduce a new attraction is to close another attraction and utilize the space. To accommodate Pooh, the Country Bear Jamboree was closed due to a lack of popularity and the area, Bear Country, was rethemed into Critter Country. The Many Adventures of Winnie the Pooh opened in 2003 to mixed reviews.

Riding around in large honey pots, guests are transported through the Disney film. Although the ride makes liberal use of visual effects, it suffers from a lack of cohesive narrative, relying on a familiarity with the film and the film's soundtrack to make sense of the scenes. The only indicator of the story is that Pooh is in search for honey, which is the motivation for many of Pooh's Disney adventures. Like Alice in Wonderland, the ride ends with a birthday party and guests are sent back into the "real world" with the gifts from his friends. The queue line exits into the Critter Country cul-de-sac, where Pooh and friends can be found for guest meet-and-greets, reinforcing the friendliness and inclusion of the Pooh franchise.

Then there's Splash Mountain. The mountain design gives balance to the park. There are two mountains to the east of Main Street, U.S.A. (the Matterhorn and Space Mountain). When Splash Mountain opened in 1989, it became the second mountain in the western half, standing alongside Big Thunder Mountain. The mountains of the park reinforce the berm, protecting the Disney skyline from encroachment of the ever-expanding Los Angeles skyline. The ride is a water flume ride that combines the story aspect of a dark ride with the thrill of a steep and splashy drop into the briar patch. Although many of the characters are repurposed from now-defunct attractions (notably, the patriotic America Sings), the story of the ride is the controversial *Song of the South*. This attraction is, for many guests, their only exposure to the *Song of the South*. Disney's notorious film has been at the seat of controversy from its earliest days.[12]

The Song of the South is a hybrid film, combining live-action with animation, based on the Uncle Remus and Br'er Rabbit stories collected by Joel Chandler Harris and published in 1881. The live-action segment centers around Johnny, who, along with his mother, are visiting his grandmother while his father does some work in Atlanta. Johnny is troubled by his father's absence, and there is some indication that his parents' relationship is strained. One night, Johnny tries to run away, but is caught by Uncle Remus. Rather than march Johnny home, Uncle Remus makes him some food and tells him a Br'er Rabbit story about running away from home, and uses reverse psychology to convince Johnny to return home. Uncle Remus keeps an eye out for Johnny, providing comfort and stories whenever Johnny gets into trouble or is confused about his place. His attachment with Uncle Remus, however, causes problems with his mother, who believes that the stories are misguiding Johnny. She tells Uncle Remus to stop filling his head with stories, and when Johnny and Uncle Remus both disobey this command, she tells Johnny to stop seeing him altogether, not recognizing the boy's attachment to the elder man (especially strong in the absence of his father). Uncle Remus packs his things to go, and Johnny runs after him across a field populated by a violent bull. The bull attacks Johnny. While he is recovering, his father returns, but Johnny asks for

Epilogue

Uncle Remus. Uncle Remus comes and tells Johnny about "the laughing place," and Johnny survives.

The animated segments tell three of the Br'er Rabbit stories: "Br'er Rabbit Runs Away," "Br'er Rabbit and the Tar Baby," and "Br'er Rabbit's Laughing Place." Br'er Rabbit is a trickster, mischievous and plotting. He is the target of Br'er Fox and Br'er Bear, who resemble live-action Johnny's bullies. Br'er Fox and Br'er Bear pursue Br'er Rabbit to try to eat him, and each time, Br'er Rabbit finds a way to escape and return home.

The problems of the film are linked with the changing nature of race relations in the United States. The film is set on an antebellum plantation, and despite being set in a Reconstruction South, the film suggests that the African American employees are no better than slaves. Although the suggestion is made in the film that they are free, their subjugated role is nonetheless reinforced through their dress and dialogue with Johnny's family. Looking at the film mythically, however, reveals Uncle Remus to be an archetypal wise old man who uses trickster stories to teach Johnny confidence and raise his self-esteem during a difficult period for his family. His father is away, working for a controversial newspaper in Atlanta. Uncle Remus fills in for Johnny's male role model, recalling a similar relationship between Mark Twain's protagonist, Huck Finn, and the runaway slave, Jim.

Because the film was released in 1946 (though probably would have been released sooner had the War not dominated the Disney studio), its portrayal of African Americans, despite its sincerity, was outdated. Hollywood and the American people had moved on from the glory of *Gone with the Wind*. Though success of Civil Rights was still in the future, the stereotyped portrayal of African Americans was no longer acceptable.

In the 1980s, Imagineers started to consider how to add some thrill to Bear Country, which suffered from low attendance, and Tony Baxter, head Imagineer for Splash Mountain, claims to have dreamt of Splash Mountain while stuck in traffic in 1983. Combining together several Br'er Rabbit stories, with focus on the "Br'er Rabbit Runs Away" segment from *The Song of the South*, the attraction constructs a narrative about life in Br'er Rabbit's world: his tension with Br'er Fox and Br'er Bear, his desire to leave home, the Tar Baby incident (replaced with a honey pot to help subdue criticism of racism). A log-flume ride, the climax of the ride is the 53-foot drop into the Briar Patch complete with a drenching splash, followed by a "Zip-A-Dee-Doo-Dah" reminder of the wonders of staying home. Tony Baxter laments in an interview that Splash Mountain is the only way that most guests will ever know the story of *The Song of the South*.[13]

Nonetheless, the film was a success and continued to experience additional success in re-issue, which also furthered the controversy about its content. The amount of controversy has been so vocal for so long, that the film was vaulted after its 1986 re-release, not to be released officially by Disney again. Although the Indian Village was closed so as to avoid propagating stereotype, *Song of the South* and Splash Mountain continue to prevail. The film's most popular song, "Zip-A-Dee-Doo-Dah," continues to be a favorite Disney tune, and the adventures of Br'er Rabbit are the basis of the Splash Mountain plot.

Mickey's Toontown

Mickey's Toontown Key Attractions
- Roger Rabbit's Car Toon Spin
- Donald's Boat
- Minnie's House
- Mickey's House

In contrast to the themes inherent in Critter Country, Mickey's Toontown addresses post-identity culture in noticeably different ways.

Who Framed Roger Rabbit (1988), a hybrid live action/animation film released under Disney's Touchstone Pictures division, illustrates the culture clash that can happen whenever two disparate groups try to co-exist in the same area. In this case, the two groups are humans and toons. What frequently happens in such situations is a case of "us versus them," or "us versus the Other." These are two groups who cannot see beyond their differences, although they try. Set in 1947, the story becomes *noir*-esque as private detective Eddie Valiant investigates a possible extramarital affair of Roger Rabbit's toon wife, Jessica, that becomes a murder investigation when Jessica's supposed lover turns

Epilogue

up dead. Valiant uncovers the complicated politics of Toontown, where all the toons live, and namely that the toons don't own the town. Rather, a corporation owns the town, and to complicate Valiant's investigation, he learns that if the will that bequeaths Toontown to the toons isn't found, the town will be sold to another company.

The toons live in their own community, separated from the people as much as possible. In the film, this is portrayed as the preference for like to live with like, conveying the message that life is better this way rather than encouraging full unity of all the residents. The toons come into Hollywood, act in films, often making people laugh, then go home. This reinforces Reganesque propaganda surrounding post-identity culture: That it's okay for two groups to come together in the work and entertainment spheres, but that they should live in their own separate places.

Since I've previously discussed race relations within Disneyland, it may be tempting to automatically assume that a discussion now about *Who Framed Roger Rabbit* is another discussion about race in America, and this may be the easy way to respond to the lifestyle of the toons. The Other is anyone who isn't like us. When there is a mainstream culture, the Other is everyone who doesn't fit into the collective perception of itself. This manifests in White Culture versus everyone else (African American, immigrant, Native American), but it can also be Man versus Woman, Rich versus Poor, Educated versus Uneducated, and so on. It is through our politics and cultural relations that determine how we respond to the Other, and because of the complexity of attributes that comprise the Other, solutions for equitable interaction are likewise complex. In studies of Disney, it's difficult to simply say that Disney is racist or sexist. For one thing, it's difficult to prove that their intention is to be any form of "-ist." Perhaps more importantly, as others have noted, Disney is in the business of entertainment and are trying to appeal to a conception of the mainstream. My intent isn't to downplay the claims of discrimination by omission, nor is my aim to convince readers to change their opinions of Disney; but it is my hope to contribute another perspective to the conversation. A theme that runs through the canons of Disney and its subsidiaries is the question of the Other. Borrowing from fairy tales, the hero or heroine may have spent some part of his or her life living with the Other and has to prove him- or herself worthy of the princess or prince. Additionally, the theme of good versus evil (the sympathetic protagonists versus the Other) runs throughout these stories. Sometimes, as with the Disney fairy tale films, the Other as evil is overt, but in other cases, such as the television show *Lost*, the Other, or Others in this case, present ambiguities as more information is revealed about their presence on the island.

This is the case with *Who Framed Roger Rabbit*. Valiant's investigation begins with the good intention of not projecting his perceptions of the toons onto his work. The story, told mostly through his perspective, reveals the process by which he comes to know the Other (the toons), and the corporate politics of Toontown. The latent message of the film, then, becomes a reminder to not take the Other for granted; that our perceptions and values about cultural differences may also impact our relationships. Valiant finds his understanding of the toons changing as he continues investigating Roger and Jessica Rabbit, realizing that they aren't elastic figures and gains a new respect for them.

Who Framed Roger Rabbit was an ambitious project. As Roger Ebert described in his review, this was the first film that successfully blended real life and animation, and made it look real:

> I've never seen anything like it before. Roger Rabbit and his cartoon comrades cast real shadows. They shake the hands and grab the coats and rattle the teeth of real actors. They change size and dimension and perspective as they move through a scene, and the camera isn't locked down in one place to make it easy, either—the camera in this movie moves around like it's in a 1940s thriller—and the cartoon characters look three-dimensional and seem to be occupying real space.[14]

Disney has a long history of trying to blend live-action and animation, dating back to the earliest Disney cartoons, the Alice shorts, in which Alice, a real girl, would interact with an animated Wonderland, in contrast to the cartoons of other animation studios in which the animated character interacted with the real world. Disney continued to use this technique throughout its repertoire, notably in *Mary Poppins*. With *Roger Rabbit*, however, they were able to perfect the technique at a time when animation was at a crossroads: *Roger Rabbit* coincided with an era of renewed interest in animated film, but arrived just before the advent of computer-generated animation. Computers made it easier to bring cartoons and live action together, and the crossover technique perfected with *Roger Rabbit* has become a central feature of recent fantasy films as computers allow artists to transcend the accepted norms and laws of traditional animation, and construct and render increasingly life-like animated elements.

To include a dark ride dedicated to *Who Framed Roger Rabbit* in Mickey's Toontown, an area of Disneyland seemingly dedicated to younger children, helps justify the area's name, but nonetheless poses some problems. *Who Framed Roger Rabbit* is more "adult" than the usual Disney fare, despite its PG rating. The themes of sex, violence, and innuendo that run throughout the film are familiar gags from the *Looney Tunes* cartoons, but are not aligned with traditional Disney offerings, which is why the film was released under the Touchstone imprint. The attraction, Roger Rabbit's CarToon Spin, removes the adult elements of the story and creates a new story that involves Weasels, villains from the film and from Disney's short film based on *The Wind in the Willows*, attempting to kidnap Jessica Rabbit and dissolve Roger in Dip, green goo that is the only way to "kill" a cartoon. Roger, along with Baby Herman (a gruff-voiced, talking baby) and the guests riding in Lenny the Cab, then go on an adventure to get her back. The most noticeable feature about this ride is that the ride vehicles can spin around, like the Mad Tea Cups, as they move along the story track.

By removing the core of the original film story,[15] the message about the Other is likewise removed. The ride story is essentially a damsel-in-distress rescue story, with Roger playing the role of the bumbling hero characteristic of a Goofy-themed cartoon. Disney favors the bumbling hero, because this character is more endearing as an Everyman sort of figure, with the comic flare of clumsiness and prone to the kinds of accidents that remind viewers that the animated world follows completely different laws of physics.

Disney had long been asked where Mickey Mouse lived and where people could meet him.[16] Despite this being one of the primary reasons behind the construction of Disneyland, Imagineers realized that Mickey didn't actually have a home in the park. To the north of Fantasyland, beyond the park boundary, they built Mickey's Toontown, mirroring Main Street, U.S.A., in that it has all of the elements of a fully-functional town, except it is a constructed cartoon.

189

Walt's Utopia

At the far end of Mickey's Toontown is a small "neighborhood" of the homes of Mickey and his friends. Guests can visit the homes, touch the possessions of their favorite characters, and at certain times of day, meet them.[17] In many ways, this brings the character to life more than their inclusion in the parade or as a streetwalker, because it humanizes them.

Mickey Mouse is significant to the Disney opus, and not just because, as Walt was fond of reminding his employees, "it all started with a mouse." Mickey functions as an archetypal Everyman of American culture. His primeval nature is automatically attractive to people of all backgrounds.[18] John Hench described this as being inherent in the circular nature of Mickey's design. The circles are inviting, warm, nurturing; the shape of Mickey's head and the position of his two ears invoke mother imagery. As Everyman, Mickey, representing the average American without pretense of a major adventure, is a gentle character of good middle–American values. He's the natural leader because he's so well put together.

What makes Mickey Everyman is that he has no clear racial indicator. He is neither black, nor white. In fact, he's both. He not only embraces "the common man," but he embraces all skin tones and all cultural backgrounds. This is significant, given that he was born prior to desegregation. Walt Disney seems to be suggesting that Mickey Mouse is all–American, and that distinction has nothing to do with race, class, or creed. Because his representation is often farm-based, Mickey is tied to an environment that all world cultures can relate to. Had Mickey's stories been set in the city, they would have lost some of their appeal. Additionally, he has transcended time and place. He is the by-product of the modern world, yet more than eighty years after his debut, he still evokes the same reactions.

As Mickey evolved into the symbol for the Disney Corporation, it became more important that he behave as an upstanding citizen, which led to the creation of other characters who could behave badly. Mickey's friends work in concert to entertain us, but they also seem to function as components of American myth. Furthermore, at any given time, any one of them can stand alone as a hero, though they often work together as a group of heroes toward a common goal. At different times in Disney's history, some characters have been more popular than others, but because each character has his or her own distinct personality, they can be used to represent different things, each bringing a component of the Everyman archetype to reinforce the Disney Doctrine.

For example, Donald is the perfect foil to Mickey, often stealing the scene from the mouse. He is temperamental, mischievous (sometimes malicious), and prone to devilish vices. Because his character was created this way, he was allowed to get away with more questionable behavior than Mickey. If Mickey was the star of the 1930s and thus the Great Depression, the 1940s and the War belonged to Donald. Donald gets drafted and we share his struggles through basic training and interactions with authority figures. This provided an outlet for some pent-up frustrations culturally, especially toward limitations on the home front because of the War. The 1950s belonged to Goofy, who was recast from Mickey's goofy and klutzy pal to the All-American Dad. He is gangly and accident-prone, a dad who works in the city and comes home to the suburbs to his wife and son. In his cartoons, Goofy struggles with weight and fitness, and was the subject of instructional comic videos on a variety of subjects.[19]

Mickey Mouse stands as a champion of Disney's utopian vision of a world without tension and negativity. Myths will precede the history. The stories have to become ingrained in our psyche before we can make them happen. Thinking about some other utopian dreams from the 1960s, such as *Star Trek*, is it possible that the Utopia that Walt dreamed about is around the corner?

Appendix A:
Key Attractions by Land

Because of the changing nature of Disneyland, ongoing attractions may have closed since the writing of this book.

Main Street, U.S.A.
• Great Moments with Mr. Lincoln (Town Square), *show* (1965–2005, 2009–ongoing)
• The Santa Fe & Disneyland Railroad, now The Disneyland Railroad (Town Square), *train ride* (1955–ongoing)
• The Main Street Cinema (Main Street), *show* (1955–ongoing)
• Main Street Windows (Main Street), *décor* (1955–ongoing)
• *Partners* (Plaza Hub), *décor* (1993–ongoing)

Adventureland
• Jungle Cruise, *boat ride* (1955–ongoing)
• Walt Disney's Enchanted Tiki Room, *show* (1963–ongoing)
• Indiana Jones Adventure, *kinetic dark ride* (1995–ongoing)
• Swiss Family Treehouse, now Tarzan's Treehouse, *walk-through* (1962–ongoing)

New Orleans Square
• Pirates of the Caribbean, *dark ride* (1967–ongoing)
• The Haunted Mansion, *dark ride* (1969–ongoing)
• Club 33, *restaurant* (1967–ongoing)

Frontierland
• Nature's Wonderland (closed), *scenic area* (1960–1977)
• Big Thunder Mountain Railroad, *roller coaster* (1979–ongoing)
• Indian Village (closed), *show* (1955–1971)

- Tom Sawyer Island, now Pirate's Lair on Tom Sawyer Island, *activity area* (1956–ongoing)
- Rivers of America, *mixed use* (1955–ongoing)

Fantasyland

- Snow White Adventures, now Snow White Scary Adventures, *dark ride* (1955–ongoing)
- Peter Pan Flight, *dark ride* (1955–ongoing)
- Mr. Toad's Wild Ride, *dark ride* (1955–ongoing)
- Alice in Wonderland, *dark ride* (1958–ongoing)
- Pinocchio, *dark ride* (1983–ongoing)
- Sleeping Beauty Castle, *walk-through* (1955–ongoing)
- Matterhorn Bobsleds, *roller coaster* (1959–ongoing)
- it's a small world, *boat ride* (1966–ongoing)

Tomorrowland

- Autopia, *car ride* (1955–ongoing)
- Disneyland-Alweg Monorail, now Disneyland Monorail or Monorail, *train ride* (1959–ongoing)
- WEDWay People Mover (closed), *train ride* (1955–1995)
- Star Tours, now New Star Tours, *3D experience* (1987–ongoing)
- Space Mountain, *roller coaster* (1977–ongoing)
- Buzz Lightyear Astro Blasters, *dark ride experience* (2005–ongoing)
- Submarine Voyage, now Finding Nemo Submarine Voyage, *submarine ride* (1959–1998, 2007–ongoing)

Critter Country

- Country Bear Jamboree (closed), *show* (1972–2001)
- The Many Adventures of Winnie the Pooh, *dark ride* (2003–ongoing)
- Splash Mountain, *log-flume ride/dark ride* (1989–ongoing)

Mickey's Toontown

- Mickey's House, *walk-through/meet-and-greet* (1993–ongoing)
- Minnie's House, *walk-through/meet-and-greet* (1993–ongoing)
- Donald's Boat, *walk-through/meet-and-greet* (1993–ongoing)
- Roger Rabbit's Car Toon Spin, *kinetic dark ride* (1994–ongoing)

Appendix B:
The Fantasyland
Fairy Tales

The following is a collection of summaries of the fairy tales presented in Fantasyland.

Snow White and the Seven Dwarfs

The Grimm version tells how Snow-White's stepmother, who is jealous of her beauty, attempts to destroy her so she, the Queen, can be the only beautiful woman in the land. First, she tries having Snow-White killed, but the huntsman lets her live. She runs into the woods and is welcomed into the dwarf's cottage. Discovering she is still alive, the queen disguises herself as a merchant woman, and on three occasions tries to sell Snow-White her poisoned wares: a lace bodice, a comb, and an apple. In all three cases, Snow-White is rescued; the first two times by the dwarfs and the final time by accident as her coffin hits a bump in the road and dislodges the apple from her throat. Because the dwarfs cannot dislodge the apple, they build Snow-White the glass coffin so as to not lose her beauty. It is in this state that the prince first meets her and takes her back to his kingdom. Along the way, this carriage hits a bump and dislodges the piece of apple from Snow-White's throat and they decide to marry. The Queen is condemned to dance herself to death at their wedding in hot iron shoes.

The Wind in the Willows

The novel alternates between the daily lives of Mr. Mole and Mr. Rat and the romanticization of nature, and the adventures of Mr. Toad that invariably involve problematic cross-overs into the human realm, embracing human technology and progress, and subsequently getting into trouble for it. We first meet Mr. Toad while Rat is giving Mole a tour of the river. Mole had just decided to relocate to the river, and Rat is taking him on a picnic. While sailing, Mr. Toad sails by in a brand new wagon-boat. Rat tells Mole about Toad:

> Once, it was nothing but sailing.... Then he tired of that and took to punting. Nothing would please him but to punt all day and every day, and a nice mess he made of it. Last year it was house-boating, and we all had to go and stay with him in his house-boat, and pretend we liked it. He was going to spend the rest of his life in a house-boat. It's all the same, whatever he takes up; he gets tired of it, and starts on something fresh [Grahame 11].

Toad's eccentricity is attractive to Mole, who wants to make his acquaintance. As a testament to Toad's character, Rat describes him as a genius, though not clever, and prone to boasting and conceit, but Toad is nonetheless one of the wealthiest creatures along the river. Toad quickly abandons boating in favor of the gypsy cart and the allure of the open road. One day into the cart's inaugural voyage with Rat and Mole, the cart is run off the road by a car and Toad catches motorcar fever. Like Pinocchio, Toad's story is about the danger of disobedience. Toad is always remorseful in the face of punishment, but will quickly change his tune when the danger has passed. The last chapter of the book, titled "The Return of Ulysses," brings the adventures of Toad to a close. The reference to Ulysses connects Toad to Homer's *Odyssey*, which best describes Toad's homecoming. While he is away, jailed for stealing a motorcar, his home is overridden by weasels. Toad and his friends sneak into the house through a secret passage and quickly dispatch the weasels. In celebration, they arrange a banquet then return to their river lives. A marked change has come over Toad, who makes amends to anyone he harmed during his reckless behavior and adopts the animals' civilized life without the temptation of the human realm.

Disney's short film removes Mole and Rat's romantic song to

nature and focuses only on Toad's adventures. The film begins at Toad Hall, where we meet MacBadger, who has taken charge of Toad's finances after it is revealed that his reckless antics have driven him almost to bankruptcy. He urgently sends for Rat and Mole to find Toad, who has run off with a canary yellow gypsy cart and a horse named Cyril. After they find him and before they can return him safely to Toad Hall, a motorcar drives by and Toad is engulfed in motor-mania. He sneaks out of his bedroom window to find a car, and is arrested for stealing it. He claims it was a fair trade, having traded the deed for Toad Hall for it with the weasels and their leader Mr. Winky, a bar proprietor. Mr. Winky denies any such trade and Toad is sentenced to jail. At Christmas, Cyril helps him escape and he returns to Rat's house. MacBadger rushes in with news that weasels in fact were living at Toad Hall, revealing Toad's innocence. Together, they sneak into the house to fight off Mr. Winky and his weasels and to reclaim the deed. Exonerated, MacBadger resumes his role as Toad's accountant and Toad takes up flying. The theme of the film rests with the importance of one's friends and home despite one's recklessness. Though the book converts Toad to follow society's norm, the film permits him to remain the same Toad, while his friends try to support him through his adventures and whims.

Pinocchio

The story of Pinocchio begins as an ill-behaved piece of wood that is bought by Geppetto, who fashions it into a marionette. Because the wood is enchanted, Pinocchio is immediately alive and behaves very badly, causing Geppetto to leave the workshop in exasperation. The Talking Cricket visits Pinocchio to advise him of the error of his ways, and Pinocchio kills him. Only afterwards does he feel remorse for his actions, though induced by hunger, and promises Geppetto to be a good boy from then on. Geppetto sells his coat to send Pinocchio to school and to buy him a schoolbook, which Pinocchio sells to see a puppet show. He is almost killed by the Puppet Master, but is paid for his performances. He intends on taking the money home to Geppetto, but encounters a fox and a cat who lure him on an adventure to multiply his five gold pieces into a thousand. That night, Pinocchio is ambushed by two bandits, who are really the fox and cat. He hides his money in his mouth and so is hanged from a tree to die, so the bandits can get the money. He is rescued by birds and taken to the home of the Blue Fairy who nurses him back to health and sends him on an errand to meet Geppetto. Instead, Pinocchio runs into the fox and cat, who take him to the magical field where he can multiply his gold. He buries it and comes back several hours later to learn that the fox and cat had tricked and robbed him. Saddened, he returns to the house of the Fairy to find it gone. He wanders through the woods, and eventually comes to a town where the people are dedicated to work. They agree to help him only if he helps them, which he refuses until out of desperation, he accepts a task from the Blue Fairy. In gratitude, he promises to be good. The next day he goes to school and acts the model student, for which the other boys bully him. A brawl breaks out, and Pinocchio's book is thrown at another boy, killing him. Pinocchio is arrested and spends four months in jail. After escaping, he is nearly fried like a fish for a giant's dinner. After he returns to the Blue Fairy, he again promises to be good. She, in turn, promises to turn him into a real boy. Pinocchio goes out to invite his friends to the party, but is tempted to accompany his friend Lampwick to the Land of Play, where every day is a vacation and boys never have to go to school. He is turned into a donkey and sold to a circus, where he is injured, then sold to a drum maker for his skin. The drum maker drowns Pinocchio, and while underwater the fish eat away his donkey skin. He escapes the drum maker, only to be swallowed by the Great Whale. Pinocchio is reunited with Geppetto and devises a plan to climb out of the whale, which has asthma and sleeps with his mouth open. Once out, they swim for shore. A Tuna, a friend of Pinocchio, helps them once Pinocchio gets tired. They go home and Pinocchio devotes himself to hard work and his studies to buy food and supplies to nurse Geppetto back to health. As a reward, he is turned into a real boy.

Disney's *Pinocchio* begins when Geppetto creates the puppet and wishes upon a star for his puppet to come to life. The Blue Fairy comes and awakens Pinocchio and charges Jiminy Cricket to act as his conscience. Geppetto wakes up to find Pinocchio and there is a lot of dancing. He sends Pinocchio off to school. On his way, Pinocchio runs into the fox and the cat, who want to sell him over to the gypsy Stromboli. They lure Pinocchio by glorifying the life of actors and Pinocchio goes with them, ignoring Jiminy's advice. Pinocchio's first show is so successful that Jiminy believes that he is no longer needed, but when he goes to say goodbye to Pinocchio, he finds him in a cage. The Blue Fairy comes to rescue them and Pinocchio races home. Nearly there, he again encounters the fox and the cat, who kidnap and take him to the Coachman. At first, Pinocchio just wants to get home, but is seduced by the prospects of Pleasure Island. He and his friend Lampwick are among the last of the boys to turn into donkeys, though Jiminy gets to Pinocchio just in time. He only has the ears and tail, and has not fully turned into a donkey. They jump off the island and return home. Geppetto's studio is empty and a fairy brings Pinocchio a note telling him that Geppetto is sitting in the belly of Monstro the whale. Pinocchio and Jiminy go to the bottom of the sea to find the whale and are swallowed. They find Geppetto and are reunited. Pinocchio devises a plan to start a fire to force the whale to sneeze them out. The whale chases them to land. They make it, but Pinocchio appears to be dead. Back at Geppetto's studio, while mourning Pinocchio, the Blue Fairy visits. For Pinocchio's brave sacrifice, she turns him into a real boy and they live happily ever after.

Peter Pan

In order to save some money, the Darlings have a nurse dog, Nana, who one night causes a ruckus that results in Mr. Darling's throwing her outside. This opens the opportunity for Peter Pan to visit the children to find his missing shadow, stowed away in the children's nursery. Peter rescues his shadow but cannot reconnect to it, so he begins to cry. His sobs wake Wendy, who, playing the mother, sews the shadow to Peter's foot. Peter and Wendy chat about how he ran away and became friends with Tinker Bell and the Lost Boys in Neverland. He lures Wendy to come with him by telling her that he and the Boys have no mother to tell them stories. Wendy wakes up her brothers and Peter dusts them with fairy dust so they can fly to Neverland. Once there, Tinker Bell, out of jealousy for Wendy, convinces the Lost Boys to shoot her down like a bird. Peter banishes Tink once he finds out about her plot, although Wendy is unharmed. The Boys build a house for Wendy and pretend she is their mother. While visiting the mermaids at Marooner's Rock, Peter and Wendy learn that Captain Hook and his pirates have captured Tiger Lily and go to rescue her. It is a trap for Peter, and he and Hook duel. Peter is wounded, but is saved by a Never-Bird, who flies him and Wendy home. Meanwhile, Tinker Bell had betrayed the Lost Boys' hideout to Hook, who kidnaps the children, but leaves a sleeping Peter. Hook poisons his medicine, but right before Peter drinks it, a remorseful Tink swoops in and drinks it instead. She is saved by the clapping of those who believe in fairies, a remnant of Barre's original play. Together, they go to rescue the children. Pan battles Hook one more time, defeating him. They then sail Hook's ship, the Jolly Roger, back to London to return the children home. The Darling family is reunited, and Wendy grows up. Peter befriends Jane, her daughter, and the adventures continue.

Alice in Wonderland

Alice's Adventures begins with Alice's first sighting on the White Rabbit and subsequent tumble down the Rabbit Hole in pursuit of him. After stretching and shrinking to acquire the key to the door, Alice enters Wonderland. She races in the Caucus-Race with Dodo, overwhelms the White Rabbit's house, recites for the hookah-smoking Caterpillar, meets the Duchess and turns her baby into a pig, drinks tea with the Mad Hatter and March Hare, plays croquet with the Queen of Hearts, hears the Mock Turtle's story, dances a lobster quadrille, and stands trial along with those accused of stealing the queen's tarts, all the while stretching and shrinking from the various Wonderland cakes and mushrooms. She returns from Wonderland when her sister awakes her. Disney, for the most part, followed this story closely, but borrowed some additional content from *Through the Looking Glass*, namely: the fiery personality for the Queen of Hearts is derived from the Red Queen and her hot-headed temper, Alice's tour through the Garden of Live Flowers, and her encounter with the rotund twins Tweedle-Dee and Tweedle-Dum. Extra note: Since Disney's 1951 film, the two queens have often been combined. No clue if this was intentional or not.

Sleeping Beauty

In Perrault's fairy tale, a daughter is born to a king and a queen. The kingdom's seven fairies are named her godmothers. Toward the end of the celebrations, an old fairy arrives who had not been invited because she was believed to be dead. All of the fairies came forth to offer their gifts of perfection on the Princess. When the old fairy's turn arrived, her gift was that the princess would have her hand pierced with a spindle and die from the wound. The seventh fairy godmother could not undo the old fairy's gift, but transformed it into a deep sleep that would last 100 years until a prince woke her. The king proclaimed all spindles illegal on pain of death, but sixteen years later the princess encounters an old woman spinning and pricks her hand, falling asleep. She is locked away in a palace apartment. The good fairy arrives and puts the entire kingdom to sleep so the princess would have familiar people around her when she awoke. Immediately following this spell, brambles and bushes grow up around the castle so that no one could enter. One hundred years later, the prince finds the castle and is instantly curious about it. Hearing a rumor about the spell, he enters the briar forest. He finds the princess and kneels beside her the minute the spell wears off. They are immediately married. The prince never informs his parents of his marriage, afraid that his mother is really an ogre. After two years, he is crowned king and brings his wife and family home. The queen reveals herself to be an ogre and dies in a trap set for the princess and her family.

Chapter Notes

Introduction

1. King, Margaret J., and J. G. O'Boyle. "The Theme Park: The Art of Time and Space." *Disneyland and Culture: Essays on the Parks and Their Influence.* Ed. Kathy Merlock Jackson and Mark I. West. Jefferson: McFarland, 2011. 6.

2. Wuthnow, Robert. *American Mythos: Why Our Best Efforts to Be a Better Nation Fall Short.* Princeton: Princeton University Press, 2006. 3.

3. Robertson, James Oliver. *American Myth, American Reality.* New York: Hill and Wang, 1980. 78–79.

4. Robertson, 299.

5. Jung, C. G. "The Complications of American Psychology." *The Collected Works of C. G. Jung.* Trans. R. F. C. Hull. Vol. 10. 2nd ed. Bollingen Series 20. Princeton: Princeton University Press, 1970. Par. 976.

6. Jung, C. G. "Flying Saucers: A Modern Myth." *CW 10.* Par. 624.

7. Graebner, William. *The Age of Doubt: American Thought and Culture in the 1940s.* Long Grove: Waveland Press, 1991. xii.

8. Kittleson, Mary Lynn. "Coming Home: Hyper-Images of the Hero and Child in America." *The Soul of Popular Culture: Looking at Contemporary Heroes, Myths, and Monsters.* Ed. Mary Lynn Kittleson. Chicago: Open Court, 1998. 102.

9. See Victor Turner. *The Ritual Process: Structure and Anti-Structure.*

10. Campbell, Joseph. *The Masks of God: Occidental Mythology.* New York: Penguin Compass, 1976. 519–521.

11. Hillman, James. "Pothos: The Nostalgia of the Puer Eternus." *Loose Ends: Primary Papers in Archetypal Psychology.* Dallas: Spring Publications, 1975. 53.

12. Hillman, James. "Senex and Puer." *Puer Papers.* Ed. James Hillman. Dallas: Spring Publications, Inc., 1979. 23.24.

13. See Robert Wuthnow, *American Mythos.*

14. As reported on MousePlanet.com and StitchKingdom.com.

15. Schickel, Richard. *The Disney Version: The Life, Times, Art and Commerce of Walt Disney.* 3rd ed. Chicago: Elephant, 1997. 325.

16. Bryman, Alan. *The Disneyization of Society.* London: Sage, 2004. 2.

17. Sammond, Nicholas. *Babes in Tomorrowland: Walt Disney and the Making of the American Child, 1930–1960.* Durham: Duke University Press, 2005. 354. Also, Richard Francaviglia. "Frontierland as an Allegorical Map of the American West" in *Disneyland and Culture.* 59.

Chapter 1

1. Gabler, Neal. *Walt Disney: The Triumph of the American Imagination.* New York: Alfred A. Knopf, 2006. xx.

2. Ibid. xv.

3. The Imagineers. *The Imagineering Field Guide to Disneyland: An Imagineer's-Eye Tour.* New York: Disney Editions, 2008. 16.

4. Quoted in The Imagineers, *Imagineering Field Guide*, 20.
5. Schickel, *The Disney Version*, 361.
6. The Imagineers, *Imagineering Field Guide*. 6.
7. Avens, Roberts. *The New Gnosis: Heidegger, Hillman, and Angels.* Putnam: Spring Publications, 2003. 55.
8. Ibid. 98.
9. Ibid. 19.
10. As most Millennials are finding out, it's difficult for *any* person, except for a lucky few, entering the job market after 2007 to find a well-paying job or to overcome the cycle of debt.
11. Avens, *The New Gnosis*, 79.
12. Andrews, Tamara. *A Dictionary of Nature Myths.* Oxford: Oxford University Press, 1998. xiii.
13. Abram, David. *The Spell of the Sensuous.* New York: Vintage Books, 1996. 8–10.
14. Roszak, Theodore. *The Voice of the Earth: An Exploration of Ecopsychology.* 2nd ed. Grand Rapids: Phanes Press, 2001. 307.
15. Royce, quoted in Roszak, 133.
16. Jung quoted in Sabini, Meredith, ed. *The Earth Has a Soul: C. G. Jung on Nature, Technology, and Modern Life.* Berkeley: North Atlantic Books, 2002. 15.
17. Barreto, Marco Heleno. "On the Death of Nature." *Spring, a Journal of Archetype and Culture* 75 (2006): 269.
18. Ibid. 262.
19. Roszak, *The Voice of the Earth*, 58
20. Ibid. 185.
21. Abram, *The Spell of the Sensuous*, 40
22. Sabini, *The Earth Has a Soul*, 11.

Chapter 2

1. Strodder, Chris. *The Disneyland Encyclopedia: The Unofficial, Unauthorized, and Unprecedented History of Every Land, Attraction, Restaurant, Shop, and Event in the Original Magic Kingdom.* Santa Monica: Santa Monica Press, 2008. 253.
2. Marling, Karal Ann. "Imagineering the Disney Theme Parks." *Designing Disney's Theme Park: The Architecture of Reassurance.* Ed. Karal Ann Marling. Paris: Flammarion, 1997. 54.
3. Strodder 253.
4. Sammond, *Babes in Tomorrowland* 193.
5. Baudrillard, Jean. *The Consumer Society: Myths and Structures.* Trans. Chris Turner. London: Sage, 1998. 49.
6. Ibid. 50.
7. Ibid. 56.
8. Svonkin, Craig. "A Southern California Boyhood in the Simu-Southland Shadows of Walt Disney's Enchanted Tiki Room." *Disneyland and Culture: Essays on the Parks and Their Influence.* Ed. Kathy Merlock Jackson and Mark I. West. Jefferson: McFarland, 2011. 119.
9. Graebner, *The Age of Doubt*, 53.
10. Watts, Steven. *The Magic Kingdom: Walt Disney and the American Way of Life.* Columbia: University of Missouri Press, 1997. 289.
11. Brode, Douglas. "Of Theme Parks and Television: Walt Disney, Rod Serling, and the Politics of Nostalgia." *Disneyland and Culture: Essays on the Parks and Their Influence.* Ed. Kathy Merlock Jackson and Mark I. West. Jefferson: McFarland, 2011. 192.
12. Robertson, *American Myth, American Reality*, 3.
13. King, and O'Boyle, "The Theme Park: The Art of Time and Space," *Disneyland and Culture*, 12.
14. Brode, "Of Theme Parks and Television," 187.
15. Robertson 6.
16. Some Disney commentary remarks that the unity of Disney projects is specifically a unity within the established white status quo, resting this critique on the lack of diversity present in the Disney opus. Indeed, the Disney subscription to a post-identity culture suggests a latent racism, but as with all myths, the intent, no matter how obscure, should be taken into consideration. Racial differences can coexist within a Utopia, one that Disney alluded to within the confines of Hollywood's

codes. The real culprit is in the nostalgia for a whitewashed America, which runs the risk of communicating a preference for this image. Jason Sperb argues in his analysis of *The Song of the South* that this was the mythos behind Reganism, and at the heart of the racial divide that continues to undermine the effects of the Civil Rights Movement.

17. Robertson 85.
18. Graebner 105.
19. Robertson 310.
20. Marling, Karl Ann. "Disneyland, 1955: Just Take the Santa Ana Freeway to the American Dream." *American Art* 5.1/2 (Winter/Spring 1991): 177–180.
21. Marling, "Imagineering the Disney Theme Parks," 50.
22. Neuman, Robert. "Disneyland's Main Street, USA, and Its Sources in Hollywood, USA." *Journal of American Culture* 31.1 (2008): 87.
23. May, Rollo. *The Cry for Myth.* New York: Delta, 1991. 103.
24. Ibid. 99.
25. Ibid. 92.
26. Ibid. 92.
27. Ibid. 93–94.
28. Robertson 11.
29. Ibid. 12.
30. See Douglas Brode, *From Walt to Woodstock: How Disney Created Counterculture.* Austin: University of Texas Press, 2004. (Brode)
31. Robertson 173.
32. Strodder 253.
33. Ibid. 254.
34. See David Koenig, *Mouse Tales: A Behind-the-Ears Look at Disneyland.* Irvine: Bonaventure, 1995; and *More Mouse Tales: A Closer Peek Backstage at Disneyland.* Irvine: Bonaventure, 2002.
35. Leonard Maltin in "Mickey in Living Color with Leonard Maltin." *Walt Disney Treasures Mickey Mouse in Living Color.* Ed. Leonard Maltin. Perf. Leonard Maltin. Disney, 2001. DVD.
36. See Henry Giroux and Grace Pollock. *The Mouse That Roared: Disney and the End of Innocence.* 2nd ed. Lanham: Rowman & Littlefield, 2010; and Carl Hiaasen, *Team Rodent: How Disney Devours the World.* New York: Ballantine, 1998.
37. Robertson 177, emphasis original.
38. Ibid 180.
39. Robertson 322.
40. Ibid 217.
41. As distinct from Epcot, a kingdom of Walt Disney World.
42. Brode, "Of Theme Parks and Television," 192.
43. See Alan Bryman, *The Disneyization of Society,* 2004.
44. Garde, Ajay. "Designing and Developing New Urbanist Projects in the United States: Insights and Implications." *Journal of Urban Design* 11.1 (Feb. 2006): 33.
45. Ibid. 34.
46. As quoted in Watts 444.
47. "The Optimistic Futurist." *Walt Disney Treasures Tomorrowland.* Ed. Leonard Maltin. Perf. Leonard Maltin, Ray Bradbury. Disney, 2004. DVD.
48. King, Margaret J. "The Disney Effect: Fifty Years After Theme Park Design." *Disneyland and Culture: Essays on the Parks and Their Influence.* Ed. Kathy Merlock Jackson and Mark I. West. Jefferson: McFarland, 2011. 225.
49. C. G. Jung as quoted in Storr, Anthony, ed. *The Essential Jung.* Princeton: Princeton University Press, 1983. 234.
50. Ibid. 236.
51. Noxon, Christopher. *Rejuvenile: Kickball, Cartoons, Cupcakes, and the Reinvention of the American Grown-Up.* New York: Three Rivers Press, 2006. 2.
52. Bryman, Alan. *Disney and His Worlds.* London: Routledge, 1995. 138.
53. Ibid. 138–139.
54. Bryman, *The Disneyization of Society,* 2.
55. Sammond 35.
56. Marling, "Imagineering the Disney Theme Parks," 54.

Chapter 3

1. Strodder, *The Disneyland Encyclopedia,* 39.
2. A word choice in accord with the release of *Alice in Wonderland* four

years prior to the opening of Disneyland and a Disney "buzz word" throughout the 1950s.

3. Strodder 38.

4. Svonkin, "A Southern California Boyhood," *Disneyland and Culture*, 112.

5. Baudrillard, Jean. *Simulacra and Simulation*. Trans. Sheila Faria Glaser. Ann Arbor: University of Michigan Press, 1994. 2.

6. Eco, Umberto. "Travels in Hyperreality." *Travels in Hyperreality: Essays.* Trans. William Weaver. San Diego: Harcourt, 1986. 44.

7. Ibid. 56.

8. The other two are Star Tours and Captain EO, both in Tomorrowland.

9. Strodder 213.

10. Ibid.

11. Legend gives credit to Walt.

12. Eco 46.

13. Tobias, Ronald. "Sex, Love, and Death: True-Life Fantasies." *Learning from Mickey, Donald and Walt: Essays on Disney's Edutainment Films.* Ed. A. Bowdoin Van Riper. Jefferson: McFarland, 2011. 166.

14. Ibid.

15. Baudrillard, *Simulacra and Simulation*, 121.

16. Ibid. 12.

17. Eco 43.

18. Ibid.

19. Leskosky, Richard J. "Cartoons Will Win the War: World War II Propaganda Shorts." *Learning from Mickey, Donald and Walt: Essays on Disney's Edutainment Films.* Ed. A. Bowdoin Van Riper. Jackson: McFarland, 2011. 44–45.

20. Ibid. 44.

21. Ibid.

22. Ibid. 45.

23. Tobias 165.

24. Eco 45–46.

25. Baudrillard, *Simulacra and Simulation*, 106.

26. See Neil Postman, *Amusing Ourselves to Death: Public Discourse in the Age of Show Business.* New York: Penguin, 2005.

27. Baudrillard, *Simulacra and Simulation*, 13.

28. As quoted in Strodder, 405–406.

29. Ibid. 408.

30. See, for instance, Henry David Thoreau's *Walden*.

31. Cowan, Lyn. "False Memories, True Memory, and Maybes." *The Soul of Popular Culture: Looking at Contemporary Heroes, Myths, and Monsters.* Ed. Mary Lynn Kittleson. Chicago: Open Court, 1998. 253.

32. Wasko, Janet. *Understanding Disney: The Manufacture of Fantasy.* Malden: Polity, 2001. 148.

Chapter 4

1. Mathes, Charlotte M. "The Soul of New Orleans: Archetypal Density and the Unconscious." *Psyche and the City: A Soul's Guide to the Modern Metropolis.* Ed. Thomas Singer. New Orleans: Spring, 2010. 158.

2. "Shadow" as it is used here refers to the Jungian concept of the shadow. According to Jung, the shadow forms over the course of identity formation and contains all aspects of the personality that were rendered off of the conscious. When applied to culture, the same attributes still apply. The cultural shadow contains beliefs and attributes that the dominant culture believes are not relevant or present in the overall society.

3. Mathes 160.

4. Ibid. 157.

5. Ibid. 156–157.

6. Graebner, *The Age of Doubt*, 111.

7. Eco, "Travels in Hyperreality," 47.

8. Ibid. 57–58.

9. The women, presumably, are the spoils of pillage.

10. C. G. Jung as quoted in Storr, *The Essential Jung*, 87.

11. Robertson, *American Myth, American Reality*, 298.

12. Graebner 103.

13. The Pirates of the Caribbean attraction theme song.

14. Master Gracey, in fact, was not part of the original story. A tombstone for Master Gracey was erected in the

Haunted Mansion cemetery as tribute to Imagineer and Special Effects wizard, Yale Gracey, who helped contribute many of the illusions in the house before his untimely murder. Many fans interpret him to be the mansion owner and thus the Ghost Host. Disney acknowledged this in the film adaptation of the attraction.

15. Surrell, Jason. *The Haunted Mansion: From the Magic Kingdom to the Movies.* New York: Disney, 2009. 17, 82–85.

16. The illusion of see-through audio-animatronic ghosts is accomplished using the Pepper's Ghost Technique.

17. Freud, Sigmund. *Jokes and Their Relation to the Unconscious.* Trans. James Strachey. New York: W. W. Norton, 1960. 119–120.

18. Ibid. 131.

19. Ibid. 181.

20. Erikson, Erik H. *Childhood and Society.* 3rd ed. New York: W. W. Norton, 1993. 406.

21. Ibid. 407.

22. Freud 180.

23. That he keeps losing it is a reflection of America's aimless rootlessness.

24. Lyric form the Pirates of the Caribbean attraction theme song.

25. If the myth paves the way for history, perhaps it is this same defiance that has helped inspire the recent Occupy movement that has become outspoken about American doubt, speaking against the leadership and policies that have had a negative impact on some major aspect of the protestors' lives.

26. Von Franz, Marie-Louise. *Shadow and Evil in Fairy Tales.* Rev. ed. Boston: Shambhala, 1995. 9.

27. Robertson 85–86.

28. Graebner 102.

29. Ibid. 61.

30. Ibid.

31. Luna, Nancy. "Secretive Club 33 sheds much of its past in major renovation." *Orange County Register.* 1 July 2014. Web.

32. You might be wondering why, as a woman, I might take a high-and-mighty stance about Masonic symbolism. True, I'm about as much of a Freemason as I am a member of Club 33. What I do have, however, is a large network of friends and family who are Masons, who have willingly shared many aspects of the fraternity with me, with the exception of the lodge's secret passwords and handshakes, and I'm not allowed to sit in in a ritual (but I have been in a lodge room during an open meeting). Having the experience of visiting lodges is very revealing, and people who write about Illuminati and conspiracy theories should be commended for their creative interpretation of their lack of knowledge.

Chapter 5

1. Frontierland has always been one of the largest areas of Disneyland, originally accounting for a third of the total space, most of which "was and is accessible only by boat, mule, or train" (Strodder, *The Disneyland Encyclopedia,* 177).

2. Francaviglia, "Frontierland as an Allegorical Map of the American West," *Disneyland and Culture,* 61.

3. Ibid. 70.

4. Ibid. 67.

5. Savage, William. "What You'd Like the World to Be: The Wet and the American Mind." *Journal of American Culture* 3.2 (Summer 1980): 304.

6. Francaviglia 69.

7. Holdzkom, Marianne. "A Past to Make Us Proud: U. S. History According to Disney." *Learning from Mickey, Donald and Walt: Essays on Disney's Edutainment Films.* Ed. A. Bowdoin Van Riper. Jefferson: McFarland, 2011. 184.

8. Ibid. 183.

9. See Douglas Brode, *Dream West: Politics and Religion in Cowboy Movies.* Austin: University of Texas Press, 2013.

10. Blonsky, Marshall. *American Mythologies.* Oxford: Oxford University Press, 1992. 20.

11. Watts, *The Magic Kingdom,* 362.

12. Blonsky 20.

13. Ebert, Roger. "Summer Movie Spe-

cial: Sequel Madness." *Newsweek* 15 May 2011.

14. Furlotti, Nancy. "Angels and Idols: Los Angeles, a City of Contrasts." *Psyche and City: A Soul's Guide to the Modern Metropolis.* Ed. Thomas Singer. New Orleans: Spring, 2010. 243–244. In 1955, when Disneyland opened, Los Angeles's sprawl had yet to engulf Anaheim.

15. "Dateline: Disneyland." *Walt Disney Treasures Disneyland, USA.* Ed. Leonard Maltin. Perf. Walt Disney, Art Linkletter, Fess Parker. 1955. Disney, 2000. DVD.

16. Francaviglia 62.

17. Nilsen, Sarah. "America's Salesman: *The USA in Circarama.*" *Learning from Mickey, Donald and Walt: Essays on Disney's Edutainment Films.* Ed. A. Bowdoin Van Riper. Jefferson: McFarland, 2011. 238.

18. Robertson, *American Myth, American Reality,* 14.

19. Francaviglia 63.

20. Robertson 114–115.

21. Savage 302.

22. Holdzkom 188.

23. Ibid.

24. Robertson 74.

25. Ibid. 72.

26. Fjellman, Stephen M. *Vinyl Leaves: Walt Disney World and America.* Boulder: Westview Press, 1992.

27. See Douglas Brode, *Multiculturalism and the Mouse.* Austin: University of Texas Press, 2009.

28. Robertson 115.

29. Ibid. 336.

30. Graebner, *The Age of Doubt,* 146.

31. Francaviglia 69.

32. The transcript of Walt's testimony can be found in Kathy Merlock Jackson, ed. "The Testimony of Walter E. Disney Before the House Committee of Un-American Activities." *Walt Disney Conversations.* Jackson: University Press of Mississippi, 2006. 34–41.

33. Holdzkom 191.

34. Ibid. 197.

35. Francaviglia 77.

36. Holdzkom 197.

37. Strodder 74.

38. Ibid.

39. Brode, "Of Theme Parks and Television," 190.

40. Weber, Max. *The Protestant Ethic and the Spirit of Capitalism.* Trans. Talcott Parsons. New York: Scribner's, 1958. 162.

41. Robertson 83.

42. Ritzer, George. *Enchanting a Disenchanted World: Revolutionizing the Means of Consumption.* 2nd ed. Thousand Oaks: Pine Forge Press, 2005. 58.

43. Robertson 79.

44. Ibid.

45. Ibid. 78.

46. Brode, *From Walt to Woodstock,* xvi.

47. Ibid.

48. Ibid.

49. Watts 326.

50. Historically, General Sam Houston did ultimately defeat the Mexican army at the Battle of San Jacinto, earning for Texas a brief period of total autonomy as the Republic of Texas.

51. Strodder 357.

52. Francaviglia 72.

53. Strodder 268.

54. Ibid.

55. Ibid. 367.

56. Francaviglia 78. Recalls that it is from Lafitte's Landing that guests set sail with the Pirates of the Caribbean.

57. Strodder 422.

58. West, Mark I. "Tom Sawyer Island: Mark Twain, Walt Disney, and the Literary Playground." *Disneyland and Culture: Essays on the Parks and Their Influence.* Ed. Kathy Merlock Jackson and Mark I. West. Jefferson: McFarland, 2011. 101.

59. Strodder 426.

60. West 106.

61. Robertson 121.

Chapter 6

1. Other dark rides in the park, New Orleans Square's Haunted Mansion and the Pirates of the Caribbean, are more cinematic in nature and are several minutes long.

2. Britton, Donald. "The Dark Side of Disneyland." *Mythomania, Fantasies, Fables, and Sheer Lies in Contemporary American Popular Art*. Ed. Bernard Welt. Los Angeles: Art Issues, 1996. 116.

3. Arguably, the point of a fairy tale is that it does not have a cultural context that is relevant to the interpretation of these stories; however, because I am concentrating on the mythic narrative of Disneyland, the cultural context of the fairy tales is taken into account to help elucidate Disney's choice of these specific stories.

4. Tolkien, J. R. R. "On Fairy-Stories." *The Tolkien Reader*. New York: Ballantine, 1996. 34.

5. Von Franz, Marie-Louise. *The Interpretation of Fairy Tales*. Boston: Shambhala, 1996. 26.

6. Campbell, Joseph. *The Flight of the Wild Gander: Explorations in the Mythological Dimensions of Fairy Tales, Legends, and Symbols*. New York: HarperPerennial, 1990. 24–25.

7. Bettleheim, Bruno. *The Uses of Enchantment: The Meaning and Importance of Fairy Tales*. New York: Alfred A. Knopf, 1997. 26.

8. Ibid. 37.

9. Von Franz, *The Interpretation of Fairy Tales*, 25.

10. Bettleheim 24.

11. Rahn, Suzanne. "The Dark Ride of Snow White: Narrative Strategies at Disneyland." *Disneyland and Culture: Essays on the Parks and Their Influence*. Ed. Kathy Merlock Jackson and Mark I. West. Jefferson: McFarland, 2011. 91–92.

12. Quoted in Rahn 92.

13. Zipes, Jack. *Fairy Tale as Myth*. Lexington: University Press of Kentucky, 1994. 14.

14. Tolkien 22.

15. Von Franz, *Shadow and Evil in Fairy Tales*, 12.

16. Strodder 324.

17. Despite being one of the preferred dark rides, it is also one of the most frustrating because, despite being as long as the others in the land, it attracts the longest lines of any of the Fantasyland dark rides giving it the illusion of being a shorter ride.

18. This film packages two thirty-minute short films into a one-hour feature. The other half of this film is based off the Washington Irving story, "The Legend of Sleepy Hollow."

19. Quoted in Strodder 329, emphasis added.

20. Though these images have inspired the conception of the hero, for example, in the modern, Western world, the lack of context has divorced the meaning from the image. The emphasis on cultural context within this discussion is to help transcend the traditional perception among academic of outdated practices that still behave as though American popular culture holds no meaning in the culture's mythology, maintaining the stance that it is from here that America's new mythology will emerge.

Chapter 7

1. A letter written by educator Frances Clarke Sayers to the *Los Angeles Times* is credited with beginning the conversation. The letter and an interview with Ms. Sayers: Sayers, Frances Clarke. "Walt Disney Accused." *The Horn Book Magazine* December 1965: n. p.

2. "Interview with David Griffiths," in Jackson, *Walt Disney Conversations*, 68–69.

3. Deszez, Justyna. "Beyond the Disney Spell, or Escape into Pantoland." *Folklore* 113.1 (Apr. 2002): 85.

4. Disney Consumer Products, responsible for the merchandising throughout the corporation, "earned $27.2 billion from licensed product sales in 2009, making it the largest licenser in the world." Stein, Andi. *Why We Love Disney: The Power of the Disney Brand*. New York: Peter Lang, 2011. 230.

5. Deszez 85.

6. Strodder 378.

7. Strodder 377.

8. Quoted in Kurtti, Jeff. *Walt Disney's Imagineering Legends and the Genesis of the Disney Theme Park.* New York: Disney, 2008. 139.
9. Strodder 377.
10. Brode, *From Walt to Woodstock,* xiii.
11. Ibid. xv.
12. Zipes, Jack. *Happily Ever After: Fairy Tales, Children, and the Culture Industry.* New York: Routledge, 1997. 6.
13. Ibid. 6–7.
14. King, and O'Boyle, "The Theme Park: The Art of Time and Space," *Disneyland and Culture,* 10–11.
15. Eco, "Travels in Hyperreality," 48.
16. Deszez 86.
17. For instance, Thomas More's *Utopia.*
18. Historian Bernard de Voto, as quoted in Robertson 345.
19. Jung, "The Complications of American Psychology," *CW10,* par. 980.
20. Strodder 427.
21. Sherman, Richard, and Robert Sherman. "It's a Small World (After All)." *The Sherman Brothers Songbook.* Disney, 2009. CD.
22. Brode, *Multiculturalism and the Mouse,* 39.
23. Campbell, Joseph. "The Hero's Adventure." *The Power of Myth with Bill Moyers.* Perf. Joseph Campbell, Bill Moyers. 1988. Mystic Fire, 2001. DVD.

Chapter 8

1. Quoted in Strodder 415.
2. Ibid. 416.
3. Ibid. 417.
4. Detweiler, Eric. "Hyperurbanity: Idealism, New Urbanism, and the Politics of Hyperreality in the Town of Celebration, Florida." *Disneyland and Culture: Essays on the Parks and Their Influence.* Ed. Kathy Merlock Jackson and Mark I. West. Jefferson: McFarland, 2011. 153.
5. Francaviglia, "Frontierland as an Allegorical Map of the American West," *Disneyland and Culture,* 80.
6. Robertson 288.

7. Ibid. 281.
8. Ibid. 198.
9. Graebner 43.
10. Quoted in Strodder 418.
11. Ibid. 419.
12. Blonsky 27.
13. McLuhan, Marshall. *The Medium Is the Massage: An Inventory of Effects.* Ed. Jerome Agel. Berkeley: Gingko Press, 1967. 72.
14. Buzz Lightyear's motto in the *Toy Story* films.
15. The Imagineers 20.
16. The other two are Tomorrowland's *Captain EO* and the Indiana Jones Adventure, which is located in Adventureland.
17. Strodder 396–397.
18. Ibid. 388.
19. Postman, Neil. *The Disappearance of Childhood.* New York: Vintage Books, 1994. 36.
20. Ibid. 99.
21. Quoted in Von Franz, Marie-Louise. *The Problem of the Puer Aeternus.* 3rd ed. Toronto: Inner City, 2000.
22. Noxon 7, emphasis added.
23. Huizinga, Johan. *Homo Ludens: A Study of the Play Element in Culture.* Boston: Beacon, 1955. 7.
24. Both Noxon and Bryman comment on statistics that demonstrate the relationship between adult play and Disneyland, and an overwhelming number of adult consumers versus the number of kids who are believed to be the primary target audience for these products or services.
25. Erikson 212.
26. An update of the original Tomorrowland attraction Mission to the Moon, updated after American astronauts landed there.
27. Robertson 334.
28. Howe, Katherine. "Vacation in Historyland." *Disneyland and Culture: Essays on the Parks and Their Influence.* Ed. Kathy Merlock Jackson and Mark I. West. Jefferson: McFarland, 2011. 204.
29. Ibid. 205.
30. Jung, "Good and Evil in Analytical Psychology," *CW10,* par. 879.

31. Robertson 201.
32. Eco 47–48.
33. Van Riper, A. Bowdoin. "A Promise of Things to Come: *Disneyland* and the Wonders of Technology, 1954–58." *Learning from Mickey, Donald and Walt: Essays on Disney's Edutainment Films.* Ed. A. Bowdoin Van Riper. Jefferson: McFarland, 2011. 95.
34. "The Disneyland Story." *Walt Disney Treasures Disneyland, USA.* Ed. Leonard Maltin. Perf. Walt Disney. 1954. Disney, 2000. DVD.
35. Graebner 78.
36. Sammond 7.
37. Ibid. 80.
38. Graebner 99.
39. McLuhan 125.
40. The counterculture movement is excluded here, as it merits its own discussion.

Epilogue

1. As of this writing, Shanghai Disneyland is still under construction.
2. Littleton, Cynthia. "Disney Promotes Tom Staggs to No. 2 Post, Positioning Him as Iger's Successor." *Variety* 5 February 2015. Web.
3. Due to the perception of a post-identity culture, Americans believe the society is "beyond" punishing people for their differences, that they do not exist, and this has thus created a generation complacent against activism and confused about how to handle acts of racism and sexism.
4. Steiner, Michael. "Frontierland as Tomorrowland: Walt Disney and the Agricultural Packaging of the Mythic West." *Montana: The Magazine of Western History* 48.1 (Spring 1998). 13.
5. Hackney, Sheldon. "The American Identity." *The Public Historian* 19.1 (Winter 1997). 18.
6. *Reel Injun.* Dir. Neil Diamond. Domino Film, 2009. Netflix.
7. Steiner 13.
8. A declaration made by Frederick Jackson Turner in "The Significance of the Frontier in American History." *The Frontier in American History.* New York: Henry Holt, 1921.
9. Strodder 116.
10. Ibid. 69.
11. The bear is also the state animal of California.
12. For a detailed history, see Jason Sperb. *Disney's Most Notorious Film: Race, Convergence, and the Hidden Histories of* Song of the South. Austin: University of Texas Press, 2012.
13. "Disneyland: Secrets, Stories and Magic of the Happiest Place on Earth." *Walt Disney Treasures Disneyland: Secrets, Stories and Magic.* Ed. Leonard Maltin. Perf. Tony Baxter. 2005. Disney, 2007. DVD.
14. Ebert, Roger. Rev. of *Who Framed Roger Rabbit?*, by Robert Zemeckis. *Roger Ebert.com* 22 June 1988. n.p. Web.
15. The film was based on the novel, *Who Censored Roger Rabbit?* by Gary K. Wolf (1981).
16. Strodder 281.
17. At other times, the character is roaming the park under a strict schedule of visibility. If Mickey is at home receiving guests, he shouldn't also be seen wandering Main Street, U.S.A.
18. Leonard Maltin in "Mickey in Living Color with Leonard Maltin." *Walt Disney Treasures Mickey Mouse in Living Color.*
19. One such video, "Motor Mania" (1950), is still a mainstay of defensive driving courses.

Selected Bibliography

Books and Articles

Barre, J. M. *Peter Pan.* New York: Aladdin Classica, 2003.
Baudrillard, Jean. *America.* Trans. Chris Turner. London: Verso, 1988.
_____. *The Consumer Society: Myths and Structures.* Trans. Chris Turner. London: Sage, 1998.
_____. *Simulacra and Simulation.* Trans. Sheila Faria Glaser. Ann Arbor: University of Michigan Press, 1994.
Bettleheim, Bruno. *The Uses of Enchantment: The Meaning and Importance of Fairy Tales.* New York: Alfred A. Knopf, 1997.
Blonsky, Marshall. *American Mythologies.* Oxford: Oxford University Press, 1992.
Brode, Douglas. *From Walt to Woodstock: How Disney Created Counterculture.* Austin: University of Texas Press, 2004.
_____. *Multiculturalism and the Mouse.* Austin: University of Texas Press, 2009.
Bryman, Alan. *Disney and His Worlds.* London: Routledge, 1995.
_____. *The Disneyization of Society.* London: Sage, 2004.
Campbell, Joseph. *The Flight of the Wild Gander: Explorations in the Mythological Dimensions of Fairy Tales, Legends, and Symbols.* New York: HarperPerennial, 1990.
Carroll, Lewis. *Alice's Adventures in Wonderland and Through the Looking Glass.* New York: Puffin, 1997.
Collodi, Carlo. *The Adventures of Pinocchio.* Trans. Carla Della Chiesa. Franklin: Dalmatian Press, 2005.
Davis, Erik. *TechGnosis: Myth, Magic and Mysticism in the Age of Information.* New York: Harmony, 1998.
Eco, Umberto. "Travels in Hyperreality." *Travels in Hyperreality: Essays.* Trans. William Weaver. San Diego: Harcourt, 1986.
Erikson, Erik H. *Childhood and Society.* 3rd ed. New York: W.W. Norton, 1993.
Fjellman, Stephen M. *Vinyl Leaves: Walt Disney World and America.* Boulder: Westview, 1992.
Gabler, Neal. *Walt Disney: The Triumph of the American Imagination.* New York: Alfred A. Knopf, 2006.
Giroux, Henry A., and Grace Pollock. *The Mouse That Roared: Disney and the End of Innocence.* Rev. ed. Lanham: Rowman & Littlefield, 2010.
Graebner, William. *The Age of Doubt: American Thought and Culture in the 1940s.* Long Grove: Waveland Press, 1991.
Grahame, Kenneth. *The Wind in the Willows.* New York: Sterling, 2005.
Grimm, Jacob, and Wilhelm Grimm. "Snow-White and the Seven Dwarfs." *Grimm's Complete Fairy Tales.* New York: Barnes and Noble, 1993. 328–336.

Selected Bibliography

Hackney, Sheldon. "The American Identity." *The Public Historian* 19.1 (Winter 1997). 11–22.

Hiaasen, Carl. *Team Rodent: How Disney Devours the World.* New York: Ballantine, 1998.

Huizinga, Johan. *Homo Ludens: A Study of the Play Element in Culture.* Boston: Beacon, 1955.

The Imagineers. *The Imagineering Field Guide to Disneyland: An Imagineer's Eye-Tour.* New York: Disney Editions, 2008.

Jackson, Kathy Merlock, ed. *Walt Disney Conversations.* Jackson: University Press of Mississippi, 2006.

Jackson, Kathy Merlock, and Mark I. West, eds. *Disneyland and Culture: Essays on the Parks and Their Influence.* Jefferson: McFarland, 2011.

Jung, C.G. *The Collected Works of C. G. Jung.* Trans. R. F. C. Hull. Vol. 10. 2nd ed. Bollingen Series 20. Princeton: Princeton University Press, 1970.

Koenig, David. *More Mouse Tales: A Closer Peek Backstage at Disneyland.* Irvine: Bonaventure, 2002.

_____. *Mouse Tales: A Behind-the-Ears-Look at Disneyland.* Irvine: Bonaventure, 1995.

_____. *Mouse Under Glass: Secrets of Disney Animation and Theme Parks.* Irvine: Bonaventure, 2001.

Kurtti, Jeff. *Walt Disney's Imagineering Legends and the Genesis of the Disney Theme Park.* New York: Disney, 2008.

Marling, Karal Ann, ed. *Designing Disney's Theme Park: The Architecture of Reassurance.* Paris: Flammarion, 1997.

McLuhan, Marshall. *The Medium Is the Massage: An Inventory of Effects.* Ed. Jerome Agel, Berkeley, Gingko Press, 1967.

McMahon, Robert J. *The Cold War: A Very Short Introduction.* Oxford: Oxford University Press, 2003.

Milne, A.A. *The Complete Tales of Winnie-the-Pooh.* New York: Dutton Children's, 1996.

More, Sir Thomas. *Utopia.* Trans. Ralph Robinson. Ed. Wayne A. Rebhorn. New York: Barnes and Noble, 2005.

Noxon, Christopher. *Rejuvenile: Kickball, Cartoons, Cupcakes, and the Reinvention of the American Grown-up.* New York: Three Rivers Press, 2006.

Perrault, Charles. "The Sleeping Beauty in the Wood." *The Blue Fairy Book.* Ed. Andrew Lang. New York: Dover, 1965. 54–63.

Postman, Neil. *Amusing Ourselves to Death: Public Discourse in the Age of Show Business.* New York: Penguin, 2005.

_____. *The Disappearance of Childhood.* New York: Vintage Books, 1994.

Ritzer, George. *Enchanting a Disenchanted World: Revolutionizing the Means of Consumption.* 2nd ed. Thousand Oaks: Pine Forge Press, 2005.

_____. *The McDonaldization of Society.* Revised New Century Edition. Thousand Oaks: Pine Forge Press, 2004.

Robertson, James Oliver. *American Myth, American Reality.* New York: Hill and Wang, 1980.

Sammond, Nicholas. *Babes in Tomorrowland: Walt Disney and the Making of the American Child, 1930–1960.* Durham: Duke University Press, 2005.

Sayers, Frances Clarke. "Walt Disney Accused." *The Horn Book Magazine* December 1965: n.p.

Schickel, Richard. *The Disney Version: The Life, Times, Art and Commerce of Walt Disney.* 3rd ed. Chicago: Elephant, 1997.

Sperb, Jason. *Disney's Most Notorious Film: Race, Convergence, and the Hidden Histories of* Song of the South. Austin: University of Texas Press, 2012.

Selected Bibliography

Stein, Andi. *Why We Love Disney: The Power of the Disney Brand*. New York: Peter Lang, 2011.

Strodder, Chris. *The Disneyland Encyclopedia: The Unofficial, Unauthorized, and Unprecedented History of Every Land, Attraction, Restaurant, Shop, and Event in the Original Magic Kingdom*. Santa Monica: Santa Monica Press, 2008.

Surrell, Jason. *The Haunted Mansion: From the Magic Kingdom to the Movies*. New York: Disney, 2009.

_____. *The Pirates of the Caribbean: From the Magic Kingdom to the Movies*. New York: Disney, 2005.

Tolkien, J.R.R. "On Fairy-Stories." *The Tolkien Reader* New York: Ballantine, 1996. 3–84.

Turner, Frederick Jackson. "The Significance of the Frontier in American History." *The Frontier in American History*. New York: Henry Holt, 1921. E-book.

Turner, Victor. *The Ritual Process: Structure and Anti-Structure*. New York: Aldine De Gruyter, 1969.

Van Riper, A. Bowdoin, ed. *Learning from Mickey, Donald and Walt: Essays on Disney's Edutainment Films*. Jefferson, McFarland, 2011.

Von Franz, Marie-Louise. *The Interpretation of Fairy Tales*. Boston: Shambhala, 1996.

_____. *Shadow and Evil in Fairy Tales*. Rev. ed. Boston: Shambhala, 1995.

Watts, Steven. *The Magic Kingdom: Walt Disney and the American Way of Life*. Columbia: University of Missouri Press, 1997.

Weber, Max. *The Protestant Work Ethic and the Spirit of Capitalism*. Trans. Talcott Parsons. New York: Scribner's, 1958.

Wuthnow, Robert. *American Mythos: Why Our Best Efforts to Be a Better Nation Fall Short*. Princeton: Princeton University Press, 2006.

Zipes, Jack. *Fairy Tale as Myth*. Lexington: University Press of Kentucky, 1994.

_____. *Happily Ever After: Fairy Tales, Children, and the Culture Industry*. New York: Routledge, 1997.

Film and Music

The Adventures of Ichabod and Mr. Toad. Dir. Jack Kinney, Clyde Geronimi, James Algar. Walt Disney Productions, 1949. DVD.

Alice in Wonderland. Dir. Clyde Geronimi, Wilfred Jackson, Hamilton Luske. Walt Disney Productions, 1951. DVD.

"Dateline: Disneyland." *Walt Disney Treasures Disneyland, USA*. Ed. Leonard Maltin. Perf. Walt Disney, Art Linkletter, Fess Parker. 1955. Disney, 2000. DVD.

"Disneyland: Secrets, Stories and Magic of the Happiest Place on Earth." *Walt Disney Treasures Disneyland: Secret, Stories and Magic*. Ed. Leonard Maltin. Perf. Tony Baxter. 2005. Disney, 2007. DVD.

"The Disneyland Story." *Walt Disney Treasures Disneyland, USA*. Ed. Leonard Maltin. Perf. Walt Disney. 1954. Disney, 2000. DVD.

"Donald and the Wheel." *Walt Disney Treasures Chronological Donald, Volume 4*. Ed. Leonard Maltin. Dir. Hamilton Luske. 1961. Disney, 2008. DVD.

"Donald in Mathmagic Land." *Walt Disney Treasures Chronological Donald, Volume 4*. Ed. Leonard Maltin. Dir. Hamilton Luske, et al. 1959. Disney, 2008. DVD.

"EPCOT." *Walt Disney Treasures Tomorrow Land*. Ed. Leonard Maltin. Perf. Walt Disney. 1966. Disney, 2004. DVD.

The Many Adventures of Winnie the Pooh. Dir. John Lounsbery and Wolfgang Reitherman. Walt Disney Productions, 1977. Netflix.

"Mickey in Living Color with Leonard Maltin." *Walt Disney Treasures Mickey Mouse in Living Color*. Ed. Leonard Maltin. Perf. Leonard Maltin. Disney, 2001. DVD.

Selected Bibliography

"The Optimistic Futurist." *Walt Disney Treasures Tomorrow Land*. Ed. Leonard Maltin. Perf. Leonard Maltin, Ray Bradbury. Disney, 2004. DVD.

Peter Pan. Dir. Clyde Geronimi, Wilfred Jackson, Hamilton Luske. Walt Disney Studios, 1953. DVD.

Pinocchio. Dir. Ben Sharpsteen, et al. Walt Disney Studios, 1940. Blu-ray.

Sleeping Beauty. Dir. Clyde Geronimi, Les Clark, Eric Larson, Wolfgang Reitherman. Walt Disney Productions, 1959. DVD.

Snow White and the Seven Dwarfs. Dir. David Hand, et al. Walt Disney Productions, 1937. Blu-ray.

Song of the South. Dir. Harve Foster and Wilfred Jackson. Perf. James Baskett, Bobby Driscoll, Luana Patten. Walt Disney Productions, 1946. YouTube.

Walt Disney Treasures Davy Crockett. Ed. Leonard Maltin. Perf. Fess Parker, Buddy Ebsen. 1954–1955. Disney, 2001. DVD.

Walt Disney Treasures Tomorrow Land. Ed. Leonard Maltin. Disney, 2004. DVD.

Who Framed Roger Rabbit?. Dir. Robert Zemeckis. Perf. Bob Hoskins, Christopher Lloyd, Charles Fleischer. Touchstone Pictures, 1988. Netflix.

Index

Index

Index

Index

Index

Index